Managing
Development Programs

Also of Interest

*Managing Development in the Third World, Coralie Bryant and Louise G. White

Appropriate Technology for Development: A Discussion and Case Histories, edited by Donald D. Evans and Laurie Nogg Adler

Development Financing: A Framework for International Financial Cooperation, Salah Al-Shaikhly

*International Financial Cooperation, Frances Stewart and Arjun Sengupta

The Economics of New Technology in Developing Countries, Frances Stewart and Geoffrey James

Implementing Development Assistance: European Approaches to Basic Needs, Steven H. Arnold

Development Strategies and Basic Needs in Latin America, edited by Claes Brundenius and Mats Lundahl

Science and Technology in a Changing International Order: The United Nations Conference on Science and Technology for Development, edited by Volker Rittberger

*Farming Systems Research and Development: Guidelines for Developing Countries, W. W. Shaner, P. F. Philipp, and W. R. Schmehl

Managing Renewable Natural Resources in Developing Countries, edited by Charles W. Howe

*From Dependency to Development: Strategies to Overcome Underdevelopment and Inequality, edited by Heraldo Muñoz

*Threat to Development: Pitfalls of the NIEO, William Loehr and John P. Powelson

*The Challenge of the New International Economic Order, edited by Edwin P. Reubens

Agricultural Credit for Small Farm Development: Policies and Practices, David D. Bathrick

*Women and Technological Change in Developing Countries, edited by Roslyn Dauber and Melinda L. Cain

Scientific-Technological Change and the Role of Women in Development, edited by Pamela M. D'Onofrio-Flores and Sheila M. Pfafflin

*Available in hardcover and paperback.

Westview Special Studies in Social, Political, and Economic Development

Managing Development Programs:
The Lessons of Success
Samuel Paul

Why do some development programs succeed while so many others fail? What role do managerial and institutional innovations play in program performance? Dr. Paul's comparative analysis of six successful development programs selected from Asia, Africa, and Latin America provides important answers to these questions. The study shows that a clear focus on a single goal or service; decentralization; the use of network structures and beneficiary participation consistent with the complexity of the program environment; and highly adaptive planning, monitoring, and motivation processes are among the common features of the six successful programs. The design and orchestration of these and other elements were facilitated by the relative autonomy of the programs and by the continuity and commitment of their leadership.

There is no dearth of studies of failure in the field of development, points out Dr. Paul, but studying failure does not necessarily lead to insights into the positive management actions and institutional innovations that have led to successful programs. This study, the first of its kind to focus on high performers, is unique in the lessons it offers on the strategic management of development programs.

Dr. Paul is professor and former director of the Indian Institute of Management, Ahmedabad, a leading center for management education and research in the developing world, and has been a chief technical advisor to the International Labour Organisation and a visiting professor and research associate at Harvard University. He also is an expert advisor to the UN Commission on Transnational Corporations. Among his publications are *Industrialization and Management* and *Managerial Economics*.

Managing
Development Programs:
The Lessons of Success

Samuel Paul

Westview Press / Boulder, Colorado

4759

M-602

RECEIVED

MAR 3 0 1984

KENNEDY SCHOOL OF
GOVERNMENT LIBRARY

Westview softcover editions are manufactured on our own premises using the highest quality materials. They are printed on acid-free paper and bound into soft-
covers that carry the highest rating of NASTA in consultation with the AAP and
the BMI.

Westview Special Studies in Social, Political, and Economic Development

Copyright © 1982 by Westview Press, Inc.

Published in 1982 in the United States of America by
     Westview Press, Inc.
     5500 Central Avenue
     Boulder, Colorado 80301
     Frederick A. Praeger, President and Publisher

Library of Congress Catalog Card Number 82-050610
ISBN 0-86531-411-X

Composition for this book was provided by the author
Printed and bound in the United States of America

10 9 8 7 6 5 4

To
MOHAN
with affection

Contents

Tables, Diagrams, and Exhibits

Tables

Diagrams

Exhibits

Preface

This book is about the management of development programs. My interest in this subject was stimulated by the opportunities I have had in recent years to observe both public enterprises and development programs in India and several other developing countries. The field experience of the Public Systems Group, a research and training group at the Indian Institute of Management, Ahmedabad, convinced me of the need to cut across the sectoral orientation so common among development planners and analysts. An opportunity to try out my ideas presented itself when I left the directorship of the Institute and took a leave of absence to work at the Kennedy School of Government, Harvard University. I am grateful to Dean Graham Allison of the Kennedy School for inviting me to undertake a research project on "Public Management in Developing Countries", financed partly through a grant from the Rockefeller Foundation to the University. The present book owes a great deal to the support of these institutions and the Indian Institute of Management.

Two colleagues provided me considerable intellectual and emotional sustenance while I was at the Kennedy School. Professors John D. Montgomery and Robert E. Klitgaard advised me on many aspects of my research, commented on my draft papers, and kept up my spirits as I moved back and forth between my extended field visits and spells of writing at the Kennedy School. Prof. Klitgaard and I jointly taught a Harvard Seminar on "Public Management Innovations in Developing Countries" in which all my new case studies and theoretical papers were tried out. I am grateful to him and my student friends who contributed much to the development of my ideas. I am deeply indebted also to Prof. James Austin and Dr. David Korten for their advice and support at different stages of this study.

To Dr. Laurence Stifel, I owe a special word of thanks. He nurtured my ideas and provided many opportunities for testing out my research methodology and findings. Persons who assisted me in the course of field visits are too many to mention by name. Needless to add this book would not have been possible without their cooperation and support.

At the Indian Institute of Management, where I did part of the writing upon return from Harvard, there are many whose support I should acknowledge. First of all, I am grateful to Dr V.S.Vyas, the Institute's Director, for granting me a long leave of absence. Several colleagues have commented on the manuscript and discussed a summary paper in a specially organised seminar. To Professors S.R. Ganesh, R.S. Ganapathy, P.N. Khandwalla, Jay Satia, and Ashok Subramaniam, I am deeply grateful not only for their helpful comments, but also for tolerating my continued demands on their time. I learnt a great deal from them. However,none of these friends in India or abroad have any responsibility for the errors that remain in the book.

Finally, I should like to thank Ravi Acharya and Revathi Srinivasan for their excellent editorial assistance, Betty Miele, my secretary at Harvard University, and Arti Sharma, my present secretary, for their efficient support in the different phases of this project, and G.D. Patel and Ajay Shah for their assistance in the preparation of diagrams. My wife,Lily, and children, Neena, Mohan,and Annie deserve a special word of appreciation for their endurance of my long periods of absence and our rather unsettled state of existence while this international project was in progress.

Indian Institute of Management   Samuel Paul
Ahmedabad, India

1
Introduction

The performance of development programs in the Third World has attracted considerable international interest in recent years. The focus of the discussion, for the most part, has been on the economic, financial and political factors relevant to these programs. In this book, we shall explore a neglected dimension - the role of management interventions in development programs. For reasons which will shortly be explained, the focus of the study will be on the high performers among development programs. The basic questions we shall investigate are two : what are the management and institutional interventions associated with successful development programs? What lessons can we learn from their experience?

It is well known that development programs and their outcomes are influenced by a number of variables of which management is only one. The environment in which a program operates, the techno-economic and human resources available to the program, and the degree of political commitment and support behind it are among the major influences in any setting. The rationale for the focus on management interventions in the present study is the growing realisation in international circles as well as developing countries (DCs) that problems of management and institutional development are hurting program performance,[1] and that this phenomenon has not received the attention it deserves. The fact that nearly fifty percent of the annual budgets of many DCs are devoted to financing a wide variety of development programs and projects adds to the significance of the study.

The basic raw materials for the analysis presented in this book have been drawn from a set of relatively successful development programs selected from different parts of the Third World. This approach is in sharp contrast to the dominant trend among students and observers of public policy and management, whose primary concern has been the study of failures. Perhaps this trend reflects the general conclusion that public programs in DCs are, by and large, low performers. In a recent study of a dozen public interventions in DCs, Grindle and her co-authors have narrated the dismal outcomes of several development projects.[2] In a survey of the rural development programs and projects in Africa, Lele has come to a similar conclusion and highlighted the environmental and policy

1

related factors responsible for poor performance.[3] A recent ESCAP report on India's rural development administration has commented on the generally unsatisfactory record of that country's numerous rural development interventions under public auspices.[4] Siffin, in an incisive analysis of the US technical assistance programs to improve public administration in DCs, has lamented the insignificant impact such efforts have had over the past two decades.[5] A recent United Nations publication has summarised the sense of pessimism that prevails in the developing world:[6]

> Unfortunately, the promised deliverance has not been achieved, or at least not fully achieved. The elusive key which would turn off the source of conditions that generate poverty has not been found, a fact which has prompted much expression of frustration and disaffection. The Economic and Social Commission for Asia and the Pacific summed up the resulting mood of countries in the region when it recently pointed out the "deep concern and moral indignation about conditions of poverty within their countries and of the limited effectiveness of existing strategies" for implementing development programmes for rural areas.

Surprisingly, the recurring theme in most studies of development programs in developed countries is also strikingly similar. Scholars who have investigated a wide variety of U.S. public programs have drawn attention to their dismal record of performance.[7] They have attributed poor outcomes to problems of both policy-program design and implementation. An important by-product of these studies is the growing emphasis on building implementation analysis into the policy-program design process.[8] It is being increasingly realised that policy choices and program designs will lead to desired outcomes only when they take into account the problems and politics of implementation. The U.S. public programs which have been extensively analysed are from sectors such as education, health, urban development and housing,and are intended to benefit the poorer sections of the society. The limited capacity of the Federal Government to influence action at the local level,problems in organising cooperative action on a large scale (the complexity of joint action), the inability of the poor to mobilise themselves in relation to programs, and over-ambitious or inappropriate program designs are among the reasons for failure identified by most analysts.[9] Similar assessments of public interventions in the United Kingdom have also been published.[10]

Are scholars and analysts in both developing and developed countries unduly harsh in their assessment of public programs? Perhaps there is some truth in the belief that failures attract more scholarly attention than successes. An anatomy of failure is unique in the opportunities it offers the critic to put forth his(her) ideas, with hind-sight of course, on what should have been done to optimise program performance. On the other hand, even if we allow for the normal human tendency to focus on failure, it is not unlikely that the dominant trend in the literature reflects, by and large, the reality of development program performance in many countries.

What accounts for the poor performance of public interventions on the development front? There was a time when in many DCs, the absence of macro economic planning was regarded as the prime cause of the malady. National planning commissions or authorities were set up in many countries to formulate development goals and programs and allocate scarce resources among the relevant sectors, aided by the use of economic models. While this approach was valuable in terms of giving a sense of direction to development efforts and setting sectoral priorities, it was soon found that allocations and targets were of little avail in the absence of well-designed and properly selected projects and programs. In a survey of development planning Waterson has observed: [11]

> By far the greatest number of failures to carry out public sector projects and programs at reasonable cost and in reasonable periods of time are traceable to inadequate project selection and preparation. Few less developed countries are fully aware of the necessity for selecting soundly conceived projects with potentially high yields, defining their scope with clarity, estimating their national currency and foreign exchange requirements with a sufficient degree of accuracy, and laying down realistic schedules for their execution; fewer yet have the administrative capacity and the political will to cope with these needs and, especially, to carry out plan projects and programs in accordance with carefully developed programs of action.

An important response to this problem was the increasing use of project appraisal methods and cost-benefit analysis in many countries. International donor agencies played a major role in promoting this approach on a large scale. International aid was invariably tied to specific projects, and it seemed logical to ensure at the planning stage that beneficiary projects were viable in socio-economic terms. Even countries which did not practise macro planning have adopted project appraisal methods with considerable enthusiasm. Project appraisal manuals were widely disseminated by national and international agencies, and special units for project analysis were set up in many countries as part of various government departments and ministries. [12]

As experience with development planning accummulated, leaders and planners in DCs began to realise that macro and micro planning were not sufficient conditions for optimal project or program performance. Even in the heyday of macro planning, it was suspected that performance had something to do with the management of projects and programs. As one observer put it: [13]

It is normal for economists to be more interested in the internal content of an economic plan than in the planning process as such. It is the plan as a document which embodies the problems that are interesting to economic theory - the form of the planning model, the handling of the variables, given assumptions, projection techniques, target and policy variables, parameters of behaviour, etc. It is in the formal preparation of plans that the particular expertise of economists is most useful.

The establishment of a planning process is an exercise of quite a different character. Here the problem is not one of producing an internally consistent and analytically elegant document. The task is to spread the planning habit, establish rational economic calculation as the common norm for decision-making, and have this accepted by those responsible for making decisions. It is a problem of organization and management.

That development tasks called for administrative reform in several areas soon began to be recognised in government reports and speeches by leaders. The growing concern about the problems in implementing and managing development programs probably reflects the wide spread frustration with poor performance on the development front and the fear on the part of governments that both macro and micro planning will remain ineffective as long as these problems persist.

A STUDY OF HIGH PERFORMERS

If public management is indeed a major problem, the exclusive focus on the study of failures may well be somewhat misplaced. Undoubtedly there is much to learn from the experience of low performers. But, by and large, such studies are more useful in identifying the errors to be avoided than the positive approaches to be adopted. The removal of obstacles does not necessarily ensure performance.[14] This is especially true in the field of management and implementation which are action oriented by their very nature. There is considerable evidence to show that successful management interventions and practices cannot be deduced or predicted from an analysis of failures or poor performance. Innovative approaches stem from discontinuties and not linear projections. That is why the prescriptions derived from such studies often fail to offer adequate guidance for action. In understanding the nature of public management and developing insights for improving the performance of development programs, therefore, there is a strong case for investigating the experiences of high performers. In the terminology of statisticians, this approach is tantamount to studying the "right tail" of the frequency distribution. In most economic and social analyses, the focus is on the "mean" of the distribution as the analyst is interested in understanding or predicting the average or representative behaviour of whatever phenomenon or population is under scrutiny. The tails of the distribution or "outliers" are treated as an aberration and the attempt is to minimise the distortions they create in estimating the central tendency.

There are, however, many problems in the study of which the right tail rather than the mean is of primary concern.[15] In agricultural research, for example, scientists typically concentrate on the best seedlings raised in the nursery and ignore the average and the poor. Their objective is to understand the features of the exceptional cases and learn how to replicate them. In drug research also, very similar methodologies are used. Psychologists study key myths in detail and not all myths as a basis for understanding more clearly the mental processes operating to a lesser extent elsewhere. Klitgaard, who has examined this question from the standpoint of educational research, argues that often the study of exceptional performers may be more meaningful than an analysis of averages when the need is to identify the characteristics of high performers in order to replicate or adapt them, understand the underlying processes which tend to be less clear in average situations, and avoid the over-simplification arising from the analysis of averages. These are reasons which seem to apply equally well to the management of development programs.

The focus of the present study will, therefore, be on the management interventions of exceptional performers in the field of development. The unit of analysis will be the individual development program. Ideally, the study should have investigated both successes and failures. Though no case studies of poor performers will be attempted as part of this study, we propose to draw upon existing studies and use available evidence for comparison wherever relevant. We suspect however, that the insights and understanding to be gained from high performers will be far more valuable than the incremental gains to be derived from further investigations of low performers about whom we already know a great deal. Our exclusive preoccupation with exceptional performers is therefore deliberate, and designed to redress an imbalance which has been a dominant feature of the literature on development.

This approach in no way implies that performance is determined solely by the quality of public management. We would readily concede that planning, both macro and micro, has a strong influence on outcomes, although it is questionable whether the tendency to treat micro planning and management at the program or project level as discrete and seperate entities is meaningful. Among other variables often highlighted as critical to performance are political support and commitment, economic resources and leadership. Again, there cannot be any disagreement as to the importance of these variables. Without strong political commitment and power sharing arrangements, no public program can go very far.[16] Allocation of adequate resources to a program often reflects political commitment at the top. The quality and motivation of the leader or top manager in charge of the program also will make considerable difference to its performance. However, we also know that these are not sufficient conditions. There are many poor performers among development programs which apparently had significant political support behind them. Many programs which were well endowed in terms of resources

(adequate capital and technology) have performed indifferently.
There are program leaders who inspite of their charisma and other
personal qualities were unable to achieve high levels of performance.
In the context of the present study, we shall treat these variables
as enabling factors. They are complementary to "management" which
is the missing link in many investigations. When programs perform
poorly, it is possible that the positive influence of enabling
factors is negated by ineffective or inappropriate management
interventions. It is equally plausible that the management interventions were appropriate, but were neutralised by the inadequacies
of the enabling factors. It would seem, therefore, that the two are
complementary and must reinforce each other in order to optimize
performance. Successful programs are likely to be located at the
intersection of these two sets of variables, namely, political
commitment and other enabling conditions on the one hand, and
management and institutional interventions on the other. A study
of the management interventions associated with high performers is
potentially more rewarding as the presence of enabling conditions
help "demask" the real managerial processes at work. The
development programs selected for study in this book have been
characterised by strong political support at the national level and
adequacy of economic resources. However, since our objective is to
isolate and understand the nature of management interventions
associated with them, we shall not probe the underlying political
and economic influences. Many others have investigated political
processes and economic efficiency issues in the context of
development programs and projects in a variety of countries. In
fact, it could be argued that the efficiency of resource use tends
to reflect the quality of management and is therefore not independent
of it.
    It is necessary at this stage to define the term "development
program". Since this is a term which will be extensively used in
this book, it is useful to clarify its meaning and scope in some
detail. We shall also briefly explain the methodology used in
identifying and selecting the exceptional performers among
development programs for study and the organisation of the book in
the concluding section of this chapter.

THE NATURE AND SCOPE OF DEVELOPMENT PROGRAMS

    Development programs are creatures of the state. Their growth
and popularity in most DCs could be directly attributed to the
increasing role of the state in development. It was the recognition
of governments that "development tasks" called for strategies and
organisational forms different from those relevant to their
"maintenance tasks" that led them to initiate programs and projects
with identities of their own. The term "development plan" has been
used in the literature to denote the total set of government
programs spelt out in the national development plan of the country.
The unit of analysis in our study, however, will be the individual
program which is a part of this total set. We shall, therefore,
use the term "development program" to denote any identifiable

program initiated and managed by the government with a view to
achieving specified development goals or outcomes. The nature of
expected outcomes may be economic, social or a combination of both.
Agriculture, industry, public utilities, health, and education
are examples of important sectors of the economy in which development
programs of a wide variety have been undertaken in DCs. Programs
have been organised by governments to promote the development of
specific food crops, industries, social services, and infrastructural
facilities such as roads, power and communication. Development
programs have also been organised with a deliberate strategy to cut
across diverse sectors of the economy. The recent trend towards the
creation of integrated rural development programs involving multiple
sectors reflects the growing dissatisfaction in many DCs with the
side effects of growth oriented development policies and the belief
that more complex program designs with a sharper focus on the rural
poor are needed to achieve growth with equity.[17] Depending on the
nature of the tasks involved, programs may assume varying degrees of
complexity in terms of their scope and organisational form. Programs
which are meant to serve large segments of the public may have
structures that work through the federal, state, and local levels of
government and organisational arrangements to cover all regions of
the country (eg., population programs and health services). A
program whose focus is the development of an isolated backward region
or the development of a crop unique to a single state may be more
limited in its scope and organisational complexity.
Development programs are usually spawned at the national level
and tend to operate through sub-programs which are designed to cover
different geographic regions such as states, or different functions
and groups of services. The sub-programs in turn may consist of a
series of discrete, interrelated or sequential projects and/or a set
of elements which together constitute a relatively permanent delivery
system. What is important to note is the fact that the implementation
of the program is expected to occur in most cases through its location
and service specific components which interface with the clients or
beneficiaries of the program in different locations. An agricultural
or small industry development program, for example, may deliver its
services through units set up in locations close to the farmers or
entrepreneurs scattered in different parts of a region or country.
Development programs as defined above need to be differentiated
from the conventional and routine operations and services provided
by government departments (eg., revenue collection), as well as
projects set up as temporary systems or experimental efforts within
government departments in developing countries. The focus of most
of the studies in development programs, for example, has been on
development projects which are of a pilot nature or confined to
limited areas in DCs.[18] One reason for the dominance of this project
orientation is the role of aid agencies which tend to design and
promote pilot projects or limited area projects, though major
institutions such as the World Bank have been involved in larger
programs of an ongoing nature. The development and management of
national or regional programs to replicate pilot project results are
usually the responsibility of the DC governments. The relatively

limited involvement of donors in the larger programs might be one
reason for the comparative neglect of the problems of their
management. Pilot projects and limited area projects are to
national programs what research and development (R&D) projects are
to a large corporation. The product that the corporation sells to
the public may have resulted from an R&D project. But the
corporation's problems of managing the commercial production and
marketing the product are distinctly different from, and often more
complex than the problems of managing its R&D project. Similarly,
the management problems of a large development program are not the
same as those of the pilot project which supplies the "product" to
be replicated by the former.

By neglecting the study of the larger, national programs of DCs,
researchers might have ignored an important class of public
management problems.[19] This leaves a gap to be filled as the
replication of project results will eventually occur only through
the medium of larger programs in most cases. The final test of the
success of pilot projects should be the extent to which they are
replicated or adapted on a national scale in DCs. In a study of
selected pilot projects in developing countries, an author once
concluded that they were successful because their technical findings
were promising. Further investigations, however, showed that
none of the countries extended, adapted, or replicated these projects.
It is difficult to attribute success to these projects when they had
failed in the final test!

Inspite of the growing role of the state in economic and social
development, we know much less about "public management" as against
"enterprise management". This paradox is in part due to some
features which are unique to the public context.[20] First of all, it
is important to note that the "bottom line" is more fuzzy in the
public context so that the search for appropriate management
interventions does not receive the sense of urgency normally present
in the private sector. Often, development programs are launched to
compensate for the existence of "market failure". But in the process,
the programs may assume monopoly power and in the absence of
competitive or market indicators, measurement of efficiency becomes
a casualty. Program performance is then viewed in terms of adherence
to procedures. Cost control and the application of efficiency
criteria normally associated with the discipline of the market place
become low priority concerns.

Second, since development programs are government supported and
initiated, they are vulnerable to political pressures and interference which may conflict with their originally stated goals or
charter. The management of the programs within the bureaucratic
structure which in turn is subject to political control as well as
public scrutiny adds to this problem. Multiple and conflicting
goals and demands get foisted on programs. Overmanning and low
productivity get institutionalised. The costs and consequences of
these trends get masked by the fuzzy bottom line feature referred to
above.

Third, development program outputs tend to be services the demand for which may have to be mobilised. Their clientele are generally unsophisticated masses who need to be organised and influenced in effective ways. Whether it is the promotion of new seed varieties and extension to small farmers or family planning and nutrition to illiterate and poor households, it often becomes necessary for the program to build credibility among clients, promote public response,and adapt the services to meet the local conditions. This is in sharp contrast to the standardised products and services promoted by enterprises operating in protected markets and the routine functions performed by the "maintenance" departments of the government. The provision of developmental services therefore calls for a setting that permits some measure of autonomy, risk taking, and personnel who are sensitive to client needs and are motivated enough to work together in well knit teams,and if necessary, with a network of organisations. These are not features one encounters in the hierarchically oriented bureaucratic setting which spawns and supervisesdevelopment programs. The means and resources required to make programs perform and the flexibility needed to adapt them to changing environmental conditions are seldom available to the public manager.

This brief discussion of the nature of development programs offers us some useful insights into the complexity of their management and the reasons why successful management interventions in this area are not plentiful. It appears that public and private managers differ significantly in the degree of control they exercise over their choice of goals, resources and environments. Those who lead development programs seem to face more severe constraints in respect of goals,means, and their ability to orchestrate the two.

In light of the foregoing discussion, we list below four distinctive features of development programs:

Policy Sanction. Normally, a specific legislative enactment would have preceded the creation of a new development program. There is thus an authoritative decision of the government behind every program.[21] In countries which have national development plans, an executive decision will suffice, as the national plan of which programs are a part already has legislative approval behind it.

Development Focus. In contrast to regulatory programs whose developmental impact might be indirect, development programs are expected to generate economic and social outcomes (measurable and immeasurable) consistent with national development goals such as income growth and distribution, and improvement in the quality of life. The nature of their tasks is such that the discipline of the market is not an adequate framework for planning and controlling their operations.

Organisational Identity. A development program will be characterised by an identity of its own in terms of an organisational structure, budget and personnel. Even though the program may be under the administrative control of a ministry or department of the government, it should be possible to identify it by reference to a relatively permanent organisation with its own structure, and

assignments of tasks and responsibilities, and reporting relationships. They could thus be differentiated from temporary systems
and experimental projects whose life cycles are short.

Replication. The program's mission tends to be the replication
or adaptation of a "developmental product" or "service" over the
entire country or some of its constituent regions for the benefit
of a specified client group. The developmental service need not be
a physical commodity. It may be a system designed to deliver a
product or service within a specified geographical area and determined by the techno-economics of the sector or sectors and the
existing geographic and organisational conditions. Thus in a health
program, the service is not the set of individual health services
(which are, of course, of direct concern to the beneficiaries), but
the system designed to assemble and deliver them at the village, sub-
district, or district level, whichever is the appropriate unit of
operation. Similarly, it may be misleading to define the output of
a dairy development program as the supply of milk. Its service
might well be the interrelated system which has been developed to
integrate the set of services for the production, processing and
marketing of milk for the benefit of specified client groups. It is
this system which a pilot project tries to test out, and a national
program usually is concerned with its replication and adaptation over
large areas.[22]

Most development programs have three distinct phases in their
life cycle, though chronological overlaps between phases is possible.
The pilot phase is the initial period when a product or service is
being designed or adapted. This may or may not precede the formal
launching of a national program. The replication or adaptation phase
begins when the program is extended from the pilot area to other
parts of the country. It is this phase which offers the maximum
challenge to the strategic and operational management of the program.
The growth in the size and complexity of the program due to spatial
expansion is not a dimension on which real experimentation is
feasible in the pilot phase. Once a program has completed its
replication phase, it moves into a maturity phase. Depending on the
nature of the service, the maturity phase may take one of three
alternative forms. (1) it may continue indefinitely as the service
is needed on a permanent basis (e.g., the generation and supply of
electricity, health services etc.) (2) it may be terminated as the
service is no longer required or because the beneficiary groups or
private agents are able to take over the functions being performed
by the program (e.g., agricultural extension and input services,
family planning, etc.) (3) the program gets diversified, taking on
new tasks, but carrying on the original services as part of its
broadened mandate. For example, a population or health program may
diversify to provide nutrition services without giving up its
original services. The problems of management tend to be particu-
larly severe during the replication phase because of the "scaling
up" from the pilot phase, and the maturity phase if the program
happens to adopt the third alternative.

METHODOLOGY AND SCOPE

In an earlier section, it was pointed out that the basic
materials for the study were derived from a set of relatively
successful public programs operating in different parts of the
developing world. We shall comment briefly on the selection of
these programs, the methods of analysis adopted, and the scope of
the management interventions investigated in the present study.

The identification of high performers is a difficult task in the
field of development. Simple, uniform,and quantifiable indicators
of performance or outcome are difficult to find. This is in sharp
contrast to the ease with which students of corporate management are
able to rank and compare enterprises by measures such as the rate of
return on investment. Development programs vary a great deal in
their goals and have multiple dimensions of performance not all of
which are quantifiable. Though we did examine quantitative data on
program performance, given the limitations of data, we concluded
that subjective assessment of performance was unavoidable.

In view of these data limitations, and other problems in attempting direct international comparisons, we asked a cross section of
international experts, observers and public managers familiar with
various sectors and development efforts in different parts of the
world to use their knowledge and experience to identify outstanding
performers among the development programs in DCs. No restrictions
were placed on the sectors and regions they were to scan in order to
identify high performers. Their choices were to be based on their
own implicit criteria for judging performance. The six programs
that we finally selected for study received unanimous or near
unanimous support from the panels of advisers concerned with the
relevant sectors and regions. That there was consensus on their
choice even when judged by differing criteria is what lends credibility to their inclusion in this study. The six development programs
identified as high performers were the National Dairy Development
Program of India, the Indonesian Population Program, the Philippine
Rice Development Program (Masagana-99), the Public Health Program of
China, the Small holder Tea Development Program of Kenya, and the
Mexican Rural Education Program (CONAFE). Without exception, all of
them happened to be programs with a heavy rural orientation. Data
for a period of eight to ten years were available on all programs.
This period covers the pilot phase and replication phase of the
programs for the most part. All of them continue to operate and are
yet to reach full maturity. Our study covers a significant phase,
but not the entirety of their life-cycle.

It is important to emphasise that our interest in this exercise
was to identify a subset of development programs which were widely
regarded as relatively successful in relation to their goals, and to
examine the management interventions associated with their performance. The selection process was not used to rank the programs. It
is significant that most knowledgeable observers agree on outstanding
performers even though there are no clear cut and uniform criteria
for assessment. Perhaps, there is a similar unanimity with respect
to outstanding failures too.

Intensive case studies of the six development programs were
attempted using secondary data as well as field visits, interviews,
and questionnaires. This approach permitted a comprehensive
analysis and understanding of the complexity of the program which
is our unit of analysis. In a study the purpose of which is to
gain insights into the nature and interaction effects of management interventions, this is a more appropriate method than a
purely statistical or quantitative approach, which, of necessity,
must use simple indicators and partial analysis. In our present
state of knowledge, intensive case studies and comparisons are a
more fruitful means of capturing the complexity of public management and generating hypotheses to oe tested through large-scale
studies in future. Other researchers have in the past employed
similar methods with considerable success.[23]

The case studies summarised in Chapters 2 - 7 of the book were
attempted within a conceptual framework that defined the nature of
management interventions and their interrelationships. While
there are numerous managerial decisions and actions that influence
program performance, we hypothesise that the key to successful
performance lies in management interventions which are of a
"strategic" nature. It is "strategic management" which sets the
pace and tone for numerous operations decisions and actions and
thus influence their outcomes. Our approach to strategic management which is presented in Chapter 8 focuses on the set of top
management interventions which influence the design and orchestration of the strategy, organisational structure, and processes of
the program in relation to its environment. The four interacting
variables which influence program performance will be called the
environmental, strategic, structural, and process variables.
Underlying a program at any given time is a combination of these
variables. It will be argued in Chapter 8 that the unique
contribution of a program's management lies in creating and sustaining a state of congruence among these variables. The guidelines for the individual case studies were thus provided by the
analytical framework of strategic management.

Chapters 9, 10, and 11 will be devoted to an analysis and
interpretation of the manner in which the top managers in each of
our programs intervened to influence and orchestrate the
strategic, structural, and process variables. Thus, the strategic
components of each program, their interdependence and "fit" with
the environment are examined in Chapter 9. The evolution of their
organisational structures, patterns of authority sharing, and
autonomy are the focus of Chapter 10. The role of participation,
human resource development, monitoring, and motivation are
viewed as processes which support the strategic and structural
interventions of the programs in Chapter 11. A set of propositions is presented in each chapter based on the evidence provided
by the six programs. The concluding chapter offers an overview of
the lessons in strategic management emerging from the study and
highlights its broader implications for public policy and
management.

NOTES

1. This point has been extensively commented upon by many authors. For example, see A.Waterson, Development Planning : Lessons of Experience (Batimore:Johns Hopkins University Press, 1965), Chapters 8 and 9; R.Chambers, Managing Rural Development (Uppsala:Scandinavian Institute of African Studies, 1974); G.U.Iglesias (Ed), Implementation : The Problem of Achieving Results (Manila:EROPA, 1976); Stifel, et.al., Education & Training for Public Sector Management in Developing Countries (New York : Rockefeller Foundation, 1977); Honadle and Klaus (Eds), International Development Administration (New York, Praeger, 1979); John Mellor, The New Economics of Growth (Ithaca: Cornell University Press, 1976); Chapter 1.

2. M.S. Grindle (Ed.), Politics and Policy Implementation in the Third World (Princeton : Princeton University Press, 1980)·

3. U. Lele, The Design of Rural Development : Lessons from Africa (Baltimore : Johns Hopkins, 1975).

4. UN, ESCAP, Rural Development Administration in India : Some Emerging Policy Issues (Bangkok, 1979).

5. W. Siffin, "Two Decades of Public Administration in Developing Countries", Public Administration Review, Vol.36, No.1 1976. Siffin also argues that public administration, which has been preoccupied with the problems of the central systems of government, has failed to grapple with the new issues emerging from the operation of field agencies. The latter, it would seem, are concerned with the problems of public programs.

6. United Nations, Public Administration Institutions and Practices in Integrated Rural Development Programs, (New York,1980), p.3.

7. J.Pressman & A. Wildavsky, Implementation (Berkeley : University of California Press, 1971); M.Derthick, New Towns in Town (Washington D.C:The Urban Institute, 1972); W.Williams and R.Elmore (Eds.) Social Program Implementation, (New York: Academic Press,1976). E.Bardach, The Implementation Game (Cambridge: M.I.T. Press,1977).

8. C.Wolf Jr., "A Theory of Non-Market Failure : Framework for Implementation Analysis", Journal of Law and Economics, April, 1979, pp.140-97. Also see the Special Issue on "Implementation" in Public Policy, Spring 1978.

9. Pressman and Wildavsky, op.cit; Derthick, op.cit.

10. B.Watkin, The National Health Service : The First Phase 1948-74 and After (London: Allen & Unwin, 1978); H.M.S.O., The Nationalised Industries (London, 1978)

11. A.Waterson, op.cit. p.320-21

12. UNIDO, Guidelines for Project Evaluation, United Nations (New York, 1972); I.M.D. Little and J.Mirrlees, Manual of Industrial Project Analysis in Developing Countries (Paris:OECD, 1969).

13. S.K. Roxas, Lessons from Philippine Experience in Developing Planning, Paper prepared for Conference on Economic Planning, Honolulu, 1965, pp.47-48.

14

14. A.O. Hirshman, The Strategy of Economic Development (Hartford : Yale University Press, 1958). Chapter 1.

15. Robert Klitgaard, "Identifying Exceptional Performers", Policy Analysis, Fall, 1978, p.531-33.

16. For an excellent review of the role of political and bureaucratic processes in public decision making, see G.Allison, The Essence of Decision (Boston : Little, Brown, 1971); C.Lindblom, "The Science of Muddling Through", Public Administration Review, Spring, 1959, pp.79-88.

17. U.N., Public Administration Institutions and Practices in Integrated Rural Development Programs (New York, 1980). p.6.

18. There are, of course, some projects which are of a continuing nature, eg., irrigation projects which are of a donor agencies in such projects tend to be for a short or medium term. Their time p rspective, therefore, tends to differ from that of the national government.

19. Interestingly enough, scholars located in DCs or who had opportunities to be in the field have paid greater attention to the problems of such national programs. Of course, if countries have not gone beyond the stage of pilot projects, opportunities for such involvements cannot possibly exist.

20. Stifel, et.al., op.cit. p.7. US scholars who have worked on public program implementation have on the whole avoided the sectoral bias as comparisons across sectors and departments have been a part of their general approach. The problem has been more serious for scholars working on DC programs, possibly because of their long term sectoral involvements.

21. The concept of policy sanction is applicable even if countries do not have development plans. The various US public programs which have been studied, for example, have appropriate legislative approval behind them.

22. The design of the individual services or end products is, of course, important. But their design is often a technical rather than a management problem. Projects and programs have to generate design, production, and delivery systems which enable beneficiaries to receive the intended services, consistent with available resources and norms of efficiency.

2
The National Dairy Development Program of India

In 1965, Government of India established the National Dairy
Development Board as the lead agency to promote and assist dairy
development in the country. This decision followed a visit by the
then Prime Minister of India, Mr Lal Bahadur Shastri to Anand, a
small town in Gujarat state, where the Kaira District Cooperative
Milk Producers' Union (AMUL) had its headquarters. He was greatly
impressed by the work of the Union in organising dairy cooperatives
for small farmers in the surrounding rural areas. Upon return to
New Delhi, he wrote to the Governors and Chief Ministers of the
state governments drawing their attention to the successful Anand
pattern of dairy cooperatives and exhorting them to take steps to
promote such cooperatives in their states. However, there was no
tangible response to his plea from any of the states. Though
Mr Shastri died shortly thereafter, Government of India (GOI)
proceeded to set up the National Dairy Development Board (NDDB) with
headquarters in Anand. The new Board was given a broad mandate to
develop the dairy sector of the country and Dr V.Kurien, the General
Manager of the Kaira District Cooperative Milk Producers Union, was
appointed as its chairman.

The newly established NDDB initiated a national dairy development program in 1970 with the assistance of the World Food
Program (WFP) of the United Nations.[1] It was called 'Operation
Flood', signifying its mission to create a 'flood' of rurally
produced milk. The major goals of the program were to (1) capture
a commanding share of the milk markets in the four metropolitan
cities of India, (2) create milk processing facilities in 18
selected rural milksheds through farmers' organisations to provide
a remunerative channel for rurally produced milk, (3) enhance rural
milk production and strengthen procurement systems by providing
technical services to farmer-producers, and (4) develop basic
transportation and storage infrastructure to link the metropolitan
milk markets to the rural milksheds. Though the program ran into
some initial difficulties and delays, and the completion of its
first phase had to be extended, it has been acclaimed internationally
as an outstanding contribution to rural development. The entry
point of the program was dairying. Yet its impact has gone well
beyond the dairy sector. Though there has been no single compre-

hensive study of the program and its impact so far, independent
studies by several authors have documented the positive effects
of the program on income generation, women's status, and receptivity
to community cooperation and change.[2] Field studies have shown an
increase in income ranging from 50-100 per cent among the members
of the cooperatives. The rate of return for an average farmer is
estimated at 31 per cent.

PERFORMANCE

NDDB's achievement of its national targets is most impressive.
Though the progress of the program was delayed somewhat for
several reasons, by 1980 when the first phase of Operation Flood
ended, 1.3 million rural families and 12,000 villages benefited
from the program as against the target of one million families and
10,000 villages respectively. To set up viable cooperative
societies in 10,000 villages was in itself a stupendous task. Milk
production capacities in the four metropolitan cities had reached
2.9 million litres as against the target of 2.75 million litres
per day. By 1980, through-put in the city dairies had more than
doubled to 2.2 million litres per day as against the target of
2.75 million. Through-put in the rural feeder balancing dairies
had reached 3 million litres while the target was 2.75 million per
day. Commercial import of milk powder into India was stopped by
1976 and the production of milk powder in the country had gone up
to 64,000 tonnes. Four regional milk grids were made operational,
linking the four metropolitan areas with the 18 rural milksheds
served by thousands of small farmer organisations (cooperatives).

While NDDB's achievement of its targets for Operation Flood was
remarkable, it was not uniform throughout the country. Its first
phase was extended from 1976 to 1980. In two states, Uttar Pradesh
and Bihar, the program did not move as effectively as it did in
other parts of the country. In some states, it was reported that
the new dairy development corporations which were responsible for
the program lacked the commitment and responsiveness characteristic
of Amul, the original district union. Some critics have pointed
out that the increased commercial sale of milk in rural areas led
to a decline in availability of milk and milk products in villages,
thus aggravating the nutrition problems of the poor. Others have
argued that the increased use of crop residue as cattle feed
reduced the fuel supply to the poor. In spite of these criticisms,
many observers are convinced that on the whole NDDB has had a
positive impact on rural development.

In economic terms, the program's contribution is regarded as
outstanding. The cost of farmgate rural milk is said to compare
favourably with the landed cost of imported milk. Taking
additional incomes generated out of the new rural milk production
as the benefit, one international donor has estimated the economic
rate of return of the second phase of the program at 25 per cent.
An internal study of NDDB using a slightly different methodology
has shown that the program's return on investment will be 35 per

cent. These estimates, however, have not considered the value of
social benefits such as the creation of farmers' own organisations,
impact on women's status, regularity of employment and pattern of
income distribution.
    A recent United Nations Inter-Agency Mission reviewed the
progress of Operation Flood in detail by visiting different parts
of the country, interviewing officials and non-officials, farmer
groups, and critics of the program. Their evaluation rated
Operation Flood as a remarkable success.

Operation Flood, the world's largest dairy development
program, is distinguished by its involvement of small
holders and landless rural milk producers. It is a
successful example of effective use of food aid and of
technical assistance for development. The program has
significantly increased the incomes of a very large
number of poor rural producers. It has also increased
the availability of good quality milk at reasonable
price for city consumers.

The Government of India and the Project Authority showed
boldness in entrusting national dairy development to the
rural milk producers themselves through their own
cooperatives. Creation of 10,000 village cooperatives
involving over 1.3 million producers and their families
in 27 milksheds in India by the end of Operation Flood
(Phase I) has been a massive achievement.[3]

DAIRYING : HISTORICAL FACTORS[4]

    Until three decades ago, dairying in India was a largely
unorganised activity. Apart from some isolated efforts to improve
breeds, dairying was left for the most part in the hands of
traditional producers, middlemen, and vendors. Cattle stables in
the cities multiplied over time and middlemen acquired milk supplies
from poor producers by advancing "loans" in anticipation of the next
lactation of their milch animals. During the second World War, some
private dairies were encouraged to produce pasteurised butter and
cheese for the British Army. One such firm in Kaira became the
major supplier to the "Bombay Milk Scheme" by shipping milk in cans
to Bombay by rail (over a distance of 300 miles). The government,
however, found the scheme too costly and soon closed it down. The
milk producers of Kaira meanwhile, had learnt one lesson during this
period. They had gone on strike against the firm which had the
monopoly procurement contract for Bombay on account of a dispute
over the price paid to them. Sardar Patel, a national leader in the
independence movement of India, had exhorted them to form a dairy
cooperative at this time. A small band of milk producers responded
to his call and the Kaira District Cooperative Milk Producers'
Union was born in 1946.

Since 1947, several steps were taken by the government to develop the dairy sector. A new milk scheme known as "The Greater Bombay Milk Scheme" with a market milk plant in Bombay was established. The Kaira District Union which had its processing plant in Anand began to supply milk to this scheme. During the fifties, the Key Village Scheme was started by the government with a view to providing purebred bulls in selected villages. In the sixties, a more elaborate scheme of "Intensive Cattle Development" projects was started in order to provide aid to milk producers for improving breeding, feeding, and management of their cattle. These schemes were administered departmentally by the state governments with technical and financial assistance by the Center.

Meanwhile, urban dairies in the larger cities were promoting yet another approach to dairy development. Led by the Greater Bombay Milk Scheme, they provided good stable facilities near the urban dairy, and cattle keepers in the city were encouraged to move their milch animals to these premises. By then, many state governments had also realised the need for coordinating the efforts of their different departments such as veterinary, agricultural, and cooperative divisions. Some states created new dairy development departments in order to plan and implement coordinated dairy schemes. Gujarat was the only exception. It never set up a dairy department, having left the task to the cooperative organisations of farmers pioneered initially by the Kaira District Union.

Thus, by the mid-sixties, India's dairy sector had developed four distinct subsectors: (1) a small number of modern, private dairies collecting milk through private or cooperative channels, (2) the traditional sector consisting of traders and middlemen linked to urban cattle keepers and rural farmers, (3) departmental dairy projects with state government owned processing facilities manned by civil servants, and procuring milk either through middlemen or cooperatives, and (4) a small number of integrated producers' cooperatives based on the Anand pattern.

Of these structures, the producers' cooperatives were dominant only in Gujarat state. Others, though varying in their relative importance, existed in about all parts of the country. The government owned urban dairy system was well entrenched in most of the states. Private milk trade was active in all urban areas though organised private dairy plants were few in number and tended to specialise in the manufacture of a variety of milk products. Interest groups had developed around each of these structures which in turn created several problems for the newly established Dairy Development Board (NDDB). It is important to note that in spite of these diverse, organised efforts, milk consumption per capita was either stagnant or declining in the country as a whole (from 139 grams in 1950 to 126 grams in 1960 and 105 grams in 1970). In other words, though India had a long tradition in dairying, the dairy sector was not moving at a pace that could be termed dynamic.

The Key Issues

NDDB had to grapple with several larger issues of the dairy sector. First of all, the efforts of the state governments in organising milk production, procurement, processing, and marketing under departmental auspices had failed to make any major impact.[5] Many of these departments were operating at 30 to 40 per cent capacity, given the low level of milk production and procurement they were able to mobilise. Coordination among the different government departments was a major problem and the manning of these schemes by civil servants who did not necessarily have any professional competence or commitment to the dairy sector might also have contributed to this state of affairs. As a result, government owned dairies were not able to obtain more than one third of the liquid milk markets in their urban territories. The aggressive strategies needed to compete in the market with private traders, and the flexibility to cope with the organisational requirements of a perishable commodity such as milk were seldom associated with these schemes.

Second, most government schemes reinforced the urban bias in India's dairy development. The focus was on building modern diary plants in cities close to the consumers rather than in the milksheds where the milk was being produced. A direct consequence of this trend was the concentration and expansion of cattle colonies in urban areas. Both cattle and feeds had to be brought into the cities, thus making milk production more expensive than it should be. The economics of urban milk production was such that the rate of slaughter of high quality cattle was accelerated, depleting the stock faster than warranted in the process.

Third, as the department milk schemes found it difficult to organise rural milk procurement, government administrators turned increasingly to the use of imported skim milk powder which was available at relatively cheaper prices then. Cheap imports enabled them to meet urban consumer market demand more easily and at relatively low prices without worrying about economy and efficiency. As a result, the alternative of encouraging milk production in the rural areas on a long term basis was ignored.

THE ANAND PATTERN

In 1965, when NDDB was established, the government had hoped that the future dairy development in India could be organised along the lines of the Anand pattern evolved by the Kaira District Milk Producers' Union. Similar milk producers' cooperatives had since been set up in five other districts of Gujarat with Amul's assistance and all of them have had an impressive record of growth. Amul got started in 1946 as a protest movement when the farmers of Kaira district resolved to organise their dairy operations on cooperative lines. The Union started with two village milk producers' societies and began pasteurising milk for the Bombay Milk Scheme in 1948. From two societies and a collection of 250 litres of milk per day in 1948, the District Union steadily expanded to nearly 850 village societies and milk collection of 8,00,000 litres per day by 1978. The movement had the support of some very important political and social leaders of Gujarat at the time of its founding. The first chairman of Amul, Mr T.K. Patel was a respected local leader who played a major role in mobilising public support and participation in the new scheme. Mr Patel was assisted in his early efforts by a young engineer, Mr V.Kurien, who provided the technical and managerial support needed by the infant organisation. Mr. Kurien, who had gone to Anand only for a temporary assignment, decided to stay on and eventually became the chief executive of Amul and the chairman of NDDB. The involvement of important and influential leaders in Amul's development ensured support for it at the state government level. Both political leaders and bureaucrats played a facilitating rather than an interfering role. The state government's cooperative department performed only an audit function in relation to Amul, unlike similar departments in other states which had powers to nominate chairmen and managing directors of cooperative societies and appoint their own officials to run cooperatives.

Amul faced a number of problems in its early years. In 1953, the Bombay Milk Scheme refused to buy all the milk supplied by Amul in the winter months. This was clearly a consequence of the seasonality in milk production, a problem that Amul was bound to run into as it stepped up its procurement. Restriction on procurement in winter months, of course, posed a serious problem for the farmer who wanted a steady and assured market throughout the year. Amul responded by putting up a new dairy factory to convert a part of the milk into milk powder and other milk products. The aid provided under the Colombo Plan for this project was repaid by Amul by providing free milk to pre-school children under an agreement with UNICEF. The new factory which was opened in 1955 enabled Kaira farmers to step up milk production and procurement significantly. In 1958, the factory was further expanded and in 1960, new products such as babyfood and cheese were added which were marketed by the Union throughout India.

Organising Farmers

While the extensive use of modern technology and marketing by Amul appears impressive, its most significant breakthrough lay in the innovations it introduced in its farmer organisation. Kaira was a district with 80 per cent of its population dependent on agriculture. The average farmer family's landholding was about three acres. Bajri, a type of millet, was the major cereal crop of this region. Bajri straw was fed to the buffaloes, one or two of which were found in almost any average household in Kaira. Dairying was a subsidiary source of income for most farmers. Buffaloes were maintained on the byproducts of the farm and the surplus labour of the farmer's family. His main problems were the low milk yield of his milch cattle and the lack of facilities for marketing the milk. The farmer generally was apathetic towards scientific practices of animal husbandry and nutrition. Quite often, the needed inputs and services were not available. Even if they were, the farmer did not find it worthwhile to invest in them since he was not sure that the returns would be adequate and stable. The market for milk was simply not dependable.

It was this vicious cycle that Amul broke in the early fifties, an endeavour in which the village level cooperative played a key role. Each cooperative consisted of farmer members, each of whom bought a share and paid a small membership fee totalling $ 1.50 per head. They also agreed to sell to the cooperative a predetermined share of the milk they produced in a year. This was to ensure that only genuine farmers joined the cooperative. The managing committee of the cooperative would be elected by the members, each of whom had one vote. The committee elected its own chairman. Depending on the volume of milk collected, a society employed three to six persons (on part time payment) for the day to day business of measuring and testing the milk and making cash payments to the sellers of milk.

When a new cooperative society is started, it receives from the District Union a hand operated fat testing machine, free of cost. Its replacement is to be financed by the society from its own funds. The society buys milk from its members (300-400 farmers) in the morning and evening daily. A sample of milk is taken from each container and tested for fat content. The price of milk is deter- mined on the basis of its fat content. Payment for the milk bought in the morning is made in the evening and for the evening's sale, a person gets paid in the morning. The District Union collects the milk twice a day from each village cooperative. Milk cans are collected by truck and the 850 villages are covered by a network of 79 truck routes.

Amul realised early that while the farmer would respond if adequate and stable returns are provided to him, the productivity of cattle could be augmented only by improving breeds, and nutritional and veterinary care. Such services were usually provided to the farmer by government agencies or private operators. The veterinary department of the state government was concerned with breeding and treatment of diseases. The agricultural depart- ment was concerned with fodder and nutrition. Private veterinary doctors also provided some of these services. The farmer's problem was that he did not have easy access to these services and often these inputs and services were not available. The concerned government agencies were not always responsive, and the private traders who bought milk from the farmers had no incentive to provide such services.[6] It was against this background that Amul decided to assume responsibility for providing certain critical inputs to farmers through the village cooperatives.

One of the early benefits provided by Amul was in respect of veterinary services. All villages are visited once a week by qualified veterinary staff who give treatment to the cattle on the spot. Today, there are 23 mobile veterinary dispensaries which provide this service regularly in the 850 villages which are members of Amul. The farmers may also call for emergency veterinary assistance at any time of the day or night by telephoning the headquarters at Anand. Members are required to pay $ 2 and non- members $ 3.50 per visit.[7] One member of each village society is

trained in first aid veterinary work and Amul veterinarians check
their work once a week. The medicines used during the week by
the local first aid workers will be replenished free of charge by
the mobile dispensaries during their routine weekly visits.
Nearly 3,00,000 cases are treated annually by the veterinary
staff of the village societies and District Union together.
Financial assistance not exceeding 75 per cent of the expenditure
incurred by a society is provided by the Amul Research and
Development Association (ARDA) towards the operation of the
village first aid veterinary center.

As part of a program to upgrade animal breeds, Amul
established Artificial Insemination (A.I.) sub centers in the
villages over the years and village society secretaries have
been trained to perform A.I. operations. Diluted and preserved
semen is shipped from Anand to all village A.I. sub centres in
milk trucks which visit the villages twice daily for collecting
milk. Though A.I. service is given free of charge, it is
supervised by the veterinary staff periodically. ARDA subsidises
every society undertaking A.I. work to the extent of 75 per cent
of the expenditure incurred by it. Experimental work on the
cross breeding of cows has also been underway at Anand for some
years and the adaptability of new breeds to local conditions is
being studied.[8]

In addition to farm residue and herbage, farmers have
traditionally fed whole cottonseeds as concentrate cattle feed to
buffaloes in milk. Research has shown that this is a rather
wasteful way of feeding. The better method of feeding concentrates to milch cattle is by mixing byproducts of oil seeds such as
groundnut cake, cotton seed cake, rice and wheat bran, and
mineral supplements. Depending upon prices, availability, etc.,
different concentrate mixtures should be prepared, keeping in
view both nutritional and economic considerations. **As it was**
beyond the capacity of individual farmers to develop the required
formulae and prepare the mixtures, **Amul set up a feed mixing plant.**
The feed concentrates manufactured in this plant are sold to
farmers through the village societies on a daily basis.
Deliveries are made through the milk trucks that carry the empty
cans to the villages. This service enabled the farmers to
supplement the crop residue available to their cattle with
ready made, nutritionally balanced formula feed which could be
procured at a reasonable price throughout the year. In recent
years, Amul has also been distributing fodder seeds to farmers
through the village cooperative societies.

Extension, training, and supervision were strong features of
Amul from the beginning. Simple accounting and information
systems were developed for managing the affairs of the village
society and systematic training was given to the officials at the
village level. Amul also provided a supervisory service to
cooperative societies to examine their operations periodically
and tone up their management. An important part of Amul's
extension related to the education of women who were actively
involved in feeding and maintaining buffaloes in the villages of
Kaira. Besides imparting training to women on scientific

practices relating to animal husbandry and cooperation, visits were regularly arranged for groups of women to the Amul Dairy, A.I. Centre, and the cattle feed factory.

Organisational Structure

The structure of the Kaira Cooperative Union consisted of a two tier system - the district producers' cooperative union at the district level and the village milk producers' cooperative society at the village level. In order to form a society, the intending milk producers in a village get together formally under the guidance of a milk supply officer of the Union. Once the decision to form a society is made, a general meeting of the members is called to elect their managing committee in a democratic manner. The managing committee appoints the different employees which include the secretary, milk collector, fat tester, clerk, inseminator, accountant, and a helper. To begin with, the Union supervisor helps the new society to organise its day to day business and become economically viable in about three months' time. After the society becomes a viable unit, the Union recommends it for registration to the state cooperative department. The Union continually monitors, guides, and supervises the progress of all member societies. The cooperative bye laws drawn up by the Union are to be observed by all member societies. There is also a continuous and concurrent audit of all the societies on a quarterly basis, conducted by the auditors of the state cooperative department. The societies' accounts are presented to and approved by its general body. Many societies have built up reserves and declared bonuses to its members. Reserves have been used to build schools, roads, dispensaries, and other common facilities in the village. The district union represents all registered milk producers' societies in the district and has a board of directors consisting of 19 members.

Studies of Amul's experience have shown how an appropriate mix of technologies has been effectively used to promote rural development with the aid of locally designed and adapted institutional mechanisms. Small farmers have been able to augment their income from dairying by 50 to 100 per cent as a result of the Amul program.[9] In areas where this pattern has worked, it is found that landless labourers receive 65-70 per cent of their total income from the sale of milk and even small and marginal farmers earn as much as 25-30 per cent of their income from dairying.[10] The farmers' participation in milk cooperatives may also have had a subtle influence on their values and social life in general. The practice of democracy at the grassroots (election and representation at the village and district levels), the impact on social barriers of the cooperative processes and economic activities, and the exposure of women to modern and scientific concepts and practices which they see in action at their doorstep are influences which hopefully will contribute to the speeding up of social and economic changes in rural India.

OPERATION FLOOD

The NDDB was not able to accomplish much in the early years of
its existence in spite of the clearly demonstrated achievement and
impact of Amul and its district union in the state of Gujarat.
The Prime Minister's letter to the chief ministers of states and
the subsequent establishment of   NDDB with Mr. Kurien as its
chairman had made it amply clear to all concerned that the replication of the Anand pattern had the full support of the Government of
India. While lip service was paid to the desirability of this
proposal, none of the state governments nor any other group took
any positive steps to implement the Prime Minister's idea. NDDB
had therefore to be content with responding to a few ad hoc requests
for assistance which came from state agencies from time to time.
It was only an advisory body and had no authority to set up schemes
independently or implement projects on its own. In addition to the
lack of response from the state governments, a major new problem
emerged on the international horizon. The EEC countries were
piling up huge surpluses of milk powder and butter and there was a
strong possibility that milk powder imports might be stepped up
through appropriate foreign aid schemes. Urban dairies were ardent
supporers of such aid which enabled them to either maintain or lower
urban milk prices and in the process also depress the milk prices
received by the farmers. Mr. Kurien and other members of the NDDB
knew that if imports were used to subsidise the urban consumers in
a big way, the prospects for dairy development in the country would
be shattered.
When Amul was founded, it had the unique advantage of having had
a strong local leadership that supported the cause of the rural milk
producer. Other district unions in Gujarat also came up largely
because there were leaders who could mobilise farmers and take
advantage of the potential benefits of the Anand pattern. There was
no bureaucratic or political opposition to such movements in
Gujarat. Other states obviously did not possess these unusual
prerequisites.
Amul had evolved over the years and had raised a good part of
the resources for its growth out of its own efficient operations.
The state governments and their urban dairies were not in such a
fortunate position. The state owned urban dairies were invariably
subsidised operations. Further, there were many claims on state
government resources. It was unlikely that they would allocate
substantial funds for dairy development out of their limited budget
in view of the general environment in which they operated.
The experience of NDDB in its early years and the emerging
environmental factors made it increasingly clear to its members that
a positive program had to be planned and implemented if dairy
development was to make any significant progress. The Government
of India and its Ministry of Agriculture had not provided any
guidelines beyond expressing a strong preference for replicating
the Anand pattern. The objectives of NDDB were stated in rather
broad terms. It was against this background that in 1969 the NDDB
proposed a national program for dairy development to the Government

of India, that came to be known as "Operation Flood". In 1970, the government approved the program for implementation with a budget of Rs.1000 million ($ 130 million).

Though Operation Flood (OF) had a number of stated objectives, the operational goal on which NDDB laid the greatest emphasis was tripling the modern dairies' capacities for processing and marketing liquid milk in the four major cities of India (Bombay, Delhi, Calcutta, and Madras) while simultaneously building up matching procurement and processing facilities for producers' cooperatives in 18 selected rural milksheds in different regions of the country. The rationale of this goal was that 6 per cent of India's expenditure on milk occurred in these four cities (accounting for 3 per cent of the total population) and that a commanding share of these milk markets had to be captured as a means to ensure demand for the milk procured from the rural hinterlands.[11] Other objectives such as improving cattle breeds through research and development were played down in OF on the basis that the gestation period involved was too long to make any immediate impact and that the markets had first to be developed before interest in improved breeds could be created. OF thus had a distinct and clear focus in terms of its primary task, i.e. achieving a dominant share of the urban milk market so that rural milk producers could be assured a stable and profitable outlet for their supply of milk.

OF was to commence in 1970-71 and scheduled to be completed in 1975-76. A major part of the funds was to be generated through the World Food Program (WFP) of the United Nations. A total of 1,26,000 tonnes of skim milk powder and 42,000 tonnes of butter oil were to be obtained as a gift. These donated commodities were to be distributed through NDDB to the selected urban dairies at prices approximating their milk equivalent value in India,[12] and the city dairies were to recombine the donated commodities into liquid milk for sale in each city.

The basic elements on which OF was based could be summarised as follows: (1) Imported milk powder and butter oil were to be used to prime the pump for the publicly owned urban dairies. These donated commodities, however, would be sold to the dairies at prices which would not have an adverse impact on indigenous milk production. (2) The funds generated by NDDB through the sale of donated commodities to the dairies would be used to support all the investments envisaged under OF, thereby insulating the program from periodic shortages of government funds for investments. OF was to use part of the funds generated by the sale of the recombined milk to increase the capacities of the publicly owned city dairies. (3) As the large state owned urban dairies captured dominant shares of the urban markets, city based milk production (cattle colonies) would be forced back into the rural milksheds close to the cities, reducing the cost of milk production in the process. Some of the funds generated would be used to finance the establishment of the Anand pattern of cooperatives in these rural hinterlands. (4) When the urban cattle colonies declined in importance, high yielding animals would cease to be drawn away from the rural areas. It would be easier then for the small farmers to support high

yielding milch cattle. Some of the program funds were to be used
to upgrade breeds through the provision of bull farms and artificial
insemination services under the auspices of producers' cooperatives.
(5) Even after the completion of OF, milk production in some
regions of the country might continue to be vulnerable to the
unreliability of monsoon rains. However, it was most unlikely that
all regions of the country would face such an eventuality in the
same time period. Some funds were therefore allocated for investment in road and rail tankers for long distance haulage of liquid
milk, and to set up warehouses for milk products to be conserved by
the cooperatives in view of the seasonality in milk production.

FINANCIAL AUTONOMY

      In the first two years of its existence, NDDB received modest
financial contributions from the Government of India in the form of
grants-in-aid. It was customary for autonomous government bodies
set up as registered societies or trusts to receive grants-in-aid
which in some cases might account for their total income. The
grants made to such autonomous bodies would appear in the
government's annual budget as line items which required the approval of Parliament even if the amounts involved were small. The
accounts of organisations receiving such grants were audited by
government auditors and expenditures could be incurred only in
accordance with the norms prescribed by government from time to
time. Although the boards of autonomous bodies were endowed with
considerable authority in the formulation of their policies and
programs, there was a widely held belief that government's
financial controls and audit practices tended to limit their ability
to implement approved programs effectively.
      The financial controls and procedural constraints which the NDDB
experienced in the first two years were found to be so irksome by
the Chairman and other officials of the Board that they began to
wonder whether they would ever be able to operate autonomously under
such constraints. Most of these officials were accustomed to a very
different manner of functioning in the cooperative sector where the
financial practices and controls had been adapted to the requirements
of their business and the unique features of its environment. Almost
instinctively, they began to search for ways in which the Board
could raise its own revenues and thus reduce its direct dependence
on government grants-in-aid.
      A major breakthrough in this direction was achieved when the
Board successfully convinced the Government of India that it should
be permitted to charge fees for the services it rendered to its
clientele (state governments, cooperatives, and other agencies).
The rationale was that clients would treat NDDB's services more
seriously if they had to pay for them and that NDDB would be more
careful about the relevance and quality of its services in light of
the signals given by clients. However, the more dominant consideration might have been that this approach would enable NDDB to raise
its own revenues.

When NDDB proposed OF and ways of financing it, issues of governmental financial control and autonomy surfaced once again. Government was receiving the United Nations (WFP) aid in the form of dairy commodity imports. Revenues generated by the sale of these commodities were therefore to be regarded as budgetary receipts of the government which could then be used for financing OF. However, this approach of financing OF meant that its budget would be subject to the same constraints and controls that departmental budgets were subject to. The kind of financial autonomy that NDDB had sought and obtained from the Government of India earlier would have been of no avail if in managing the much larger budget of OF, it were to be subject to the conventional budgetary norms, and audit and control procedures of the government.

In light of the arguments put forward by NDDB on this issue, the government agreed to establish a new organisation under the Ministry of Agriculture to perform functions such as trading (import and export), financing, and investment in relation to dairy development. Thus, the Indian Dairy Corporation (IDC) was created in 1969 to perform these functions and to collaborate with NDDB, the state governments, and cooperatives to further dairy development in the country. As a corporation, IDC was empowered to import dairy commodities, equipment, cattle, and other needed items, and engage in any other commercial transactions relevant to the implementation of dairy development programs. IDC was also authorised to create the "Operation Flood Fund" to which the sale proceeds of imported dairy commodities were to be credited. A major part of the fund was used to finance the different sub-programs under OF and advance loans to state government agencies and cooperatives engaged in approved dairy development schemes. Whenever NDDB provided technical services to these organisations it was eligible to receive fees for services rendered.

The advantage of this institutional arrangement was that the basic commercial transactions needed to facilitate NDDB's operations could be accomplished through a sister public corporation without NDDB having to sacrifice its financial autonomy. Close coordination between NDDB and IDC was expected to be achieved by appointing a common chairman for both organisations and physical proximity in terms of location. As a corporate body with its own board of directors, IDC had greater flexibility in operation than departmental (ministry) undertakings and agencies. On the other hand, as a corporation owned by the Government of India, it was subject to governmental audit and related financial controls which did not apply to NDDB.

ORGANISATIONAL STRUCTURE

The organisational structure of the milk producers' unions in Gujarat had a remarkable degree of compactness and functional coherence that was seemingly easy to replicate. The two tier organisation of cooperative at the village and district levels, the tight control of the Union over the village societies through the network for input delivery and the linkages in terms of processing

and marketing, and the neat and complementary division of labor
between the district and village level organisations constituted
the basis for a viable management system. A major task of NDDB
in OF was to assist in the creation of such viable organisational
structures in each of the 18 selected rural milksheds.

Each rural milkshed and milk market had its own unique
ecological and environmental characteristics. The climatic
conditions, dietary preferences and patterns of people, the quality
of milch animals and infrastructural facilities varied widely from
one region to another. These peculiarities made it imperative
to create a framework in which decisions on dairying will be made
on the spot, by persons who know the local conditions and have a
stake in what happens in the region. NDDB could not possibly have
developed the required intimate knowledge and capacity to make the
right decisions for the simple reason that the milksheds were
scattered all over the country. The most relevant decision makers
in each milkshed would have been the milk producers' representatives, leaders, and managers. But in most places, there did not
exist a structure which permitted such local decision makers to
influence the shape that dairy development in their area should
take. There was clearly a major institutional gap to be filled.

What emerged eventually was a three part institutional
structure which assumed responsibility for implementing OF and in
the process to lay the foundation for developing a viable cooperative organisational structure in the selected milksheds. First, in
the absence of farmer organisations, a local implementing agency
had to be identified in each participating state to take responsibility for setting up or expanding dairy plants and facilitating
the organisation of milk producers' cooperatives. As has already
been pointed out, many states had several departments dealing with
different aspects of dairy development causing serious problems of
coordination in the process.[13] The civil servants who were already
engaged in operating dairy plants were not enthusiastic about
NDDB's proposal of cooperatives owning and managing the dairy
schemes. The chief ministers and other political leaders in the
states were not certain as to what these farmer organisations might
do to their power and influence. A crucial task of NDDB leaders
was to persuade the key persons in the political and bureaucratic
environment that it was in the interests of each state to create
a dairy development corporation as an implementing agency responsible for working jointly with NDDB on Operation Flood. The state
corporation had to dovetail the program with the overall food and
agricultural policy of its state government while acting as a
proxy for the milk producers' representatives, managers, and
technicians who did not as yet exist.

The bargaining that took place between NDDB and the states led
to certain compromises. While state governments agreed to
coordinate their efforts through a dairy development corporation,
NDDB had to reluctantly agree to the proposal that the corporation
would own and control the dairy plants until district milk unions
were formed and gained experience in running milk procurement
operation. There was, of course, the risk that the bureaucratic
control over dairy processing and marketing might never be given up

and that the Anand pattern might not get replicated in its entirety
in some of the states. However, the formal agreement was that the
State dairy development corporation (SDDC) would be the first owner
of the dairy plants constructed in the state under OF and that
ultimately they would be owned by the milk producers' union. There
was also mutual acceptance of the role of the corporation in
promoting, assisting, and monitoring the establishment of Anand
pattern rural cooperatives under the guidance of NDDB.

A second element in the institutional structure was the newly
created Indian Dairy Corporation (IDC), a public sector enterprise
set up by the Government of India to perform the role of a
"finance cum investment house" for the dairy sector. NDDB was only
a technical advisory body and, being a non-profit organisation,
was not permitted to engage in commercial activities such as import
and export and lending. The institutional form of a corporation
was more appropriate to this task and hence the government's
decision to create the IDC as a sister organisation to NDDB. The
new corporation was authorised to import dairy commodities as and
when required and sell them to the different dairies in the
country. It was expected to use the sale proceeds to finance the
new dairy schemes and related projects being planned under OF.
IDC was also expected to make use of NDDB's technical services and
advice in relation to the specific projects it financed and to pay
NDDB for its services. Mr. Kurien was appointed chairman of IDC
and its head office was located in Baroda, a city just twenty miles
away from Anand.

The third part of the structure was NDDB itself. As an
autonomous technical service agency, it was to provide certain
services to the state governments such as design and turnkey
erection of rural dairy plants, bulk procurement of dairy equipment,
design and manufacture of dairy and cattle feed plants, and the
organisation and development of village cooperatives.

Evolution of NDDB Structure

The creation of engineering division and management and manpower development division took place in the early years when NDDB
followed a passive policy of responding to state government
requests for technical advice and assistance in dairy development.
At that time, the primary task was perceived to be the design,
erection, and commissioning of dairy plants, the focus of which was
on engineering. During the first three years, NDDB discovered that
this approach merely reinforced the past pattern of dairy development and did little to replicate the Anand pattern. OF represented
the first major effort by NDDB to offer a positive program for the
country's dairy development. It soon became clear that an important
requirement for the success of OF was the strengthening of NDDB in
terms of its size and expertise and a restructuring of its
organisation in order to perform the new tasks effectively. Among
the new tasks which emerged in the context of OF were two for which
additional divisions were created. A division of planning was
created to undertake feasibility studies and formulate

project proposals for clients in consultation with other divisions
leading to recommendations on market demand, milk procurement
potential and strategy, technical input programmes for enhancing
milk production, and the techno-economic viability of projects.
The state governmentsused these recommendations as inputs in
negotiating with IDC for financial assistance.

A new division was also created for farmer organisations and
animal husbandry. The primary task of this division was to assist
and guide milk producers in setting up cooperatives on the Anand
pattern in the districts which had approved projects. The main
organisational device used for this purpose was the "spearhead
team", a multi-disciplinary group of five or six professionals
consisting of veterinary doctors, dairy technologists, and extension workers who worked alongside a "shadow team" deputed by the
state dairy development corporation in each district. They set up
cooperatives, organised technical input services, trained cooperative workers, and assisted in milk procurement. The teams would
also stay in a district for several years, if necessary, to ensure
that the cooperative and milk procurement systems ran smoothly.
The shadow team which worked with the spearhead team was to be the
core group for the state implementation agency to continue this
work in other parts of the state once NDDB's spearhead team was
withdrawn.

Within the NDDB structure, the work of this division was
considered to be the most difficult and sensitive, as it concerned
the most fundamental aspect of the Anand pattern, namely, organisation of farmers. As conditions varied a great deal from one part
of the country to another, and the responses and problems of
farmers and other relevant groups in different locations could not
always be anticipated, this division permitted a great deal of
local adaptation and dealt with its spearhead teams with considerable
understanding and flexibility. While the teams worked within a
framework of policy and action guidelines laid down by the
division, the team leader was always given a fair measure of
autonomy. For example, he enjoyed some degree of flexibility in
operating his budget. His accounts were audited only on a monthly
basis. He had powers of hiring and firing, which officials of
comparable status in his head office did not have. His performance
was monitored through regular reports and frequent reviews by his
superiors who visited the districts periodically.

Since the division's focus was on organising farmers and
mobilising public response to the program, it placed considerable
emphasis on training activities. The shadow teams as well as
groups of farmers from the districts were brought to Anand for
orientation and training when the spearhead teams got ready to
mount their campaigns. Amul was used as a live laboratory for this
purpose.

In addition to the four divisions described above, two more were
added as NDDB's operations expanded in the early seventies. A
purchase division was created to manage the growing volume of
procurement of materials, especially in relation to engineering

design and erection of plants, and dairy equipment. A sixth functional division was created to streamline and supervise information services and systems applications (IS&SA). The six divisions were supported by the administrative division, accounts division, audit section, the monitoring unit, and the management and economics unit. NDDB had a total staff of over one thousand in 1979.

Restructuring the organisation has been a continuous process at NDDB. Adaptations were made taking into consideration the changed nature of tasks and also anticipating future needs. The decentralisation of functional tasks through the expansion of regional offices and cells is an illustration of this trend. As NDDB's activities spread to different parts of the country and the number of milksheds and dairy plants to be assisted increased, it became clear that a good deal of the operations had to be decentralised and integrated in different regions closer to the projects under implementation. Over the years, regional offices were set up in Delhi, Calcutta, Madras, Bangalore, and Bombay. In respect of engineering, for example, major design work and production of layout drawings used to be the responsibility of the engineering division at headquarters. The regional offices, however, took over the dairy plant designs and some of the division's technical staff were posted to work at the project site. The head of each regional office was administratively responsible for such staff as well as all other personnel located in his region.

Similarly, the three institutions (NDDB, IDC, & SDDCs) of the dairy sector had to cope with their own evolving problems of differentiation and integration. None of these organisations had any formal control over the others. Finance and imports were used by the IDC to influence the behaviour of SDDCs. Technical assistance and mobilisation of farmers were the two instruments of NDDB to exert power over SDDCs. A common chairman for NDDB and IDC was a mechanism that was used to induce close coordination and integration between NDDB and IDC. Nomination of state government representatives on the boards of IDC and NDDB was a device by which state agencies were able to exert some influence on these two federal organisations. The integration of the structure was facilitated by the interplay of all these forces and the subtle coordinating role played by NDDB as the locus of policy making and expertise in the field of dairy development.

IMPLEMENTATION OF THE PROGRAM

Though NDDB was often referred to as a technical advisory body, in reality it played an active role in both policy and program planning as well as program implementation. The Ministry of Agriculture had delegated to NDDB the responsibility for formulating policies and programs concerning dairy development. Since dairying was a state subject, it was understood that public or cooperative agencies at the state level would actually implement the programs and projects. NDDB was to provide technical advice and assistance to these implementing agencies as and when required.

The case of OF demonstrated the manner in which NDDB played an active and somewhat aggressive role in integrating policy formulation and program implementation, though formally maintaining its stance as a technical advisory body. OF was a strong move towards the replication of the Anand pattern and away from the urban cattle colony model. Not only did the NDDB formulate and promote OF, but also conceptualised and developed an organisational structure for implementing the new program. Since NDDB did not have any authority over the implementing agencies in the states, it could not command compliance. Instead, persuasion, bargaining, and negotiation were the processes it had to deploy in order to agree upon operating goals and the resources to be allocated for specific activities. The spearhead teams working at the district level provided significant inputs to facilitate these joint planning efforts. The NDDB leadership was actively involved in negotiating with state governments to set up their own dairy development corporations and to accept spearhead teams to help organise milk cooperatives in their districts. It was NDDB that thought through an innovative approach to financing OF and with IDC negotiated with external donors on dairy commodity imports. The instruments of financial and technical assistance were used by NDDB to influence and integrate the implementors on a continuing basis.

The orchestration of policy planning and implementation that NDDB was able to practice enabled it to make the necessary mutual adaptations and adjustments between the two parts as the program moved along. The usual problems of slow feedback, delays in decision making, and conflicts associated with the dichotomy between design and implementation were minised in this case because of the voice and flexibility given to NDDB by the Government of India in both areas. Its active role in the design and promotion of OF gave NDDB a strong stake in its implementation. Its continuing involvement in implementation enabled it to appreciate the field problems, correct any design errors brought to light through feedback, and adapt the program and its components to the emerging environment expeditiously. Compromises made on the delayed transfer of state sponsored dairy plants to cooperative unions, creation of spearhead teams, etc., are examples of adaptations made possible by the integration of the design and implementation processes within the NDDB.

Commitment and Leadership

Many observers have commented on the high degree of commitment shown by the employees of NDDB. It is possible that the integration of design and implementation within the NDDB created an environment that heightened their sense of responsibility and achievement. The sense of frustration and indifference that would have been felt working in organisations marked by the dichotomy between planning and implementation was less likely to occur in NDDB.

Four important factors seemed to have contributed to the high commitment and morale that prevailed among the NDDB staff. First, the sense of mission and commitment that characterised the staff operating at different levels in the organisation appeared to have been influenced by the feeling of participation that they enjoyed in their job situation. The sense of participation within the organisation and the autonomy they enjoyed in organising their work might have acted as incentives, motivating them to perform better. Second, the desire to work together to fight common enemies and vested interests, a goal frequently highlighted by the chairman of the board, seemed to have increased their motivation to the pursuit of organisational objectives. Amul's own history of having had to fight vested interests and the urban-bureaucratic elite was an ever present influence in NDDB, and a dimension that was emphasised in the process of inducting new employees. Third, the sense of dedication, commitment and integrity associated with NDDB leadership lent credibility to the system as a whole. Mr. Kurien was seen by his people as the key figure behind the success of Amul and as a person who was influential both within government and outside. His aggressive and domineering tendencies were balanced by his personal warmth and support for his staff. Thus the leadership of the chairman, who was a pioneer in the movement, had given stability and continuity to the organisation and evoked considerable support and loyalty from other employees. The fourth factor was the success and prestige associated with NDDB and its programs. Mr. Kurien had received several national and international awards for his services to Amul and NDDB. NDDB had also received awards for its design and development work which had led to successful import substitution. Thus it is possible that good performance instilled pride in the employees and reinforced their urge to excel.

The autonomy enjoyed by NDDB did enable it to be a bit more flexible than other government organisations in matters of financial remuneration to the staff. However, in terms of magnitude and degree, the variations were not really significant. First of all, the salary scales adopted by NDDB were practically the same as those of the central government. In some respects, the perquisites given to employees might have been marginally better than those enjoyed by the civil servants. One area in which the autonomy of NDDB helped was in evaluating and promoting the staff. It was more flexible in its procedures and practices than government departments and more effective in linking evaluation and career advancement. There was, however, no attempt to link performance and financial incentives at the level of the individual employee.

Recruitment and Development

In understanding the phenomenon of commitment, one should turn to NDDB's policies on selection and development of staff more than to financial incentives. It is customary for new government organisations and autonomous bodies set up by government to appoint persons with experience in government. A well known practice in

India is to staff the new organisations with "deputationists" (deputed by the parent departments) who bring with them the operating culture and practices of their old departments, but do not have any stake in the new organisation, as they would still retain their permanent jobs elsewhere. NDDB did not use the government as a nursery. The major nursery it drew upon was Amul and a few other professional institutions. Most of the new recruits were young and could therefore be moulded in ways which were appropriate to the mission of NDDB.

Induction and training were given a great deal of emphasis in NDDB. Not only was its own staff given opportunities for development, but considerable attention was paid to the processes of orienting and training the personnel who were to plan, manage, or implement the programs, and create cooperative organisations in the states. Farmer induction programs represented an important effort in creating a supportive and receptive environment in the village where the spearhead teams were expected to work. The concept of the shadow team was another example of staff development and training to serve the needs of state level organisations. A good deal of learning and development of the staff also occurred on the job, as a result of working together and being given added responsibilities in a manner that does not happen in conventional government organisations.

Monitoring Performance

At the district level, Amul had developed an extremely fast, but simple information system that helped it keep track of the operations of its village societies. The village society secretaries and district union officials were trained in the use of this system. It had similar systems for monitoring its dairy plants, cattle feed plants, input services, and marketing. Replication of these systems and their adaptation to the needs of the rural milksheds in different regions were part of NDDB's technical assistance program. In addition, NDDB had its own information system for monitoring the progress and problems of the different components of OF. The creation of a monitoring unit as a part of the office of the chairman and secretary of NDDB was evidence of the priority allocated to this function.

The monitoring process was not confined to formal reporting of information. Field visits by the NDDB officials for supervision and discussion of problems constituted an even more important form of monitoring. Through formal and informal channels, they were able to observe the progress and problems of projects and very often solved the problems on the spot. The autonomy of the organisation and the commitment on the part of the staff were conducive to the operation of such organisational processes. The decentralisation of the NDDB structure over time which encouraged problem solving at the regional level also tended to reinforce these processes.

There were subtle differences between the control or
compliance systems NDDB used in dealing with farmer organisations
(whose members were the primary beneficiaries) and its own
employees. The use of economic incentives (pricing of milk that
gave a high and stable rate of return to the farmer, cash payment
that improved liquidity, subsidised technical inputs) in order to
elicit compliance dominated NDDB's approach to farmer organisations.
On the other hand, in motivating its own staff and eliciting
cooperation from state level implementing agencies, there was a
relatively greater use of non-economic incentives. The staff and
other implementing groups were exhorted to work for social change
and to fight vested interests. The training and induction given
to them emphasized that they were "servants of the farmers".
Public speeches by the chairman of NDDB invariably stressed the
new values being developed and the key role of his organisation
in the uplift of the rural masses rather than economic incentives.

NDDB's performance in turn was monitored by the Ministry of
Agriculture. In the early years, there were conflicts between
Mr Kurien, Chairman of NDDB, and senior officials of the Ministry
on the nature of control and supervision by the latter over NDDB
operations. The program leaders felt that the Ministry was
inclined to question operational decisions and ignore the more
basic issues of performance and accountability. It was against this
background that NDDB sought and obtained an unusually large measure
of autonomy, especially in financial matters. Mr. Kurien maintained
the view that the Ministry's function was to plan and allocate
resources to NDDB to achieve the objectives that were agreed upon
mutually and then to monitor its performance through periodic
reviews. In 1978, the Ministry set up a steering committee to
perform this role.

36

NOTES

1. The case studies presented in chapters 2-7 are based on both published and unpublished documents, field visits, and interviews with program officials, specialists, and independent observers.

2. S.M. Patel et al., Impact of Milk Cooperatives in Gujarat Ahmedabad, 1980; A.H. Somjee and Geeta Somjee, 'Cooperative Dairying and Profiles of Social Change in India', paper presented at the International Dairy Congress, New Delhi, 1975; Devaki Jain, Women's Quest for Power,(New Delhi : Vikas, 1979); World Bank Reports have also confirmed these assessments.

3. IDC,press release on the UN Inter-Agency Mission's Report, Baroda, 1981. The 27 milksheds include those added to the original 18 through a World Bank Project.

4. This section has drawn upon several publications and reports made available by NDDB.

5. The reference here is to the government owned and operated dairy schemes which were subject to the normal government rules and procedures.

6. In any case, the investments involved were rather large and small traders would find it difficult to organise them. Large private firms might have undertaken such investments; but they could not count on reaping the full benefits of such investments.

7. It is claimed that a farmer can expect to get emergency aid within two hours of his call in any part of the district.

8. Kaira farmers have traditionally kept buffaloes. Cows are not popular as milch animals in this part of the country.

9. SIET, Spread Effects of Dairy Enterprises (Hyderabad, 1971).

10. R.K. Patel, "The Role of Dairying in Increasing Employment Potential for Unemployed Marginal Farmers & the Landless," Indian Dairyman, Nov, 1972. D.S. Thakur, "Impact of Dairy Development through Milk Cooperatives," Indian Journal of Agricultural Economics, July-September, 1975.

11. Urban milk demand was expected to grow at 6% per year during the seventies.

12. This was a departure from the earlier practice of transferring the donated items free of cost or at low prices to the dairies.

13. Such as animal husbandry, cooperatives, dairying, and veterinary departments.

3
The Philippine
Rice Development Program

In the year 1972-73, the major rice growing areas of the
Philippines were hit by the most severe flood in its history.
Coming as it did in the wake of a vicious outbreak of the tungro
disease in 1971-72 and a series of 28 typhoons in 1970-71, the new
disaster shook the fragile foundations of the country's agricultural
economy.[1] Rice was the staple diet of the people and the severe
drop in rice production that followed these disasters resulted in
imports of rice at high prices, for the first time since 1969. The
rice shortage in 1972-73 was estimated at 7,00,000 tons, over 25 per
cent of the production in the country during that year. The foreign
exchange resources of the country were under severe strain and the
procurement of large quantities of rice in international markets
seemed difficult. It was against this background that in 1973 the
Philippine government launched a new program to achieve self-
sufficiency in rice. The program was called "Masagana-99".
Masagana means "bountiful" in the local language. The number 99
signified the nominal target of 100 cavans (1 cavan = 44 kilograms)
of rice per hectare that the program set out to achieve.
   President Marcos called the new rice development program "a
program for national survival". It was an endeavour involving more
than a million farmers scattered in the 57 provinces of the
Philippines and designed to grow enough rice to feed the 50 million
people in the country. Though Masagana-99 (M-99) was born out of a
crisis and seemed like an instant response to a national emergency,
it was by no means the first public intervention to attempt self-
sufficiency in rice in the Philippines.

HISTORICAL BACKGROUND[2]

Rice production had always received a great deal of public
attention in the Philippines. The legislation on a new Rice and
Corn Production Program in 1958 was the first major public effort
to modernise the rice economy of the Republic. This development
took place during the administration of President Carlos Garcia who
created for the first time an administrative machinery to coordinate
the work of the different bureaus of the Department of Agriculture

37

and Natural Resources (DANR) and other agencies relevant to rice
production. The Rice and Corn Production Coordinating Council
(RCPCC) was established in 1958 with the Secretary (Minister) of
DANR as its chairman and all important bureau heads as members. The
new council was not able to accomplish much, largely because of the
inter-agency conflicts and rivalries that emerged. The Council was
weakened by the exclusion of the price support and stabilisation
agency of the government from its membership. The rice problem
seemed to have been viewed at this stage as a production problem
in the narrow sense.

The next administration headed by President Macapagal shifted
its priority to a new land reform legislation enacted in 1963, thus
diverting the attention of DANR away from the rice program. Adequate
financial resources were not provided for the program with the
result that its progress was seriously hampered in the early
sixties. Low levels of rice production and productivity thus
continued to persist and national self sufficiency in rice was
nowhere in sight. The average rice yield per hectare increased
from 23 cavans in 1958 to 28 in 1965, a modest increase which
necessitated heavy imports of rice during this period.

The First Self-Sufficiency Program

President Marcos seized the opportunity opened up by the
technical breakthrough of the new high yielding variety (HYV) of
rice to initiate a self-sufficiency program for rice in 1966. The
RCPCC at this time launched an experimental rice program in a small
area to test viable input packages and work out a coordinated
program involving a variety of public and private agencies. It then
designed a four year rice self-sufficiency program with sub-programs
for components such as seed, irrigation, soil management, fertiliser,
credit, and procurement of raw rice. High priority was assigned to
this program by the President who declared that self-sufficiency in
the production of food should be attained in the shortest possible
time.

The country was divided into three priority regions for the
operation of the program. Eleven out of the 57 provinces were
classified as priority I. Availability of irrigation facilities
was the dominant criterion followed by other considerations such as
adequacy of roads, banking facilities, etc. A novel feature of the
new program was the quedan system which permitted the farmer to
deposit his produce in any approved warehouse and collect a receipt
based on government supported price levels. He could then cash
this receipt at any central bank approved rural bank.

The RCPCC was further enlarged to involve additional agencies
which were critical to the planning and implementation of the
program. The Budget Commission, for example, was included in order
to facilitate fund release. The Council was given the sole power
and responsibility for implementing the Rice and Corn Production
Program. An executive director and assistant executive director
were appointed at the center to oversee all activities relating to
implementation. The field organisation structure consisted of

provincial directors and deputy directors in each of the priority
provinces assisted by provincial committees composed of representatives of the cooperating agencies in the field.

In order to ensure that the implementation of the program
received the highest priority, President Marcos asked Executive
Secretary Salas to oversee its operations. His involvement was
designed to strengthen inter-agency cooperation, to supervise
financial allocations and efficient control of the field operations.
He toured different parts of the country frequently, solved problems
on the spot, and made use of ad hoc committees to investigate
problems and propose answers. He strengthened the feedback and
evaluation systems and invited the provincial directors to attend
the monthly council meetings.

In spite of his high stature and personal leadership, the yield
per hectare increased only to 31.6 cavans in 1968 from 28 cavans in
1965. It was reported that the extension and credit systems made
rather slow progress and that the quedan system had not operated
fully in many areas. Some of the key personnel of RCPCC resigned or
left for other jobs. Even so, in 1968, the government announced
that self-sufficiency in rice had been achieved and that a part of
the surplus was being exported to other countries.

The apparent success of the 1966 program encouraged the government to use the same approach to enhance the production of other
food crops. In 1969, RCPCC was enlarged and transformed into a new
organisation called the National Food and Agriculture Council (NFAC).
Instead of focusing on rice alone, NFAC was to diversify its efforts
by creating five seperate programs for rice, corn, vegetables and
fruits, livestock and poultry, and nutrition. Rice thus became one
of the five programs, a holding operation which had to compete with
several other new programs. Rice output in 1969 fell below that of
1968 and though it recovered in 1970, both production and productivity declined drastically by 1973 in the face of a series of
natural calamities. It seemed as though the achievement of self-
sufficiency was a short lived affair and that the capacity to
generate surpluses to tide over severe shortages was yet to be
developed.

The series of natural disasters that struck the Philippines and
created a major political and economic crisis was only one of the
features of the national environment in 1972-73. A number of other
significant developments had taken place about the same time in the
Philippines which had an impact on the manner in which M-99 was
designed and implemented. One noticeable event was the imposition
of martial law on the Republic in 1972 by President Marcos, who
seized the emergency situation to effect a radical change in the
political and administrative structure of the country. The new
system which immobilised political opposition and enforced law and
order concentrated political power in the President's hands and
gave him a far greater degree of control over the administrative
apparatus of the country than ever before.

The land reform movement which was activated by President
Macapagal in the sixties was given a further push by President
Marcos under his martial law regime. The tenant was decreed the
owner of the land and the transfer process began to be implemented

seriously. An immediate consequence of the reform was that the
traditional role that landlords used to play in providing technology,
marketing, and credit to their tenants became a casualty of the
change process with no substitute arrangements available to fill
the void. The farmer had acquired a new sense of dignity and
motivation, but was unable to take advantage of his new opportunities as there was no one to play the supportive role abdicated by
the landlord. The small farmer certainly did not have the means
and capacity to procure the needed inputs and integrate them on his
own.

Evidence of this trend was visible in the statistics on
productivity and the diffusion of technology. The excellent work
done by the International Rice Research Institute (IRRI), the
University of Philippines College of Agriculture and the Bureau
of Plant Industry of DANR had resulted in the development of high
yielding varieties (HYV) of rice which were being increasingly
adopted by farmers from the mid sixties. In 1972, it was estimated
that nearly 56 per cent of all rice lands were planted with HYVs,
exceeding the anticipated national targets.[3] Between 1959 and 1972,
irrigated areas had virtually doubled from 6,64,000 to 1,119,000
hectares. This was an important factor in the increased production
due to HYVs. The use of traditional varieties of rice had declined
significantly during the same period. Yet many observers had noted
that farmers were not able to exploit the full potential of HYVs in
actual practice. Farm trials had shown a proven yield potential of
at least 5.5 tons of paddy per hectare, whereas farmers in 1970 had
produced less than half this potential. The problem was clearly not
the non-availability of the new rice technology nor the lack of
awareness of HYVs on the part of the farmer.

The Bulacan Pilot Project

In 1969, NFAC and the Agricultural Credit Administration (ACA)
had initiated, through the IRRI, a five year research and extension
program of intensive grain cultivation on upland rice growing areas.
The thrust of the program was on utilising modern farming techniques
along with traditional farm equipment to minimise the farmer's
capital investment. The attempt was to evolve and test viable
patterns for integrating new rice varieties with timing of the
growth cycle, seeding, transplanting, and related farm management
practices and the application of water, fertilizers, and pesticides.
The research results of the first two years were so impressive that
IRRI decided to launch a full scale farm extension program in 1972.
The objective was to determine the extent to which small farmers
cultivating 1-5 hectares of upland rice could replicate the results
using a 16-step package of technology under the supervision of
properly trained extension personnel and to measure the degree of
supervision needed. A deliberate effort was also made to involve
the rural banks to provide credit to the farmers in the pilot
project area. Technicians of the Bureau of Agricultural Extension
formed the core of the extension staff of the project.

The project was designed to cover a target area of 20,000 hectares. In reality, only 300 farmers covering 1,000 hectares were persuaded to participate. A major constraint in IRRI's effort to meet the land area target was the reluctance of rural banks to advance loans to farmers. This was not surprising, as the average yield in the project area was only 1.3 tons per hectare, leaving a profit of only $ 13.40 per hectare for the farmer. With input costs of $ 89.30 per hectare, the rural banks considered the rice farmer a credit risk. Eventually, two rural banks agreed to join the scheme and the other 13 followed suit. Interventions by the Central Bank and the DANR were instrumental in accomplishing this feat.

Severe flooding in the vicinity of the project area in the wake of the drought in the first month after transplanting threatened to abort the whole experiment. However, only a small portion of the crop was damaged as the farms were on the upland areas. Despite these problems, the harvest was truly bountiful, having yielded an average of 100 cavans per hectare. The farmers' net income rose to $ 155 per hectare in spite of increased input costs of $ 180.50. For the next season, entire villages pledged to join the project and adopt the prescribed package.

The Secretary of Agriculture, Mr Tanco, and other high ranking government officials reviewed the results of the Bulacan pilot project with considerable interest. Adaptive trials were set in motion in different regions of the country. There was, however, little time to attempt full scale pilot projects in different parts of the country. The recommendations for a national program made by the IRRI group on the basis of the Bulacan experience were accepted with enthusiasm by Mr. Tanco.

KEY INTERVENTIONS

At the core of the new program which attracted strong political support from President Marcos was the new rice technology and the 16-step package of practices developed out of the Bulacan pilot project experience. The band of extension technicians involved in the pilot project became the core group that trained other technicians recruited to provide extension in the national program. The new technological package was designed to acquaint the farmers with the new technology (HYV seeds, application of inputs, and sequence of practices), deliver it to them and facilitate its adoption through supervised farming.

In persuading farmers to adopt the new package, an important instrument used was the supply of agricultural credit. The strategy was to provide farmers non-collateral, low interest loans with which to buy the inputs (fertilizers, seeds, pesticides,etc.) prescribed by the new technology. The 420 rural banks, 102 branches of the Philippines National Bank and 25 branches of the Agricultural Credit Administration were mobilised to participate actively in the new program. The Bulacan project had revealed important lessons on the critical role of credit and the attitudes of rural bankers. A great deal of negotiation as well as pressure were applied on the rural banks from the highest quarters to gain their support to the program. These banks were used to lending to the large commercial farmers,

especially the sugar plantations, and not to the small rice farmer.
The security orientation of banks, the high cost of servicing small
loans to far too many small borrowers, and the risks attached to
farm credit in a typhoon prone economy were factors which reinforced this trend. Mr Tanco and other officials involved in the
design of M-99 clearly saw a need to provide special government
incentives in order to encourage banks to participate in the
program. Using a government fund of $ 12 million and the redis-
counting mechanism of the Central Bank, conventional collateral
lending was discouraged, and response to the credit needs of the
small farmer by rural banks was facilitated. Rural banks were
permitted to rediscount 100 per cent of their loans to small
farmers. The rediscounting rate used to be 7 per cent and the
rural bank lending rate was 12 per cent, leaving a spread of
5 per cent. In order to compensate for the high service costs and
risks, the rediscounting rate was now reduced to 2 per cent on
loans to small rice farmers, thus allowing banks a spread of 10
per cent. Similarly, banks were guaranteed losses due to
calamities and adverse weather conditions upto 75 per cent of the
face value of loans. Hundreds of mobile teams of credit analysts
and bank clerks were mobilised to go to villages in jeeps, motor-
cycles and on foot where no bank branches existed nearby. "Bank
on Wheels" thus became a visible symbol associated with M-99 in
many parts of the country.

While banks were being mobilised to lend to small rice farmers
on a large scale, efforts were also under way to prepare the
farmers to receive credit. This was part of the work expected of
the new breed of production technicians (extension staff). The
latter were to assist the farmer who had agreed to participate in
the program to prepare his farm plan and budget and recommend his
loan applications to the bank. Certification by the technician
was enough for the bank to process the loan request and no approval
by higher authorities was required. In order to minimise risks and
create a measure of "peer influence", farmers were asked to
organise themselves into small groups (5-7 in number) who agreed to
be jointly and severally responsible for each other's production
loans. These informal groups were known as seldas and usually
consisted of relatives, friends, etc. Part of the credit was
provided in cash and the balance in kind through a chit system. The
chit contained a prescription of inputs and the authorised amount
of production inputs that could be purchased from an authorised
dealer. A number of public and private agencies were involved in
the supply of inputs (fertilizers, seeds, pesticides, equipment,
etc.) through dealers located in different parts of the country.
For the professional service of the technician, the bank paid him
a small incentive allowance per farmer per month during the growing
period and an additional payment per farmer when the loan was
fully repaid.

Water was an important requirement of HYVs. NFAC closely coordinated M-99 plans with the National Irrigation Administration
(NIA) for the timely supply of water to participating farmers. The
program was deliberately directed towards farmers in the irrigated

areas to facilitate optimal use of inputs and achieve higher levels of output in the shortest possible time.

A price support system was introduced as part of the program to assure farmers of a reasonable return on their investment, even during harvest periods when prices tended to decline sharply. The support price for rice administered by the newly created National Grains Authority (NGA) was to be constantly reviewed and adjusted so that it continually served as an incentive to increase production. The NGA was ready to buy and store rice whenever the market price fell below the declared support price. This national system of procurement based on a fair floor price and the distribution system that moved surplus rice from farms to consumption areas were designed to motivate farmers to participate in M-99.[4] The NGA also maintained a ceiling price for milled rice and distributed the rice it procured and stored in private bonded warehouses directly or through private retailers. The use of post harvest technology in linking up farms and consumer markets through the medium of both public and private channels was an integral part of M-99.

The task of mobilising farmers to participate in M-99 was not left solely to the production technicians. The biggest broadcasting campaign the country has ever known was organised to disseminate information about the program to the farmers through local radio stations. Advice and instructions on the use of the new rice technology were provided through spot announcements in the local languages. Fifty-eight local half hour radio programs on M-99 were on the air before dawn every day, conducted by the local field technicians familiar with the area, language, and conditions. The radio campaigns were supplemented by thousands of printed brochures and articles providing illustrated instructions on the program and signboards and other information materials on bank loans without collateral. The publicity campaigns thus aided the work of the extension technicians who were the hub of the credit and technology transfer mechanism.

ADAPTATION OF ORGANISATIONAL STRUCTURE

During the national emergency that confronted the Philippines in the wake of the catastrophic floods in 1972, Agriculture Secretary Tanco and senior officials of NFAC were asked by President Marcos to formulate a strategy for Masagana-99. A great deal of time was spent by the NFAC officials and Tanco personally in discussion with the scientists of IRRI and the University of the Philippines College of Agriculture (UPLB), the different agencies and bureaus of the government whose cooperation was essential to the program, and the Central Bank and the network of commercial banks. The detailed plans and the definition of tasks and roles that emerged from these discussions became the basis for implementing M-99.

Over the years preceding the catastrophe of 1972, the membership of NFAC had expanded from 23 to 31 agencies so that practically all the major government departments were involved in the Council. The expansion was necessitated by the government's decision to diversify NFAC's functions to cover several food crops of which rice was only one. The launching of M-99 in 1973 once again restored the focus on rice and so NFAC had to reorganise itself to perform its role as the nodal policy making and implementing body for the rice program. While the involvement of 31 agencies in the Council was essential to integrating plans and gaining commitments for policies and action plans, other mechanisms were required to enable NFAC to play its implementation role. The new features which were introduced in the post-1973 period brought about some important changes in NFAC's structure.

The focus on implementation led to the creation of a national management committee (NMC) for each crop within the Council with the Executive Director of NFAC as Chairman. The executive director was a former head of one of the bureaus within the ministry. His deputy came from the College of Agriculture (University of the Philippines). In point of fact, the most active NMC was that for rice simply because of the urgency and priority attached to M-99. The NMC consisted of senior technical officials of the departments and agencies whose heads sat in the Council. A new unit for Management Information System (MIS) was created in NFAC to assist the NMC in its monitoring and control function. Similarly, a technical committee consisting of scientists and other technical experts provided advice on the technology components of the program and the adaptations needed in the light of the feedback from the field.

The NFAC structure was also modified to strengthen the planning and implementation functions at the regional, provincial, municipal and village (barangay) levels. A regional coordinator was appointed (from one of the bureaus) to coordinate the work in the provinces in his jurisdiction. Provincial Action Committees (PAC) composed of public and private sector representatives relevant to M-99 were set up as a counterpart to the NMC. The Provincial Governor served as chairman of the PAC and the Provincial Program Officer for rice (PPO) as its vice chairman. Municipal Action Teams (MAT) had mayors as chairmen and the production technicians as vice chairmen. In some provinces, villages action teams (BAT) were organised, headed by a barangay captain and serviced by a technician. The chairmen were the political heads in the area and were expected to help resolve conflicts and enlist the cooperation of the agencies and officials involved more effectively than the NFAC staff in the field could have done on their own. The NFAC officials did all the staff work, but the governors and mayors were given a formal role in the implementation process and were told by President Marcos to give the highest priority to M-99. Similarly, the PPOs in the provinces and other field staff of M-99 were told that the governors and mayors were responsible for the program and that they should take instructions from the latter in matters concerning the program's management within their jurisdiction .

Of these, the concept of the "regional coordinator" really did not become operational in the field. The regional coordinator was literally bypassed and remained as a "fifth wheel" as the program got going. He was to have coordinated the program operations in the provinces in the region and acted as a layer between NFAC and

and the PPOs. In reality the governors dealt directly with NFAC and thus the chain of command and reporting between the center and the field became more direct.

The Production Technician

The key to the field operations of M-99 was the production technician (PT) in the village whose basic task was to provide extension to the farmers and facilitate the provision of farm credit in his area as well as the repayment of the loans by the farmers. Since the program was national in scope, a large number of new PTs had to be recruited and trained in addition to those detailed from the Bureaus of Agricultural Extension (BAEX) and Plant Industry (BPI)[5]. The PTs worked as co-chairmen with mayors in municipal areas and also with barangay captains (village heads) in some cases. They were the program's "barefoot bureaucrats," the functionaries with whom farmers had to interact on a continuing basis. Administratively they reported to the PPOs, though, technically, the bureaus to which they belonged controlled their long term career progress and other personnel matters. The dual control to which they were subjected did generate conflicts and interagency squabbles from time to time. It was to re-emphasise their role in the program that the involvement of the local political leadership in the program was formalised and M-99 field staff were made responsible to governors and mayors for performance. Each PT was assigned to a specified area so as to enable him to provide assistance to and effective supervision over a specified group of farmers.

Though he was at the lowest level in the hierarchy, the PT had certain powers which other extension staff belonging to the bureaus did not have. Apart from his advisory work in terms of extension, he was the designated authority to recommend the farmer's loan request to the bank. He was authorised to prescribe inputs on the basis of which chits would be issued to the farmer for the purchase of farm inputs. He was to recommend farmers to be sent for the training programs organised by the PPO. In making these decisions, he was expected to take the local circumstances, and the special needs and problems of farmers into account, as he was operating at the village level.

Thus NFAC, which was charged with the responsibility for the planning and implementation of M-99, had to work with a structure over which it did not have complete control. Bureau heads were not directly under the control of NFAC, though the Secretary of Agriculture being the chairman of NFAC did help. Governors and mayors were not answerable to NFAC, though they were given the formal responsibility for the program in their respective jurisdictions. The three-way control to which the PT was subject at the bottom of the hierarchy truly reflected the organisational dilemma facing NFAC.

SOME ASPECTS OF IMPLEMENTATION

M-99 was a time sensitive program. The planting to harvesting cycle of rice was about 90 days. Action plans and all field operations had to be synchronised and completed within this period. The leaders of NFAC had, therefore, to evolve processes and systems of management to enable them to achieve program goals within the constraints imposed by a difficult organisational structure.
A senior official of NFAC commented on this problem as follows:[6]

It is true that we have little direct control over the many agencies whose actions we **are** supposed to coordinate. However, there are many ways in which we improvised and innovated our internal processes and systems to compensate for this lack of control. For instance, our planning exercise for each phase (season) was an effective process for integrating the different public and private sector agencies involved in our committees at different levels and gaining the commitment of the governors and mayors. Though we do not control bank credit, the active involvement of the Central Bank and allocation of funds for the program on special terms are developments we have influenced. That the funds for the program are channelled through NFAC has given us some clout. Unlike other government agencies, we have greater flexibility in reallocating our budget. Even the government auditors go along with us when we exceed certain limits of spending in view of the priority of the program.

Attracting good people and motivating them to work hard is extremely important to us. Presidential support is not enough to motivate performance at all levels. We have, for instance, the flexibility to hire high level personnel on contract terms which are better than what most government officials get. Similarly we are able to give our PTs a special incentive allowance. They were upgraded as "technologists" so that they got not only more money, but also status. Even when their own bureaus pull them, they know who the boss is. We provide inputs to the President on the performance of governors in respect of M-99 which I am sure will have some impact on the way they treat our program. We have an information system which gives us feedback on what is happening in the field. Thus, in spite of the limitations of our structure and the seeming conflicts and ambiguity underlying it, there are a few levers we can pull to tilt the balance in our favor.

Some of the key linkages needed to facilitate close coordination have been institutionalised. For instance, the Ministry of Agriculture had direct control only over extension. Credit and technology which are critical to M-99 were beyond its purview. When M-99 was launched, a Presidential Committee on Agricultural

Credit was created with the Central Bank Governor as chairman and the Secretary of Agriculture as vice-chairman. The committee had its own full time technical staff and met regularly to review credit problems relating to rice and other crops. Similarly, the newly created Philippine Council for Agricultural Research pulled together the key research agencies and focused their attention on national priorities. The head of the National Science Development Board was its chairman and the Secretary of Agriculture was the vice chairman. It allocated government research funds to institutions and was thus able to influence the direction and pace of research relevant to agriculture.

In preparing operational plans, overall guidelines were provided by NFAC. The decentralised structure of the program permitted a good deal of planning at the grass roots though in the early years NFAC had played a more dominant role. The Province was the key unit for this purpose, with the PPO acting as the nodal point for the process. He asked the PTs in the villages to indicate what targets were feasible and would goad them to aim higher if he thought the estimates were low. The PPO was asked by NFAC to propose goals, estimate input needs, loaning rates and solutions to the problems he foresaw - solutions which he would be responsible for implementing. The PAC was used as a forum for deliberating plans, targets and problems and to gain commitment from the Governor and the participating agencies. The PPO then entered into a negotiation with NFAC and reached a mutual agreement on the provincial plans for the forthcoming phase. The NFAC thus built up a national operational plan and derived from it the input requirements which needed to be planned on a national basis. The management information system of M-99 was a valuable source of field data for this purpose.

Management Information System

The MIS designed for M-99 was meant to generate timely data and reports on the progress of implementation of the program in order to facilitate mid-course correction and control. The basic data were collected by the PTs and the banks financing the farmers, collated by the PPO for each province, and processed by the MIS unit in NFAC headquarters. The national analysis of M-99 was furnished to NMC by the MIS unit and feedback copies were sent to the governors and the PACs for necessary follow-up action.

The PT would normally deliver his monthly field report personally to the PPO. The primary means of transmission of the report from the province to headquarters was by radio. A hard copy report was also sent by mail for file record purposes. The time lag for radio and telegraphic reports was usually about three days. When communications broke down, as happened during the rainy season in some regions, reports used to be delayed by more than a month. Despite these problems, NFAC usually would transmit its monthly summary report by the fifteenth of the following month to the NMC.

The reports were brief and related to data from which certain key indicators of progress could be readily estimated. The worksheets and reports of the PTs and PPOs were simple and brief. Computerisation of the central processing of data at NFAC was introduced only in 1976. The MIS data related not only to quantitative indicators such as loans and areas planted and harvested, but also to problems being faced in the field. The PTs and PPOs were given formal training in data collection and collation. Most of the data were to be gathered not by direct measurement, but by questioning others and making estimates on a judgemental bias. Some measure of personal bias was thus bound to be reflected in the information being reported. NFAC therefore had a system of periodic audit by teams which toured the country to observe, inspect and assess information in the field regarding program implementation.

Training, Development and Incentives

Given the nature of the technology to be diffused and the mobilisation of farmer response that was aimed at, it is not surprising that the program leadership devoted considerable attention to the training of personnel. To begin with, the core group of extension technicians involved in the Bulacan pilot project were used as trainers to acquaint the newly assigned PTs with the M-99 package of practices and supervised credit. Short training programs were organised at IRRI and UPLB for the large number of PTs recruited in the first year. Both IRRI and UPLB were involved in the preparation of training kits and extension materials. These institutions were also used extensively for the training of specialists in the program and the PPOs.

That many of the newly recruited PTs were young people, mostly trained in agricultural schools and colleges, was an advantage. They were receptive to new ideas and willing to try out different methods. They were perhaps more responsive to the challenge that the nation faced in the wake of the disaster of 1972-73 than older people used to the slow pace of the bureaucratic machinery. It is possible that their sense of commitment was strengthened by the higher status and remuneration made possible by the upgrading of their salary scale and designation. The incentive allowance and motorcycle loan given to the PTs would have reinforced their motivation to perform. While the publicity campaign through the media was used to attract the farmers towards the program, training, development and incentives may have been instrumental in motivating the field personnel to take advantage of the farmer's new awareness and mobilise his participation in the program.[7]

In Masagana-99, there was a critical need to win commitment from local governments. Traditionally, it was difficult for national programs to obtain this commitment because of the seperation of the national agency structures from those of the local bureaucracies. Often, they were in direct competition for the people's attention. The local government executives exercised no direct supervision over the field staffs of the national agencies

Though tea was a new crop to the small African farmers, many of them had become acquainted with tea growing and its income potential by working on the white settlers' estates. The pilot project had created a "demonstration effect" among the African farmers living in the Kenyan highlands which were extremely suitable for tea cultivation. Unlike annual or seasonal crops, tea was a "tree crop" which took three years from the time of planting to harvest and generate an income for the farmer. Thereafter, the tea plant was capable of yielding a regular income for several years continuously as tea leaves could be plucked regularly. The initial gestation period, however, meant that the farmer had to make a long term investment from which he could receive returns only after a lapse of at least three years.

Small farmer tea development was initiated in Kenya at a time when the international demand for tea was strong and the reputation of Kenyan tea was extremely good. Kenyan tea fetched premium prices in the international market though Kenya's market share was quite small. In 1955, Kenya produced only 19 million pounds of tea, whereas India and Ceylon produced 680 million and 380 million pounds respectively. By 1962, however, Kenya had doubled its production whereas India's tea output had increased only by 12 per cent, and Ceylon's by 20 per cent.[5] Since Kenya's share of the international tea market was relatively insignificant, its extremely high growth rates did not cause any major impact on the export front. The tea growers and companies in Kenya had found tea export extremely profitable and a source of steady and rising income. The average annual growth rate of production of all tea growing countries taken together was around 20 per cent during 1955-62.

In Kenya, the highlands on the eastern and western sides of the "Rift Valley" in the central part of the country were found to be well suited for tea growing. In all, KTDA identified 12 out of the 57 districts in the country as areas for the promotion of smallholder tea. Its program was confined to these 12 districts located in five provinces. These were also the areas where the large scale tea estates existed.

Detailed information on the strata of farmers who joined the KTDA program was not available. The legislative order which established KTDA defined smallholding as "a piece of land in any area on which a grower proposes to plant or to cultivate or is cultivating tea." No specification was laid down in terms of the acreage of the holding or the income levels of the farmer. It was known, however, that even a poor farmer had several acres of land on most of which he cultivated subsistence crops. The richer the farmer, the larger the proportion of his land that would be set apart for the cultivation of cash crops. Since cash crops were relatively new to the African farmer, the major goal of SCDA and its successor KTDA was to encourage farmers to grow tea on a one acre plot in his farm. Anything less than one acre was considered as unviable, both in terms of servicing the farmer and his costs of cultivation relative to the income earning capacity of the tea farm. An important step taken by the government in the fifties was to consolidate fragmented holdings. Considerable progress was made

in this direction by the time KTDA had come into being. A major
hurdle in the farmer's adoption of tea as a viable cash crop was
thus eliminated well in time.

KTDA's Services

The new government of Kenya was solidly behind the KTDA program.
The program was an important symbol of indigenisation, and economic
and political power. Its significance lay in the "access" provided
to the Africans to benefit from the modern agricultural sector. At
this stage, the government seemed little concerned about the relative distribution of benefits among the different strata of farmers
who responded to the program.

The most basic service provided by KTDA to its registered tea
growers was the supply of planting materials. KTDA had its own
nurseries from which it distributed tea "stumps" to the farmers in
different districts. In 1964, when the program was expanded, the
price per stump was 30 cents.[6] Farmers however were asked to pay
only 6 cents per stump, the balance being recovered through
deductions from their sales proceeds over a period of years. This
credit was available to the farmer only on the first 3,000 stumps
he bought. This was the number required to plant one acre of land.
Farmers were to prepare the land, space plantings, apply manure,
prune the plants, and pluck tea leaves according to the instructions
given by KTDA field staff. In the initial period, the minimum
number of stumps a farmer had to buy was 500. This would have cost
him Ks.30. The expectation was that he would continue to buy
stumps until he reached a minimum of one acre of tea. KTDA also
supplied fertiliser to the growers under credit. This amount again
was adjusted against his sales of tea to KTDA. Farmers were not
required to put up collaterals for receiving credit from KTDA.
Each grower was issued a license in respect of his plantings. KTDA
was anxious to control the number of growers and the extent of
their plantings. This control was considered important for two
reasons. First, unplanned expansion of supply could upset the
market and reduce Kenya's favourable international position.
Second, unauthorised expansion could hurt the economic viability of
tea cultivation and destroy the confidence of small farmers in the
new cash crop and its economic potential. The one acre norm was
also designed to discourage uneconomic holdings which were bound to
depress the farmers' profit margin.

Leaf collection operations were also organised and supervised
by KTDA through a network of buying centers. These centers were so
located that no farmer would have to carry his leaf collection for
more than $1\frac{1}{2}$ miles. After inspection, the leaf was purchased by
the field staff and transported to the factory for processing.
Growers were paid quarterly for their leaf at the beginning. From
1965, payments were made monthly. KTDA maintained an individual
account for each grower who received cash after deduction of cess
(levy) and repayment of credit received for fertiliser purchases.
An important role of the inspecting staff was to maintain quality
control. KTDA's policy was to purchase "two leaves and a bud",
the best quality of leaf. Leaf collections were transported by

lorries to the factories, all of which except one were privately owned in the sixties. KTDA negotiated the price of leaf with them, collected the sales proceeds and paid the farmers their share of the proceeds.

Field supervision was carried out by officers of the Department of Agriculture who were on full time attachment to the Authority. The latter reimbursed the government the entire cost of the seconded staff. The arrangements for the attachment and reimbursement of staff were set out in a supervision agreement between the government and KTDA. The only item of expenditure that the government incurred for KTDA was the construction and improvement of roads in the tea growing areas. This was done through the Ministry of Public Works. In 1965, the Authority opened two tea training schools which were designed to provide training to growers (one week courses) and also the training staff. The field staff, though seconded from the Ministry, could not be transferred without KTDA approval. The Authority thus had full control over the staff, even though technically they belonged to the Ministry.

CHANGES IN THE SEVENTIES

When KTDA was set up, both processing and marketing of tea were performed through private tea companies.[7] New factories were soon established with KTDA and CDC as equal shareholders. For this purpose, KTDA took commercial loans from private tea comapnies which in turn were appointed managing agents for the factories. There was also a provision for shareholdings by growers in these factory companies. Marketing of tea was the responsibility of the managing agents.

Eleven new factory units were set up by KTDA in the seventies. By 1979, practically all the factories which processed KTDA tea were owned by the Authority, CDC and growers. Marketing of tea was also taken over by KTDA. Thus by the late seventies, procurement, processing, and marketing of smallholder tea in Kenya were fully integrated and managed by KTDA. The locational decision concerning factories were made by the KTDA Board and growers were assigned to different factory units. The opening of new factories entailed hiving of green leaf producing areas from existing factory units or the transfer of leaf from estate factories to new KTDA factory units. In general, a new factory started with a minimum out-turn of .5 million pounds of made tea.[8] Each factory was ultimately to reach a throughput of 1.2 million pounds of made tea from plantings in its area.

Each factory unit was operated as a seperate financial undertaking. It had its own board of directors on which KTDA was represented. The factory made a first payment monthly to the Authority in respect of the leaf delivered to it. The Green Leaf Agreement between KTDA and the factories specified the rates of payment.[9] In respect of KTDA factory units, the surplus left after paying a dividend on the share capital (an average of 8 per cent) was passed on to the Authority which in turn distributed

this amount to the growers as a second payment. The financial
structure and dividend policy of KTDA factories were designed to
make them servicing units for the Authority so as to minimise the
conflict between dividends and second payments. Within the KTDA
framework, the factory units operated as profit centers with
accountability for results. KTDA had a trading relationship as
well as an ownership relationship with its factories.

KTDA was established as a corporate statutory body responsible
to the Minister for Agriculture and subject to his general or
specific directions. The field operations of KTDA were financed
in part by loans raised on commercial terms (from the Colonial
Development Corporation, later on known as the Commonwealth
Development Corporation)and in part by self generated revenues
through the levy of cesses on growers. Factories established for
processing tea were self contained units which were seperately
financed (in part by KTDA). Except for road construction, the
entire complex of tea development under the Authority was designed
to be a self financing entity. Though under the administrative
control of the Ministry of Agriculture, it received no funds from
the government budget. The Authority's accounts, however, were
examined and audited annually by the Controller and Auditor General
or any other person appointed by the Minister. The Minister was
required to lay the Authority's report, accounts and auditor's
report annually before the National Assembly.

ORGANISATION

As has already been noted, the Authority was managed by a Board,
the Chairman of which was appointed by the Minister. The General
Manager (chief executive officer) of KTDA, however, was appointed by
the Board. Growers were represented on the Board through a process
that involved the election of representatives at the divisional,
district, and regional levels. These committees were formalised
only after some experience was gained in operating the Authority.

The Working Party and other officials involved in setting up the
SCDA believed that careful and effective control was an important
consideration in managing any development program. They reasoned
that if African tea was to compete in the international market,
strict quality control was essential. Tea growing also required
careful husbanding and systematic harvesting and transportation.
Standardised practices could be planned and demonstrated, and
farmers could be trained to adopt them. Control was fundamental to
the entire process.

In the initial report that led to the creation of the smallholder
tea program, farmer representation at the Board level was mentioned
only briefly. When the Authority was created, however, the
importance of setting up committees with grower representatives was
better appreciated. Several reasons have been mentioned in this
connection.[10] First, there was a need to generate enthusiasm among
farmers for tea growing especially since the Authority wanted to
cover large areas previously untouched by the pilot project. Second,
the self financing nature of the new program meant that the policies

concerning the cess to be levied on green leaf had to be communica-
ted to and accepted by the farmers. The pilot project had been
heavily subsidised and it was feared that farmers would be upset
by the new financial arrangements. Committees would be a useful
forum to explain these changes. Third, grower representatives
could play a useful role in decisions on the number of plants to
be sold to each farmer and the selection of new growers. In other
words, in implementing the Authority's planting program, the tea
committees could play a consultative role.

Tea Committees

The tea committee system was introduced in 1961. The
divisional tea committee was set up at the sub district level where
registered growers would elect their representatives. This
committee was expected to be run with a minimum of official representation. Divisional committees would forward names of suitable
candidates for appointment to the district tea committee which had
the District Agricultural Officer as Chairman and the Tea Officer
as Secretary. The provincial tea board had both official and
growers' representatives proposed by the district tea committees.
Its Chairman was the Provincial Commissioner. Two members would
be selected from the provincial tea boards to represent growers on
the Board of the Authority. The selection process was compromised
somewhat by the Minister for Agriculture having the power of
appointment.

The view of the management of KTDA from the outset was that the
committees were purely advisory to the Authority. The functions
assigned to the committees were limited and the official members of
the committees (tea officer, etc.) tended to set the agenda and
structure the deliberations. The general view was that the committees were a means of communication between the Authority and
farmers, but that policy discussions were not within their purview.
The role of the committees and rules governing their conduct were
more clearly defined over the years. Thus in 1963, the composition
of the committee was widened to include both elected representatives and members coopted by the committee. The Divisional
Assistant Agricultural Officer was made a member of the divisional
tea committee. In 1964, the Authority further clarified the
functions of the committees. They had no jurisdiction over the
employment of staff, siting of factories, etc. They were to furnish
information on the views of growers to the Board and communicate
KTDA policies down to the growers. This division of labour, of
course, caused constant tension between the assertiveness of the
committees on the one hand, and the Head Office's determination to
play a dominant role on the other. The committees' central role
was in assisting the field staff in local allocations of stumps,
locating buying centers, mobilising farmers for sale of planting
materials, and enforcing regulations within their area. The
Authority also used the committees to test the feasibility and
acceptability of new ideas and often used their resources to
strengthen the case before the Board for proposed changes. KTDA

insisted all along that the committees were the only recognised channel for dealing with grower grievances. Whenever external pressures and interference appeared threatening, the support of committees could be used to neutralise them.

Though the committees were dominated by the Authority and its officials in the initial years, from 1964 onwards, a greater degree of openness prevailed. Africans became chairmen of the committees with the officials remaining as secretaries. The balance of power shifted to the elected as against coopted members and elections themselves determined the successful candidates. The tea election and cooption processes, however, meant that local chiefs, leaders, and the larger and more progressive farmers dominated the committees. The smaller, illiterate subsistence farmers were seldom elected or coopted nor were they organised enough to assert their interests. All members of the tea committee met together annually. Similarly, there was an annual conference of growers attended by thousands of farmers from different centers.

Organisational Structure

When KTDA was established, its primary task was the provision of stumps, extension, and credit to the farmer, leaf collection and transportation. The organisation was therefore divided into three divisions headed by a Chief Technical Officer (CTO), an Assistant General Manager (AGM) and a Chief Accountant (CA). The CTO was in charge of all field operations with tea officers and leaf officers reporting to him. The AGM was responsible for administration in the head office. The CA was in charge of all financial services including payments to farmers. The three heads reported to the General Manager who was the chief executive of the Authority. These positions were held by British officers at the outset, but most of them were filled by Africans in the early seventies. By 1978, there were only a handful of expatriates and they were in specialised technical jobs such as supervision of factory maintenance, design, and repairs.

The decision to set up tea factories and engage in export marketing was soon followed by important organisational changes. In addition to the CTO, a new AGM was created to look after leaf collection. The posts of a chief factory superintendent and a marketing officer were created to organise the new functions which the Authority had taken over. The new structure thus reflected a further differentiation of tasks within KTDA. Under the CTO, there were two senior tea officers to cover the tea districts east and west of the Rift Valley. They were responsible for all KTDA staff in their areas. There were 11 tea officers responsible for tea development in one administrative district.[11] Each tea officer had agricultural assistants reporting to him, one for 800 acres of tea planted. Below them were junior agricultural assistants, one for every 400 growers. The latter moved about on bicycles whereas the agricultural assistants went about on motor cycles. The tea officers were given land rovers to supervise their operations. The integration of the functions involved in tea development, leaf

collection, processing and marketing took place in the head office
through the General Manager. Training of the staff was given high
priority. KTDA had two well equipped training schools and research
facilities.

Centralisation and decentralisation

Towards the late seventies, several changes were introduced in
the organisational structure of KTDA. A major reform was the
creation of "group managers", one for every six factories. They
were to be located in the regions to help supervise the factories,
thus reducing the growing administrative burden on the head office.
The regional or group manager concept, however, was not adopted for
the leaf officers in the districts. As the General Manager
explained:

First of all, a great deal of standardisation is possible in
tea cultivation and processing - hence the limited degree of
decentralisation we have introduced so far. Once the cultural practices for different tea-growing climatic and soil
conditions do not change significantly. Our field staff can
teach the necessary practices to the farmers who then merely
follow the instructions on a repetitive basis. The leaf
officer's job again is highly standardised. We have a
centralised information system on leaf collection which enables
us in the head office to monitor and feed back to the field
staff relatively easily. There is, therefore, no need for
regional managers to supervise the leaf officers. The senior
tea officers are adequate for this purpose. Monthly reports
are received also from the tea officers and factory managers.
Central monitoring is an important function. Our reporting
formats are simple, yet efficient.

The problems at the factories are more complex. Though tea
processing also is standardised, there are problems of quality
variations, feedback from the market, prices and inventories,
etc., - matters which require consultations from time to time.
With 29 factories, coping with these problems from the head
office is not easy. Group managers therefore visit the
factories in their regions once a week to meet the factory
managers and solve any problems that crop up. The factory
manager is still in operational control of his establishment.

Once the number of tea growers stabilises and our extension
staff have done their job of training the farmers, there is
really no need to keep the field staff in the same strength.
The farmers will need only minimal assistance. Our hope is
that we can then revert most of the field staff back to the
Ministry of Agriculture from where they came in the first
place. KTDA may then focus chiefly on leaf collection, processing and marketing of tea. The Ministry may look after the
routine field operations needed by the tea growers.

Leaf officers were appointed, one for each KTDA factory base. Officers were appointed as new factories were erected or where the volume of leaf production in an area justified an earlier appointment. If an area was without a leaf officer, the local tea officer performed inspection and collection duties also. Under the leaf officers were inspectors, buying clerks, and lorry drivers.

The extension staff in KTDA were seconded from the Ministry of Agriculture where they held permanent positions. Some have since left government service and have joined KTDA as regular employees. Those on secondment from the Ministry were paid an incentive allowance by KTDA which also reimbursed the government their normal salaries and other benefits. The administrative control over the staff remained with KTDA which could ask the government to recall employees whose performance was found to be unsatisfactory. Though the secondment practice has caused some problems for KTDA, no serious effort to change the system has been considered. The fact that most of the staff have stayed on with KTDA was regarded as evidence of their long term commitment.

PERFORMANCE

On KTDA's progress and performance, Mr Karanja, General Manager spoke as follows:

Though we have been set up as a semi-autonomous body, it is not difficult for the government to interfere if it wants to. We do not need government funds, but still require government support and facilities for many of our tasks. The fact that our performance is good is a factor that minimises the need for interference. Also the support of farmers is a key element. Our focus has been on servicing the small farmer. He recognises the benefits of KTDA. He is solidly behind us. This is a major source of strength. We in Kenya have had a lot of problems with cooperatives. Our tea committees play only an advisory role, yet they have operated better than cooperatives. We emphasise farmer training a great deal. We hold national exhibitions and present awards to the best farmers. We recognise and encourage merit.

The presence of the CDC representative has been a positive influence on our autonomy. CDC is our major creditor and has no parochial interest. More recently, the involvement of the World Bank has reinforced the same trend. Within the organisation, the loyalty and team work of our officers have been a great help. On the whole we have been able to create a result oriented approach and develop a good system for monitoring performance. As we expand, greater strains are felt in the organisation. Our monetary benefits are somewhat better than in Government, but nowhere near what the private sector provides.

Mr. Karanja, who has been General Manager for several years, joined the KTDA in 1964 as an engineer. He was held in high regard by his colleagues for his technical competence, leadership, and organisational commitment. He was the **second** African General Manager of KTDA.

External evaluation of KTDA as well as market indicators provide mutually reinforcing data on the program's performance. A report by the World Bank says: [12]

The smallholder tea project in Kenya which IDA helped to finance not only had a very high rate of economic return, but also allowed a large number of subsistence farmers to participate in the market economy. This success is especially remarkable in light of the difficulties experienced by this type of scheme in some other countries.

Many other observers also regard the KTDA as a highly success-ful agricultural program. The following testimony is by a scholar who has done considerable research on KTDA and other rural programs in East Africa:[13]

The Kenya Tea Development Authority is one of the most successful agricultural development programs in sub-Saharan Africa. Unlike resettlement schemes such as the Gezira in the Sudan or the Ujaama villages in Tanzania, the Authority has introduced a new cash crop among widely scattered small farmers within the former African reserves of Kenya. Its achievement seems all the more remarkable in that it has introduced a technically demanding estate crop as a viable smallholder enterprise. Utilising an integrated approach to agricultural development, that is the provision of a wide range of services for the farmer within one institutional framework, the Authority has staked a leading position within the world tea industry.

KTDA's success has many facets. It has contributed to the reduction of rural poverty. The average annual income of a typical KTDA grower (who owns 0.32 hectares of mature tea) is about K.Sh.1,300 ($185) compared with an average agricultural income of about K.Sh.420 ($60) in Kenya. At the same time, KTDA achieved an estimated 28 per cent return on investment. KTDA contributed technological and organisational developments now being copied by other development agencies. Until recently, tea has been essentially an estate crop. To make it a viable smallholder crop, KTDA had to determine the right size plots for smallholders; develop a complex network for leaf collection and transport with tight scheduling; establish appropriate incentives, controls and payment systems for out-growers; determine the right size and location of factories; develop better tea plants; and set up an effective, disciplined extension service.

62

Quality, which is reflected in the premium paid over average
world market price, had to be controlled. In 1959, Kenyan teas
were 14 per cent below the London average price; in 1966 they
surpassed the average, and in 1971 were the world's highest (6 per
cent above the London average). Since then they have been in the
top three. To achieve such improvements, KTDA management had to
emphasise quality control at many points in growing, plucking,
transporting and marketing its tea.

Also significant is its record of planned growth. It has hit
or exceeded its targets with remarkable consistency. It grew from
1,000 hectares in 1959 to 50,000 hectares farmed by 130,000 growers
in 1980. While Kenyan tea estates continued to expand each year,
KTDA moved from 6 per cent of Kenyan tea exports in 1959 to 50 per
cent in 1979.

NOTES

1. T. Eden, Tea, Longmans, Green & Co., London, 1965, p.3.
2. Ibid. Tea has been used as a beverage in China for nearly
2,000-3,000 years.
3. One interpretation was that the British wanted to create a
sense of goodwill among the Africans on the eve of the transfer of
power. Tea was a crop with a future and a program could be
developed to introduce African farmers to the new crop which white
settlers could no longer monopolise in independent Kenya.
4. For details of the legislation, see the Agriculture (Kenya
Tea Development Authority) Order, L.N. 42, 1964, and amended in
1965, 1966 and 1967.
5. Eden, op.cit.
6. One Kenyan shilling equals 100 cents. One US dollar is
equal to 7.5 K.shillings. Stumps are grown in nurseries by
germinating tea seeds.
7. Except for Ragati factory which was owned by the Authority.
The CDC was the first international lender to KTDA. In later years,
the World Bank also gave major loans to the Authority.
8. Made tea is the technical term for processed tea.
9. The initial rate was 40 cents per pound of green leaf.
10. J. Steeves, Structure of Participation in Agricultural
Development, (mimeo, undated)
11. One officer had two districts in his charge. However,
these officers had no formal control over the Lead Officers in
their areas. The latter reported directly to an AGM in the Head
Office.
12. International Bank for Reconstruction and Development :
Performance Audit of the First Kenya Tea Project (Report No.343,
Washington DC, 1974, p.12). IDA refers to the International
Development Association of the World Bank.
13. J. Steeves: "Farmers, Stratification and Tea Development
in Kenya" (mimeo., undated). A similar view has been expressed
by J.R. Moris; see his paper "Managerial Structures and Plan
Implementation", in D. Leonard (ed.), Rural Administration in Kenya
Nairobi, 1973.

5
The Indonesian Population Program

The early initiative for organising a family planning program in Indonesia came from community leaders and influential women's groups. In 1957, the Indonesian Planned Parenthood Association came into being as a voluntary organisation mainly confined to the provision of family planning services in urban areas. It expanded its activities despite the lack of government support, but had to cease its operations during the political and economic convulsions that gripped the country in the mid sixties. With the transfer of power from Sukarno to General Suharto in 1966, a major shift took place in the attitude of the government towards population control. The two decades of government disapproval of family planning thus came to an end, paving the way for adoption of family planning as an official government policy in 1970.

There are three criteria by which the performance of a family planning program could be judged. First, there is the creation of a distribution network through which the program establishes contact points. The second criterion is the program's success in attracting contraceptive users, and the third is its impact on the reduction of fertility. There is considerable evidence today that the Indonesian Population Program has done outstandingly well on all three counts.

By 1978, the Indonesian Program had created an impressive number of outlets in the country for the supply of modern contraceptives (2,750 clinics and 7,000 field workers). At the village level, supply depots were created and 25,000 village family planning groups organised in order to provide services to users in the rural areas, far away from the clinics. By March 1979, these contact points had recruited nearly 13 million new acceptors, resulting in over 5.5 million current users. This represented 30 per cent of the married women of reproductive age in Indonesia. The reliability of this estimate has been checked by the independent World Fertility Survey which revealed that in 1976 the proportion of married women of reproductive age who were users of contraceptives was 23.4 per cent. For the same year, the Program Agency's estimate was 20.8 per cent. As regards the methods in vogue, nearly 25 per cent of acceptors used IUD. About two thirds were users of oral pills and the remaining used other methods such as condoms.

63

An independent estimate based on the World Fertility Survey data has shown that about 25 per cent of the decline in fertility in Indonesia (a decline of 23 per cent of the crude birthrate) is due to an increase in the marriageable age. Though it is difficult to attribute the remaining 75 per cent of the fertility decline to the family planning program alone, observers believe that the latter has had a major impact since the explanation had to be sought in reductions in fertility within marriage.[1]

In a period of five years, the average rate of child-bearing (the total fertility rate) had dropped by over a third in Bali. The comparable percentages in Central Java and East Java were 17 and 15 per cent respectively. The proportion of married women of reproductive age who reported current contraceptive use ranged from West Java's 17 per cent to 30 per cent in Bali and 43 per cent in Yogyakarta. By 1979, nearly three fourths of all women of reproductive age seem to have registered as acceptors at some time or other in the course of the program's operation. Very few countries at similar levels of socio-economic development have achieved such remarkable results in so short a time.

A comparison of population programs in Asia has shown that the per capita average expenditure of the Indonesian program during 1970-77 was 14 cents.[2] Both Bangladesh and Thailand had lower costs with 10 and 9 cents respectively. India had a per capita cost of 14 cents, whereas Pakistan, Korea, and Philippines had costs of 19, 24, and 34 cents respectively.

THE BEGINNING

Indonesia is the world's fifth most populous nation and a 3,400 mile long archipalego made up of five major and numerous smaller islands. It is located in the humid tropics, stretching from the Indian Ocean to the Pacific, and has a population of 135 million people whose per capita income is $ 200. Two thirds of the country's predominantly Muslim population live on the island of Java, which has less than 7 per cent of Indonesia's land area. The adjacent island of Bali, with a predominantly Hindu population of 2.4 million and a population density of 1,100 per square mile is another overcrowded part of the country. All other islands (known as Outer Islands) are sparsely populated, but have not so far provided any relief to the overcrowding of Java in spite of the transmigration policy of the government (redistribution of population) during the colonial and the post-colonial periods. The annual population growth rate of Indonesia has been estimated to be 2 per cent or more for the past quarter of a century. An Indonesian demographer predicted in 1970 that even a net out-migration of 2,00,000 Javanese annually (more than ten times the actual figure for 1970) would put Java's population in 1991 only 7 per cent below the total to be expected in the absence of out-migration.

An important turning point in Indonesia's population policy came in 1967 when President Suharto and 29 other world leaders signed the United Nations Declaration on Population which recognised the determination of the number and spacing of children as a basic human right. In his Independence Day speech in the same year, the

President declared that Indonesia would pay serious attention to the challenge of population control. The Planned Parenthood Association reopened and expanded its services, encouraged by the positive signals emanating from the highest levels in government.

The government set up an ad hoc committee in 1968 to recommend action in respect of population control. The Committee recommended the establishment of a national family planning program with emphasis on contraceptive distribution in Java and Bali, the most populous islands of the country. It further proposed that the program should begin with the large cities, then proceed to cover the smaller urban areas and only then take up the rural areas. This proposal, however, was ignored by the government which decided that the program would move simultaneously into the urban and rural areas of Java and Bali. This decision was influenced by the belief that the rural poor had the highest fertility.[3]

In pursuance of the ad hoc Committee's recommendation, the government established a National Family Planning Institute (LKBN) in 1968, as part of the Ministry of Health. Organized as a semi-official agency with public and private sector representatives and leaders as members of its council, it soon began to take over the activities of the voluntary Planned Parenthood Association which, henceforth, devoted its attention increasingly to training, research and evaluation, and promotion. By 1969, LKBN was in full control of all family planning services in Java and Bali. The focus, however, was on the role of family planning in mother and child welfare rather than fertility control.

A New Coordinating Board

An important influence on government policy during this period was the report of a mission of experts in 1969 sponsored by the UN, the World Bank, and WHO. The mission pointed out the limitations of the existing program, especially its deficiencies in terms of organisation and administration. It recommended a more ambitious program and the involvement of government on a massive scale through a central agency with branches at regional and local levels. Many of these recommendations were accepted by President Suharto who then proceeded to transform LKBN into the National Family Planning Coordinating Board (BKKBN) reporting directly to him and fully responsible for all government activities in family planning. BKKBN was thus established as a full fledged government agency of an inter-ministerial nature through a series of presidential decrees in 1970. Family Planning was now seen as an integral part of Indonesia's development strategy, a program with strong commitment and support from the President.

Deliberate attempts to win over Islamic leaders were among the early actions taken by the new family planning program agencies set up by the government. In the late sixties, LKBN published endorsements of family planning from Islamic religious leaders. The first national symbol of the program featured a father, mother and four children (two boys and two girls) and LKBN highlighted the "welfare of mother and child" as its major theme. There was no

mention of fertility control during this period. A group of
provincial governors and ulamas (Islamic religious leaders) were
sent to Tunisia and Egypt to get acquainted with their family
planning programs. It was felt that the approaches of these two
Islamic nations would have a positive influence on the thinking of
the Indonesian Muslim leaders. In 1972, the BKKBN organised a well
publicised conference of ulamas who declared that family planning
was not against the teachings of the Koran. Special efforts were
made by BKKBN officials to meet the local religious leaders and
teachers in different regions and to give them a place in the local
activities of the Board. Similarly, BKKBN had consulted and
involved local leaders, officials, and elders in planning and
implementing its local programs.

The choice of contraceptive technology in the early seventies
also reflected similar concerns. No attempt was made to popularise
sterilisation. IUD's adoption was encouraged in Bali which had a
predominantly Hindu population. The program's mainstay was oral
contraceptives as they were more acceptable, and easier to use,
though there were problems in ensuring their supply on a regular
basis over widely scattered areas. There were voluntary efforts
to encourage sterilisation, but BKKBN had deliberately kept away
from this movement. The focus on "fertility control" as an explicit
goal of the program was given visibility only after assurance of
adequate support from Islamic leaders.

Though family planning activities were initiated in urban areas
at the outset, they soon covered rural areas too. However, BKKBN
decided as a matter of policy, to concentrate its efforts in the
six provinces of Java and Bali to begin with. These were the areas
which were most overcrowded and seemed more ready to yield results.
In 1974, BKKBN extended its program to ten outer islands.[4] Though
geographically larger, they were much less populated and the
infrastructure facilities were less developed. In 1979, it was
decided to extend the program to the remaining eleven outer islands
also. Thus, by the end of the seventies, the program had expanded
significantly and covered the entire country.

Field Experiments

BKKBN did not go through a formal pilot project phase. The only
experience in the country came from the work done by the Planned
Parenthood Association in its 116 clinics, most of which were urban.
The general approach adopted by BKKBN from the beginning was to
conduct field experiments, the results of which were fed into the
program as it expanded. Thus, the use of field workers was first
tested in pilot areas across Java and Bali. This permitted the
program to try out high risk ideas and fine tune the program to suit
local conditions. When an experiment generated useful innovations,
they were replicated on a national basis. It is significant that
the program did not make use of any large pilot project conceived
outside of Indonesia.

Undertaking field experiments in different regions involved
extensive use of and speedy availability of funds. Though there
were government constraints on the use of public funds, an arrange-

ment was worked out with USAID whereby aid funds were provided for this purpose expeditiously. This permitted BKKBN to respond to local ideas and initiatives quickly and speed up the pace of in-house research and development. In all these R & D experiments, a common feature was the strong support provided by the national program to local initiative and the close linkages with regional offices maintained by the central office of BKKBN.

BEYOND THE CLINIC

LKBN, the predecessor of BKKBN, was created as a part of the Ministry of Health. BKKBN, on the other hand, was set up as a coordinating board outside the Ministry of Health. Population and family planning were no longer interpreted as health problems in the narrow sense. Health was treated as one of the ministries to be coordinated by BKKBN along with several other ministries such as Education, Information, Religion and Interior whose inputs were regarded as critical to the success of the family planning program.

In its delivery of services, however, BKKBN followed the conventional practice of operating through the health clinics in the field. Clients were expected to visit clinics in order to receive family planning services and supplies. Family planning "field workers" attached to the clinics would move out into the villages to motivate couples to seek services at the clinics. To some extent, use was also made of "travelling medical teams" which visited remote areas in jeeps to offer family planning services. By 1974, these services were being provided through 2400 clinics across Java and Bali.

BKKBN officials noticed several important developments during the early phase of the program. In Java, the most populous island, couples were increasingly turning towards the pill and to a lesser extent the condom. The use of IUD, on the other hand, was declining rapidly.[5] Eventhough field workers and clinics were paid an incentive to attract IUD acceptors, this method was selected by fewer acceptors. Both the pill and condom, however, were methods critically dependent on "resupply" for effective use. Resupply to large numbers of users scattered over wide areas was bound to be extremely difficult as the clinics were limited in number. Given the magnitude of eligible couples to be reached (14 million in Java and Bali in 1974) and the number of villages (22,000) to be served, it would have been an uphill task for the government to provide the needed services exclusively through the official structure and personnel. The funds and trained manpower required would be immense, whereas the resources available were limited. To cap it all, field reports began to show evidence of a rate of decline in new acceptors. This tendency to "plateau out" was similar to what had been observed in other national programs. BKKBN meanwhile had set for itself the ambitious goal of reducing national fertility by 50 per cent by the turn of the century ! A new strategy to move beyond the clinic was clearly in order.

Community Participation

The establishment of village contraceptive distribution center (VCDC) in 1975 provided an important response to the challenge faced by BKKBN in its first phase of operation. The concept emerged out of field experiments in which several alternative answers were tried out. The initial success came from Bali where the provincial BKKBN started in late 1974 by training the leaders of 50 banjars (village community organisations) in family planning tactics. In addition to extending their outreach, BKKBN officials hoped to improve follow up and record keeping by involving the banjars. As the village communities became more aware of and involved in fertility control issues, it was hoped that banjar members would identify new acceptors, mutually assist in case of side effects, and generally make family planning part of their own common activities. And it worked!

In 1975, BKKBN extended training to 400 more banjars. By 1976, all 3,700 banjars in 564 villages had been involved in the family planning program. During the monthly meetings of the male heads of households, community issues such as taxes, irrigation, disputes, and festivals used to be discussed and resolved through group consensus. Now family planning was also added as an additional topic for community deliberation and increasing responsibility was placed on the hamlet's administrative structure for managing its own family planning services. Each head of a household, for example, was required to report publicly the family planning and pregnancy status of every married woman in his household. Banjar registers were compiled listing all eligible couples, their location, use of contraception, and information of their receipt of pill and condom resupplies. The actual provision of resupplies became a banjar responsibility and an item for discussion at the monthly meeting.[6] Maps of the banjar were drawn which identified each household according to its eligibility for and use of contraception by method, and these were prominently displayed in the banjar meeting hall.

In West Java, resupply was a serious problem because of the limited number of clinics and the widely scattered location of villages in remote areas. In 1974, a small R&D project was launched in West Java to test a variety of methods for introducing contraceptive resupply in the village. The most workable solution was found to be a resupply depot set up in the home of an acceptor who was also an informal village leader.[7] The field worker would bring the monthly supplies from the clinic and deliver them to the depot and also review the depot holder's record keeping and any complaints received during the preceding month. By 1976, 1,600 VCDCs were established in West Java.[8] From the village, supplies were taken to the kampongs (hamlets) by leaders (volunteers) elected from each kampong. These volunteers provided their services free, whereas a small honorarium was received by the depot holder on a monthly basis.

VCDCs were established in East Java by the order of the
provincial Governor in 1974. The VCDC operator was usually a
member of the village headman's staff. His duties were contraceptive resupply and acceptor follow up and maintenance. In some
villages, a "pill day" was organised each month when women would
assemble for resupply. Each woman would receive her monthly
supply of pills from the operator for a payment of 35 Rupiah
(about 9 U.S.cents). She would be asked if she had any problems.
If she needed help, she was then turned over to the nurse-midwife
who visited the village on pill day.

Of the 35 rupiah taken from an acceptor, 10 were left for the
costs of record keeping and the balance was added to a lottery
fund. One person won a prize each month out of the fund and every
one got her turn to win. In this system, the luckiest got her
full investment in the very first month. The lottery thus acted
as a magnet for new acceptors, especially younger women.

In Central Java, VCDCs expanded rapidly in 1975 with central
funding. The village distributor was usually a member of the
village headman's staff. This person would assume responsibility
for contraceptive resupply and maintaining records which were
coordinated with the clinic. The field workers played an important
role in getting the supplies to the VCDCs and supporting the
distributors' efforts. In Central Java, if a woman failed to
appear for her monthly supply, the VCDC operator would sometimes
deliver the supplies at her home. Both in Central Java and West
Java, sub-village level family planning groups of women were
organised around the concept of sending a volunteer to the VCDC to
obtain monthly contraceptive supplies. These groups have ventured
into other common activities such as sewing, cooking, nutrition
courses, and poultry cooperatives.

The VCDCs or family planning posts and hamlet acceptor groups
thus became the basic building blocks around which BKKBN tried to
create a community awareness of the benefits of the small family
norm and develop the local capability to manage family planning
activities. While the official program with its fieldworkers at
the grass roots was able to develop and guide community participation in family planning activities in Java and Bali, a similar
approach was not attempted in the outer islands where field workers
were not employed. Here the responsibility for the program was
vested in the government structure, the focal point being the sub-
district leader whose task was to get communities involved in the
program's activities. BKKBN mounted a massive training program
for teams of officials from the outer island provinces to secure
their commitment and orientation to their new tasks and roles.

With Bali in the lead, nearly 45,000 VCDCs and sub-village
contraceptive outlets had been set up by 1978. The role of the
field workers had also undergone a major change in the process.
His role in supervising the village volunteers began to assume
greater importance. The village family planning model was by no
means a standard innovation. It had been adopted in different ways
to suit local circumstances. But in all cases, the contraceptive
outlets in villages were linked to a "mother clinic" which was thus

able to exercise some control and supervision over program
activities in the villages.

Contraceptive Supplies

The expansion of the program through the massive network of
VCDCs and hamlet depots had important implications for the
logistical system for contraceptive supplies. Adequate quantities
of pills, ·condoms, etc., were imported and stocked at the
provincial, clinic, and village levels. It has been estimated
that six months stocks were maintained at the provincial and
clinic levels. Studies have shown that stocks in villages were
low and that clinics supplied VCDCs on a regular basis. The in-
country inventory of supplies were adequate for 18 months'
consumption at any given time.[9] USAID was responsible for providing assistance to BKKBN in its planning and stocking of contraceptive supplies. Plentiful supplies, on the whole, averted
crises due to shortages common in many programs. More importantly,
adequate inventories helped avoid what has been termed "the cookie
jar phenomenon". Like children who hesitate to take a handful of
cookies when the jar is nearly empty, short stocked central
officials would normally be reluctant to send supplies to the
provinces for fear of depleting their own stocks. On the other
hand, the "overflowing cookie jar" encouraged the officials to
speed up supplies to the provinces and clinics. Local officials
and clinics did not have to make routine requests for supplies.

ORGANISATIONAL STRUCTURE

The establishment of BKKBN in 1970 signified important changes
not only in the country's strategy for planning population
activities but also in the organisational structure for implementing them. Unlike LKBN, the new Board was set up as a semi-
autonomous government board with its chairman reporting directly
to the President of the country and with strong linkages with the
key ministries through which the family planning program was to be
implemented. The ministries involved were Health, Education,
Information, Interior, and Religion. The Presidential Decrees of
1970 designated BKKBN as the agency responsible for the government's family planning activities and services, authorised it to
plan and finance all these activities and services, and enjoined
other ministries and public and private agencies to cooperate with
BKKBN in this national endeavour.

The Decree also established an Advisory Council to the President consisting of the chairman of BKKBN, the ministers in charge
of the departments/ministries involved in the implementation of
the program as well as the chairman of the National Planning
Agency (BAPENAS) and the head of the Planned Parenthood Association. The Decree provided that BKKBN would have two deputy
chairmen, one to look after training, research, information, and
motivation, and the other with responsibility for contraceptive
services, logistics, and reporting. There were three bureaus

under each deputy responsible for the different functions mentioned above.

BKKBN had its offices in the provinces and districts. The provincial chairmen of BKKBN were responsible for the program in their jurisdiction and reported directly to the chairman of BKKBN. They liaised closely with the governors and officials of the cooperating ministries in the provinces and provided them technical support and advice as required. BKKBN officials in the district had a direct reporting relationship to their provincial chairman, but worked closely with the district authorities in the same manner as the chairman did at the provincial level. In other words, the field officials of BKKBN acted as staff advisors to the provincial governor and district head who had overall responsibility for the family planning program in their jurisdiction.

At the sub-district level where the clinics existed, BKKBN was represented by the field workers. The latter were attached to the clinics which belonged to the Ministry of Health. At this level, there was only one BKKBN official to supervise the work of the field workers in the area. A district office typically had a staff of 25 whereas the BKKBN provincial offices had on the average a staff strength of 90. The bureaus in the head office provided technical support and advice to the field staff through the provincial offices.

In the mid seventies an important change took place in the field structure of BKKBN. The village contraceptive distribution center (VCDC) was set up and a new breed of field operators known as "volunteers" joined the program. In many provinces, the volunteers linked the clinic and VCDC to "acceptor groups" at the sub-village level. The program at the grassroots moved away from the clinic to the interface between the VCDCs and acceptor or community groups mediated by the volunteers and reinforced by the village level field workers. Meanwhile, at the BKKBN head office, a third deputy chairman was added by a Decree in 1972 who would be responsible for dealing with the management problems of the expanding national program.

The Presidential Decree of 1978 modified the structure of BKKBN still further. The functions of the deputies and their bureaus were reorganised so that one deputy could look after all activities concerning the family planning program. Another deputy was put in charge of the new population activities beyond family planning such as nutrition. Two other deputies were made responsible for common administrative and management services and general affairs. The post of a vice-chairman to assist the chairman who had meanwhile become the Minister for Health was also provided for by the Decree.

In this rather complicated structure, BKKBN had to operate with several ministries, provincial governors, district authorities, and community organisations over which it had no direct control. It did, however, provide the funds needed by the collaborating agencies (both public and private) and functionaries who were responsible for different aspects of the program. Thus the contraceptive supplies distributed through the clinics were under BKKBN's control.

It provided the funds and the logistical support needed by the
governors and also finance for educational materials and information programs organised by the Ministries of Education and
Information. The key instrument for mobilising public response at
the grassroots, namely, the village field workers, were employed
and paid for exclusively by BKKBN.

Nature of Autonomy

Though BKKBN was a full fledged government agency, it was
characterised by some features not found in other government
organisations. It was one of the few organisations which was
permitted by the government to directly receive funds from international agencies without having to go through the cumbersome
procedures for approval. As a result, BKKBN was able to utilise
foreign donor assistance without operational control by the
planning ministry. The response of the donor agencies also
facilitated this process and enlarged the flexibility that BKKBN
already enjoyed. One of the donors, for example, through a
careful delegation of powers to its local staff, enabled BKKBN to
devise and operate an extremely fast and flexible funding
procedure. It was able to respond speedily to requests from the
provinces to undertake field experiments largely because of the
availability of donor funds which could be moved directly to the
provinces at short notice. Dependence on government funds and
procedures for clearance would normally have delayed this process
considerably.

The use of donor funds for importing contraceptive supplies
in bulk also was a move in the same direction. These imports were
used to maintain seemingly high inventory levels of contraceptive
supplies in the provincial headquarters and clinics. Normal
government import procedures and stocking practices were not
followed by BKKBN as it was anxious to maintain a strong and
decentralised supply system to serve its national program.

Normally, BKKBN would have had to recruit its staff through its
parent ministry (in this case, the President's office), as its
chairman did not have the rank of a minister. However, as a
special case, the chairman was given the authority to select and
appoint the staff of the agency without having to get the
approval of any other ministry. The constraints in the government's salary scales applied to BKKBN also. However, special
incentive allowances were permitted in order to attract the
required quality of staff.

BKKBN was subject to the discipline of the Planning Ministry
(BAPENAS) for receiving government funds. Budgetary allocations
were made on the basis of its plans, proposals, and their
rationale. It was customary for BAPENAS to cut budgetary requests
and delay approvals as it had to deal with a multitude of requests.
It was believed, however, that BKKBN generally tended to receive
most of what it wanted, largely because its careful planning and
good record of performance impressed the planning agency and
facilitated a positive and speedy response to its requests.

A number of the professionals who assumed leadership positions were young persons drawn from a variety of backgrounds. Also, most of them had field experience as they came from the private Planned Parenthood Association which was an active and highly committed organisation. The chairman of BKKBN, Dr Suwardjono, was an experienced doctor from the army who had worked in the field of family planning earlier. He was known for his ability and willingness to delegate and encourage colleagues to try out new ideas. The training of village midwives in family planning services, the incorporation of family planning ideas in the stories of puppeteers of traditional drama and the condom-by-mail service were evidence of the experimental approach he nurtured in BKKBN.

In 1978, Dr Suwardjono was appointed Minister of Health by President Suharto. In the same year, BKKBN initiated a program to improve the nutrition of children. The government felt that BKKBN with its vast network of field workers and close links with village communities could play this role better than an entirely new organisation created for this purpose. A number of pilot projects on nutrition were in progress in 1979.

COPING WITH IMPLEMENTATION

One of the more controversial aspects of BKKBN's operations was its target system designed to guide and motivate its personnel to achieve rising levels of performance. BKKBN's head office, which played a key role in this process, had been criticised for creating a "target fever" that sent its village level officials rushing down to collect acceptors towards the end of the financial year. There had been comments from field workers and clinics on the insensitive pressures being put on them by the higher authorities. These reactions led to some rethinking on the manner in which planning was to be done.[10]

Planning and Control

BKKBN's more recent practice has been to negotiate with the provincial authorities on the annual target to be achieved. There is an annual planning conference wherein commitments are made by the governors and the provincial BKKBN officials on the operational goals for the forthcoming year. The provincial officials would have consulted with the district and village functionaries and sized up what is achievable. BKKBN, on its part, wouldhave estimated the number and percentages of the new acceptors of pills, IUDs, etc., needed to achieve the stated aim of a 50 per cent national decline in fertility by the year 2000. This method mix target had given the BKKBN a basis for negotiating with the governors and other local officials. The final agreement on targets arrived at, however, was the result of a "consensus building" process for which Indonesians are reputed. There was clearly a certain degree of bargaining, but finally, all the participants would have committed themselves to a mutually agreeable goal.

The same approach was used for the review of performance.
There was an annual meeting at the national level to review progress
and modify targets. No special sanctity was attached to targets.
They were used more as a guide to action. Thus, there was a great
deal of flexibility at the village level where the headman and
community leaders played a major role in determining what could be
achieved and then proceeded to take necessary action. Apart from
the information system, frequent field visits were the means used
by BKKBN officials to understand operational problems, modify
targets, and take timely corrective action. At the national level,
President Suharto had followed the practice of asking questions
about the family planning program at his cabinet meetings.

Information and Monitoring Systems

The basic data source of BKKBN was the monthly clinic report.
The major items on which clinics reported were new acceptors by
method, and contraceptive supplies distributed. Based on these
reports, the BKKBN Reporting and Evaluation Bureau would estimate
the number of current active users of oral contraceptives and
condoms. Similarly, an estimate of active IUD users would be made
by applying province specific continuation rates derived from the
acceptor survey data.

The Central Evaluation Bureau had a staff of 20 members, and
computerised data processing was contracted out to a private firm.
The Bureau had been producing a variety of reports and high
priority was attached to the dissemination of findings to the
provinces and clinics within one month. To ensure speedy processing, the Bureau would watch the timeliness of clinic reporting
closely. In February 1979, for example, 96 per cent of the clinics
in Java and Bali and 78 per cent of the clinics in the Outer
Islands had sent in their reports within 12 days after the end of
the month. Non-reporting for the year was only 1 per cent and 7
per cent respectively.

The volume of data collected and processed by the Bureau was
kept deliberately small and the focus was on a small set of
variables. The information system was designed to generate client
specific information and not for extensive demographic analysis.
BKKBN with the cooperation of the Indonesian Postal Service had
also introduced prepaid stamped envelopes to be used by clinics in
order to simplify and speed up the dispatch of clinic reports from
the field. The village family planning resupply posts did not
submit monthly reports to the clinics. It was assumed that the
oral contraceptives distributed to the users were actually delivered to the users. Each village post volunteer, however, maintained
a register of the village's eligible couples and a month-by-month
record of pregnancy status and contraceptives received.

The orientation of the information system to the needs of the
program could be gauged from the manner in which its output was
being used. Each administrative level received reports which
described the performance of all the lower level units under its
authority. The reports showed subordinate units ranked by

performance, maintaining the focus on results. Review meetings
at different levels would then make use of these reports. The
basic reliability of the data system was substantiated by the
findings of the World Fertility Survey which corroborated BKKBN's
estimates for 1976. Field visits and cross checks by higher level
officials were undertaken both to keep false reporting under
control and to facilitate problem solving on the spot.

A special feature of the reporting system was the checking of
clinic reports against the tear off sections from each acceptor
record card which were also sent monthly to the central office.
This practice enabled the central office to reprimand clinics which
made exaggerated claims about a larger number of acceptors than
could be accounted for by the tear offs received. As for the local
officials, the system permitted them to compare their district's
progress with that of others and provided them a basis for
requesting more resources and other assistance.

The information system had provided the basic data needed by
BKKBN to engage in an ongoing monitoring and evaluation of the
program. Thus periodic publication of new acceptor characteristics
such as age, number of children, education, etc., was used to
monitor the trends in the type of acceptors participating in the
program. This had been supplemented by ad hoc research surveys
and publication of their results. BKKBN officials once became
concerned about the charges that the influential Chinese minority
(2.5 per cent of the country's population) was resisting family
planning. Field workers believed that Chinese neighborhoods were
difficult to penetrate. Special surveys soon revealed, however,
that the Chinese were in fact more likely than indigenous groups
to use contraceptives, but received their supplies from private
physicians or drug stores. These findings were widely publicised
to allay unhealthy rumors and led BKKBN to hire Chinese field
workers to work in the more difficult Chinese neighborhoods.

Training and Development

In 1979, BKKBN had a permanent staff of 5,000 people in the
head office and regional and district offices. In addition, there
were 7,000 full time village level field workers who were treated
as temporary workers. The program had begun in 1970 with 150
field workers in pilot areas in Bali and Java. Though temporary by
appointment and receiving rather low wages, the field workers have
been described by observers as an enthusiastic and hardworking lot.
Equipped with field uniform, raincoat, umbrella and bicycle, they
moved about daily in search of "acceptors". Generally, they were
local people working in their own areas and therefore acquainted
with local needs and problems. Their lack of job security might
have had both positive and negative consequences for the program.

Training has been an extremely important part of the development of field workers. Initial training as well as refresher
courses were organised for them in different parts of the country.
Training was imparted not only to field workers, but also to the
corps of village volunteers and other functionaries who were not

employed by BKKBN.

Training was an important component of the development of the higher level personnel of BKKBN. Foreign aid had all along been used for the training of professional staff in selected institutions abroad. The majority of the medical personnel in the provincial BKKBN offices, however, had been trained in Indonesian medical schools. Training when linked to career development could be a powerful tool for development. In the Indonesian program, training had also been linked to performance appraisal. High performance had been elicited through rewards in terms of promotion and career development in which training had played an important role.

From the outset, BKKBN had enjoyed autonomy in the recruitment of its staff. There was a mix of medical and non-medical personnel on the staff who complemented the skills of one another. Those who joined the organisation did so on a permanent basis. The practice of "deputationists" from different ministries "colonising" the new organisation had been avoided by BKKBN. Employees of BKKBN were full fledged civil servants.

Motivation and Commitment

BKKBN is part of the bureaucracy of Indonesia and so the use of monetary incentives to motivate its staff has had a rather limited role. Officials of BKKBN did receive an incentive allowance. Field workers were paid a fixed honorarium. The village volunteers did not receive any payment. The operator of the VCDC received a nominal payment. In the early years, there was a special incentive scheme linked to performance for field workers. This, however, was abandoned as criticisms about coercion began to be voiced by the public. On the whole, the extent to which direct monetary rewards have been used by BKKBN to stimulate performance has been limited.

However, other attempts have been made to strengthen both cooperation and competitiveness among all parties involved in the program from the President down to the small acceptor groups in remote areas. Villages, clinics, districts, and provinces were encouraged to out-perform each other. The visibility given to the program and the performance of its constituent units tended to stimulate this behavior. In order to outperform each other, integrated and cooperative efforts were needed. The recognition given to the groups and individuals who excelled in their performance was built into the program.

Staff incentives have taken different forms. Outer island midwives who performed well were offered trips to go to Bali for IUD-insertion training. High performing village chiefs in Bali were awarded visits to the successful East Java program. The President distributed awards to field workers and volunteers who performed exceptionally well. Successful program managers derived a sense of accomplishment from being able to receive additional program funds to improve services of benefit to their constituencies. Managers in the head office as well as in the field enjoyed a fair measure of autonomy to experiment with new ideas and could expect speedy response to their proposals from their supervisors.

BKKBN had in the past, experimented with direct material incentives for family planning acceptors and found them ineffective. Some villages had been happy to receive communal awards for high performance such as sewing machines or television sets. These small community reward systems were, in all cases, locally generated ideas.

There were criticisms in the earlier years that the program's success was due to the use of coercion in some areas. These allegations were made especially about the East Java program where the strong government commitment to fertility reduction and the rather authoritarian local culture led to cases of "special drive" tactics that some observers characterised as coercion. Surveys of "special drive acceptors", however, have shown that where the program was able to mobilise a wide range of formal and informal leaders in motivation and information, people felt, by far, that their acceptance was voluntary.[11] Where there was little participation by village leaders and the headman merely transmitted the program aims, the message came to be perceived as an order backed by force. Overall, almost half of the special drive acceptors who were interviewed in four sample villages in East Java reported that they felt a sense of coercion.

Surprisingly, the continuation rates of acceptors have been high in spite of allegations of coercion. Field surveys, the World Fertility Survey data and service statistics have all shown that high continuation rates and low fertility were found even among pill acceptors where the possibility of using coercion was limited and the opportunity for individual subversion of the government program was extensive. On the basis of field evidence and other reports, many experts have concluded that the allegation of coercion is exaggerated and that the Indonesian program's success is, on the whole, due to voluntary acceptance and participation.[12]

NOTES

1. Hull, Hull, and Singarimbun, Indonesia's Family Planning Story : Success and Challenge (Washington : Population References Bureau, 1977)

2. Jain, S.C., and Asayes, K., "Foreign Assistance and Population Programs", mimeo, University of North Carolina, Chapel Hill, 1979.

3. Recent studies have shown that there are no significant differences in fertility rates between the urban and rural populations of Indonesia.

4. Such as Sumatra, Kalimantan, and Sulawesi.

5. This was not so in Bali where IUD was the most popular method used by clients. See, H. Suyono, et al. Village Family Planning : The Indonesian Model (Jakarta : BKKBN, 1976)

6. As Bali had largely adopted IUD, the problem of resupply was not as severe as in Java.

7. 84 per cent of the acceptors in West Java used pills.

8. West Java's improved performance was also due to the deployment of teams of health workers and field workers who were authorised to visit women in the villages, examine them and prescribe and distribute pills - an adaptation to the shortage of doctors and clinics.

9. See Heiby, et al., AID's Role in Indonesian Family Planning (Washington D.C.1979)

10. Hull, Hull, and Singarimbun, Indonesia's Family Planning Story : Success and Challenge (Population References Bureau, Washington D.C., No.6, 1977)

11. Heiby, et.al., op.cit

12. Hull, Hull and Singarimbun, op.cit. Heiby, et.al., op.cit

6
The Public Health Program of China

"In medical and health work, put the emphasis on the country-side", said Chairman Mao in his celebrated declaration on health policy in June 1965. This statement threw the health system of China right into the middle of a major political controversy which has not yet been resolved. However, long before the Cultural Revolution was launched in 1965, major changes had taken place in the Chinese health system. Mao's statement heralded even more radical changes and called for an acceleration of the reform movement which he had initiated in the 1950s.

The People's Republic of China was established in 1949 as a socialist state. Public health was a major concern of the Revolutionary Government from the outset. The new rulers had inherited a country which was not only among the poorest in the Third World, but also deplorably backward in respect of public health and hygiene. The infant morality in the pre-Liberation days was 200 per 1000 births.[1] Parasitic diseases such as schistosomiasis (caused by snails in rivers and fields), malaria, hookworm and kala-azar were rampant, and cantagious diseases such as plague, cholera, gonorrhea, tuberculosis, and smallpox were common throughout the country. Most deaths in China were due to infectious diseases, complicated by some form of malnutrition.

Modern medical resources and trained medical manpower were extremely inadequate during the pre-Liberation period. At the time of Liberation, China had approximately 20,000 trained doctors, one for every 50,000 persons.[2] Hospital facilities were shockingly scarce (90,000 beds in 1949) and were concentrated only in a few urban areas. It is no exaggeration to say that most peasants were born and died without ever having received modern medical attention. Preventive medicine was almost non-existent. The bulk of the medical services available to the population was provided by the half a million practitioners of traditional medicine. There was a great deal of hostility between these practitioners and those who practised western medicine.

By the early 1970s, China was being quoted as an example to the developing world of what could be done through social and organisational change in the field of public health. In 1959, it was reported that the national infant mortality had declined to 70 per

1,000 births.[3] Smallpox, cholera, and plague were virtually
eliminated by 1960. Though dealing with parasitic and water borne
diseases was more difficult, considerable progress had been made
in the reduction of schistosomiasis and malaria. By 1963, it was
estimated that each of the 2,000 counties in China had a hospital.[4]
During the Cultural Revolution which was heralded by Mao's famous
statement, a strong movement towards equalisation of access to
medical care in the rural areas was initiated, leading to a
narrowing of the urban-rural gap in health care. First hand
scientific studies of these developments are not available.
Several scholars and experts on health care, however, have observed
that the Chinese Health Program is among the most successful among
the public health programs in the developing world.[5]

THE CHINESE ENVIRONMENT

China has been the home of an ancient and complex system of
medical theory and practice for over 4000 years.[6] Chinese medicine
was the first school of empirical medicine to differ substantially
from the traditional systems based on superstition and ignorance.
Acupuncture and herbal remedies formed part of the ancient
techniques and cures for many ailments and disorders. Western
medicine was first introduced into China with the arrival of
foreign traders and missionaries. As western interests in China
grew, medical schools were established, one of the most well known
among them being the Peking Union Medical College set up by the
Rockefeller Foundation in 1915. The focus of these schools was on
curative and specialist medicine, with hardly any attention given
to preventive medicine or primary health care for the masses. The
services provided by the western trained health personnel during
the pre-Liberation period were totally inadequate in a poor country
where 80 per cent of the people lived in villages steeped in
poverty, squalor, and illiteracy. The problem was further aggravated when in 1929 the Ministry of Health decided to abolish
traditional medicine altogether and declare its practice as
illegal.

It was against this background that a number of new and innovative ideas on social organisation and the role of health in the
community were generated by the Chinese leaders engaged in the
dangerous years of protracted fighting in the 1930s and 1940s.
During the "Long March" and after, health care along with land
reform and mobilisation[7]of peasants had become a major preoccupation of the leadership. The rudiments of the post-Liberation
health system were formulated, tested and practised in northwest
China during these years of struggle. The new measures, involving
communicable disease control, prevention, sanitation, and health
education were first designed to protect the armed forces and the
local population during the struggle. As the benefits of these
efforts became apparent in areas such as Kiangsi and Yenan, the
leadership decided to propagate this approach with an official
call to "promote physical culture and build up people's health".
A well known example of the new approach was that presented by

the Canadian physician Norman Bethune who worked in the Eighth Route
Army's medical service during 1938-39 and died while operating on
wounded soldiers. Bethune has ever since been a hero in China.

Decision Making Processes

In China, the Communist Party is responsible for the development
of basic policies and national leadership. The Party is represented
at every level and in all sectors of national activity. The Party's
chief organ is the Central Committee that nominates the Political
Bureau responsible for the formulation of national policies and
directives. These policies are generated through a process of
interaction between the Party and the masses. A key element in this
process is the "Revolutionary Committee" which functions from the
state to the provincial, municipal, county, district and street
levels down to the commune and the production brigade in the rural
areas. The committee consists of the representatives of the workers,
peasants, and soldiers in the organisation who in turn may also be
members of the Party. In the health sector, revolutionary
committees exist in the municipal and commune hospitals, in the
health bureaus of the province, municipality, and commune and in
the Ministry of Health itself. Each committee reports to that above
it and elects representatives to the next higher level. The
revolutionary committees are based on the principle of "democratic
centralism" by which the ideas of the masses are permitted to
influence policy through the recognition of the validity of the
"mass line". These ideas are studied and transformed into
decisions of a practical nature. These in turn are fed back to the
local group which test and review them through a further process
of discussion. Thus policies and priorities are formulated through
a process that enables the masses to participate actively at the
local level and a central coordinating authority charged with
setting national goals.
In the first five years after Liberation, however, the Ministry
of Health was quite independent of the Party political apparatus.
The Ministry was dominated by western style doctors whose military
backgrounds enabled them to resist the imposition of political
controls. Under these conditions, the Ministry's institutional
structure, its leaders' perceptions and resources determined the
directions of health policy.[8] During this period, for example,
there was a strong influence of consultants, technology, and
organisation from the Soviet Union on the Ministry. Medical
education was largely moulded upon the Soviet pattern. Incentive
awards and even preventive medicine were borrowed from the Soviet
Union for a country vastly different in respect of diseases and
socio-cultural characteristics. The emphasis on higher and middle
level medical education reflected the Soviet bias. The health
bureaus of the administrative regions were dominated by doctors.
Quality work and professional excellence were the dominant themes
which governed the thinking of leaders within the country.
An important feature of the Chinese society in the 1940s was
the growing pursuit of self reliance. Its genesis could be traced
to the Long March (1934-39) under conditions of great hardship, but

marked by a strong political commitment to regeneration through one's
own efforts. Civil disharmony, foreign intervention, and subsequent isolation of China combined to reinforce this trend which was
widespread in the country after Liberation. An important implication of this development was that at lower levels, tasks were
undertaken through local initiative and for the most part without
depending on approval or funds from higher levels. From the mid-
1930s, there was evidence of experiments in China which made
maximum use of available human and material resources, taking
advantage of local initiative and involving the community. The
role of local participation is reflected in the traditional
structure of Chinese cities and towns.[9] Cities are governed by
committees which are formal government bodies. The next lower
level is a district, which has also a formal committee. The
district is subdivided into streets or neighborhoods which are the
lowest level of formal governmental organisation in the city. The
smallest unit in the city is the "lane" with 1,000 to 8,000
residents. Some lanes are further divided into "groups". The lane
is governed by a committee elected by and from among the people
living in the lane. This committee is a "mass organisation" rather
than a governmental body. Traditionally, a number of common tasks
have been performed by these local groups in urban areas. Group
and lane committee leaders have served as links to higher levels of
urban government, mediated disputes among families   and provided
social services for those in need.

THE GUIDING PRINCIPLES

In 1950, the first National Health Conference held in China
promulgated four guiding principles which have had a decisive
influence on the national health strategy through the years. They
were:

1. serve the workers, peasants, and soldiers;
2. put prevention first;
3. unite doctors of both traditional Chinese
   and western medicine; and
4. integrate health work with mass movements.

A fifth postulate was added in 1965 when Mao exhorted the nation
and the Party to put the stress on rural areas. These principles
constituted the framework within which the development of health
care took place in China in spite of some set-backs and internal
conflicts during the past 30 years.

The primary focus of the national health program in China has
been on serving the people. The traditional bias of the Ministry
of Health, as in many other developing countries, was towards the
urban and elitist classes. Medical facilities were concentrated
in urban areas and medical education, research, and services were
oriented to meeting the needs of the richer classes in society.
The first principle thus called for a radical shift in this
orientation. The masses who were denied health care in the past

were to be the favored target group of the new health system. The
Communist Party considered health care as a human right and
essential for the wellbeing of all people, but also recognised its
basic economic role in increasing the productivity of the people.
Health problems were, therefore, the concern of not only the
medical profession, but also taken into account in the national
economic and social strategies as an integral part of development
plans.

New Directions

This shift in emphasis had important implications in terms of
the approach to the types of health services to be provided, their
organisation and financing, medical education and research, and
the linkages of health services to other activities and programs
promoted by the government.
The Ministry of Health dispensed medical services to the rural
areas where 80 per cent of the population lived. In 1950-52, teams
led by doctors were sent to the countryside to establish epidemic
prevention centres, maternal and child health services, and programs
for health education and vaccination. The focus of attention
shifted to the diseases prevalent among the masses.
A major move in this direction occurred in 1956 when health was
explicitly linked with agricultural development. By 1958, the
commune had become the cornerstone for implementing economic
policy. Communes were organised in China for the sake of the
peasant who cultivated land collectively with his neighbors. A
commune has a population of 10,000 to 60,000 people and organises
agriculture, small scale industries, and educational and welfare
services for its members. Medical services were also added to its
range of activities with the commune playing an active role in the
planning and delivery of these services. The revolutionary
committees of the commune and the levels below were made responsible for financing, manpower development and mobilisation of
resources for health care in their respective areas. Their tasks
included responsibility for outpatients, direction of mass
campaigns, control of communicable diseases, and delivery of
medical care.
Since the population to be served was extremely large, several
unconventional steps were taken to man the expanding health
network. The practitioners of traditional medicine, for example,
were enlisted in large numbers. An academy of traditional medicine
was set up and the theory of traditional medicine was introduced
into the medical schools. Urban doctors were asked to lead
mobile teams in rural areas. The duration of higher medical
education was cut from six to three years and highly skilled
doctors were posted in rural areas to serve the masses. Several
new technical institutions were established throughout the country
to solve medical problems affecting the masses and assist in
implementing policy in light of local conditions. New categories
of auxiliary health workers such as the barefoot doctors and health
aides were created. The barefoot doctors were peasants who were

trained locally in health work and who, along with their normal
agricultural work performed community health services on a part
time basis.[10]

The Chinese rural oriented services were designed to eliminate
diseases most prevalent in the countryside and thus facilitate
increased farm production. In some areas, land had been reclaimed
or opened up partly as a result of eliminating diseases such as
malaria and schistosomiasis. The rural areas did not have access
to sophisticated treatment, but the majority of the population was
effectively protected against infection and chronic parasitic
diseases and had access to medical care for their common ailments
which in turn improved their productivity and morale.

The WHO Report claims that the resource cost of the Chinese
system is lower than that of the more intensive curative urban
based health systems in other parts of the world. The decentralisation of the burden of service delivery, cost sharing between the
state, commune, and individual coupled with a readily available
pool of skilled, semi-skilled, and un-skilled personnel, consumer
as well as state involvement and the use of local resources, have
allowed the health system achieve the objective of providing health
care for the vast majority of the population at relatively low
cost.[11]

Put Prevention First

Prevention was the major theme in the mass campaigns that began
in the 1950s and has been reiterated ever since in the fields of
communicable disease control, vaccination and immunisation, environmental health and general sanitation. This approach has ensured
improved maternal and child health services, higher standards of food
hygiene and nutrition, adequate water supply, and correct disposal
of sewage and nightsoil. It has created a greater national awareness of the need to guard against contagious diseases with the help
of a nationwide surveillance and warning system involving all
health workers.

One field in which China has made a major effort in prevention is
environmental health. Special stress has been laid on environmental
sanitation. The barefoot doctor and his aides, as well as the
physicians in the county and commune hospitals, allocate much of
their time to this task. Few sanitation engineers were involved.
The patriotic mass movements have been the key instrument in this
field. The epidemic prevention centers were the source of technical
advice in respect of sanitation.

Surveillance of communicable diseases has been organised on the
basis of an extensive health network. Efforts for disease control
have focused on health education and vaccination. These activities
were undertaken with the technical support of special institutes and
the health services network and with the active participation of
local communities. For example, in 1958, pilot projects on venereal
diseases were organised in eight different provinces and lessons
learnt from their experience were applied in all provinces. Large
numbers from the local population were trained to detect, report, and

treat infected individuals. Information on disease control was
disseminated through films, radio, and wall newspapers and the
cooperation of people was sought to eliminate the disease. By
1961, venereal diseases were eliminated or controlled throughout
the country.[12]

The maternal and child health (MCH) services have been well
integrated into the community organisation. In all aspects of
health, and in MCH in particular, local solution to problems
varied a great deal. The system was decentralised and services
were provided at the local level through the barefoot doctors, who
made it possible for women to have access to them through home
visits and the network of health stations in the rural areas, in
production teams, and production brigades. In urban areas, MCH
care was provided at the periphery of nursery schools by the health
teacher and voluntary health aides. Immunisation programs were
organised on a large scale throughout the country.

The government's decision to provide primary health care and
preventive services for the entire population presented a formida-
ble challenge in terms of finding adequate manpower. It was
natural, therefore, to pull the traditional practitioners into the
health system in view of their numbers, and their rapport with the
people. In 1955, the Peking Traditional Medicine Research
Institute offered its first training course in which western
oriented doctors participated. The mass orientation of medical
colleges, the reduction in medical curricula and emphasis on
practical work and the spread of medical knowledge throughout the
country were developments which followed in the wake of this movement. During the Cultural Revolution, the dilemma posed by the
determination to extend health care to the masses and the critical
shortage of manpower was resolved through the following radical
changes: (1) intensive mobilisation of existing medical personnel
through the creation of mobile medical teams to serve rural areas;
(2) discontinuation of formal medical education pending its
complete reform; (3) real unification of traditional and western
medicine so that resources available could be used more
effectively; (4) dissemination of medical knowledge to the population through massive training and induction of barefoot doctors and
health aides.

The last step alone resulted in the creation of a cadre of
four million health workers who represented an extension of health
services under the immediate control of the people. At the same
time, research on traditional medicine was expanded considerably,
and in the rural areas, the health network began to use traditional
medicine more often, reducing the cost of services and improving
the availability of drugs in the process.[13] Most of the health
centers had small plots of land where medicinal plants were grown
under the supervision of barefoot doctors. The Research Institutes
collaborated with hospitals in identifying and testing the curative
properties of plants.

Dissemination of knowledge on the causes and symptoms of
diseases and ways of preventing and curing them were part of local
health activities. With the assistance of medical teams, local

health workers had been able to organise preventive and curative
work including immunisation, family planning, and treatment of
minor diseases. Health education and community organisation and
participation have been identified by WHO Missions to China as the
key factors responsible for the improvement of health and living
standards. Mass campaigns were normally integrated with agricultural production. Inspection and reporting at the end of campaigns
were tasks to be performed by the leaders.[14] The mass campaigns in
China represented a unique application of medical knowledge and
socio-political concepts to achieve significant results in community
health with a minimum of scarce resources.

Focus on Rural Areas

From the early 1950s, the thrust of the public health strategy
of China was to redress the rural-urban imbalance in health care.
It was the slow pace of the implementation of this policy and the
periodic setbacks faced in achieving the declared goal of servicing
the masses that prompted Chairman Mao to make his famous declaration of June 1965 which endorsed the fundamental right of the
rural masses to receive medical care and sought to correct the
tendency evident since the time of the Great Leap Forward (1958) to
regroup health efforts in urban centers at the cost of the rural
areas. A further correction came with the dispatch of mobile
medical teams from the cities to the countryside where they were
most needed. Since 1968, the mobile medical teams have brought
nearly 7,00,000 medical personnel from the cities to the villages
for varying periods. What is remarkable is the decentralised
provision of health services in remote areas simultaneously with
the training of personnel to man these services, having mobilised
them from among the people themselves. The decentralisation to
rural areas in all the 22 provinces and five autonomous regions was
carried out with speed, relying heavily on commune and county
hospitals, brigade health centers, and the barefoot doctor network.
The service operated at four distinct levels : the production
team, the production brigade, the commune, and the county. At the
lowest level of the production team (100-200 people), health
services were provided by the health aide who worked on a voluntary
basis. He would administer first aid, give health education,
vaccinate, and report on diseases to the next level. At the level
of the production brigade, preventive and curative tasks were
integrated and some degree of specialisation was achieved. Each
brigade had at least one barefoot doctor who concentrated on MCH
while another was engaged in environmental health tasks. They
operated in a simple outpatient clinic which used both western and
traditional medicines. The barefoot doctors were also responsible
for the referral of patients to the commune hospital. At the
commune level, both preventive services and in-patient care were
provided. The commune hospital manned by doctors supervised the
health stations at lower levels and trained the barefoot doctors
and aides. At the county level, the hospital was larger with
400-500 beds accommodation, and was the initiating and inspiring

center for preventive health work. Medical teams were sent out of
this hospital to the rural areas.

To pay for the health services in the rural areas, a system of
cooperative medical schemes was evolved. These schemes operated
at the production brigade level where each member paid an annual
fee. Additional funds were provided by the brigade's budget. Some
brigades were able to pay for their members' medical expenses in
the commune or county hospitals whereas others were able to meet
only a part of such expenses. In addition, members participated
in local health activities and campaigns as a group. Barefoot
doctors who generally came from local peasant families and were
trained for three to six months provided the leadership in these
matters along with the local revolutionary committee.

An important achievement of the last two decades was the
progress in rural sanitation by motivating people through political
ideology, participation, and creation of public awareness. With
technical and financial support from the county and commune
authorities, sanitation programs were carried out by the people
themselves through the production brigades and teams. The methods
used were simple, labour intensive, and therefore cost effective.
The programs were normally carried out on instructions from the
higher levels of administration though they could also be
initiated at the brigade level to suit local needs. Each program
was discussed with the villagers, wherever possible, so that they
understood the nature of work involved and agreed to the various
steps in implementing it. Health education campaigns have been an
important part of the rural strategy.

SHIFTS IN POLICIES AND STRUCTURES

The Ministry of Health, under the direction of the Central
Committee of the Chinese Communist Party, is responsible for broad
policy, technical direction and financial support of training and
research institutes, hospitals, and health services. The Ministry
was the dominant force in the early 1950s when the Party was rather
ineffective in influencing the direction of health policy, allocations, and programs. In 1949, when Mao and his comrades came to
power, the Party was ill prepared to cope with the complex range of
administrative demands which confronted it. The Ministry was led
by medical doctors for whom professional competence, independence,
and scientific knowledge were the dominant values.

Divided Policy Making

In 1955, Mao observed that the Ministry of Health was more
responsive to urban than to rural curative health needs. An
important decision arising out of his dissatisfaction was the
setting up of the Nine Man Sub-Committee on Schistosomiasis under
the supervision of the Party Central Committee and almost completely beyond the control of the Ministry. The Sub-Committee
leaders were political personalities with no medical background.
In 1958, on the eve of the Great Leap Forward, commune health

centers were created under the party local committees with little
operational control by the Ministry. The communes were made
responsible for health work below the county level. The Ministry
was left with the major educational and research programs and
administration of the larger hospitals. Responsibilities for the
key health interventions were thus divided into three seperate
arenas, each of which had little formal relationship with the other.
The Sub-Committee and communes were being led by political cadres
with non-professional values and rural interests. The Ministry,
on the other hand, was dominated by doctors who valued expertise,
quality, and research.

The divided policy making structure of 1955-60 had important
consequences for health care. A great advantage of the three part
structure was that it enabled the total range of health programs
to be responsive to a broader spectrum of inputs than would have
been possible otherwise.[15] For example, until the mid-1950s, the
preventive and curative needs of the rural masses had not been
given systematic attention. The Sub-Committee and communes were
effective structures to meet these needs. The Ministry on the
other hand, was more responsive to urban needs and better equipped
to deal with higher medical education and manpower development.
The main problem with the divided system was its inability to
achieve coordination. The interdependence among the parts was
lost sight of and there was no organisational mechanism which
ensured that proper linkages were forged. Thus while the communes
increased the need for health manpower, the Ministry was expanding
the curriculum and duration of training in the medical schools. The
step up in referrals from rural areas strained the resources of the
unprepared urban hospitals. Similarly, drug production which was
controlled by the Ministry was not coordinated with the pharmaceutical
demand generated by the new rural programs.

When China faced a major agricultural setback in the early 1960s,
leaders of the communes and the Sub-Committee were unable to
mobilise the masses and extract the needed resources to finance the
local health programs and campaigns.[16] Farmers were reluctant to
contribute when their income from agriculture declined. At the same
time, urban centers resented the deterioration in the municipal
health facilities. The Sub-Committee work slowed down during this
period and many commune health centers were closed down. By 1965,
the rural thrust had weakened considerably and the regime of bureaucratic control by the Ministry with its specialist bureaus was
restored.

The Cultural Revolution

Mao's statement of June 1965 reaffirming the stress on rural
areas was a reaction to the recapture of control by the Ministry and
its adverse consequences for rural health care. During the Cultural
Revolution that followed, the party leaders once again wrested
effective control over health policy and programs from the bureaucracy. By 1968, the Ministry of Health had become virtually
irrelevant to the formulation of basic health policies in the

country. A series of purges and internal conflicts immobilised the Ministry and major policy directives began to be issued in the name of Mao himself. In spite of the disruptions it created, this shift facilitated the process of policy change and centralised coordination, especially in three areas that were of primary concern to Mao, namely, medical education, health delivery, and rural financing which was lacking in the 1955-60 period. First of all, the medical schools were closed for a certain duration. When they reopened, major curricular reforms were introduced and the length of education was reduced to 3 years. They incorporated traditional medicine in the curriculum. Second, the rural bare-foot doctors program was strengthened and promoted as a national policy. The training of these health workers was stepped up and medical mobile teams provided instruction to them in the rural areas. The expansion of the paramedic based system was based on the thesis that it was the most efficient way to conserve scarce medical manpower, and minimise costs, and provide timely treatment to a vast and dispersed population. It was during this period that the rural health delivery system linking county hospitals to the commune health centers and production brigades was firmly established. This was the policy makers' response to meeting the medical needs of the peasantry while trying to cope with the financial and production constraints facing them.

Third, a cooperative health care system was introduced to solve the problems of financing rural health care. Commune members were to pay a small fee each year. This along with a contribution from the commune itself constituted a cooperative medical fund. Basically this was a scheme of subsidised insurance with limited benefits for those requiring referral to higher level hospitals. There were several variants of this scheme in different parts of the country.

The chief merit of the centrally coordinated system was its capacity to integrate diverse, but related policies. The new system was able to restructure medical education to match the requirements of the expanded rural delivery services while simultaneously evolving financing schemes to support the proposed changes. There was no such integration during the 1950s. On the other hand, the integration was achieved over a narrow range of goals and concerns. Important areas of medical policy such as research and professional development of doctors received scant attention. The single minded focus on limited goals during the Cultural Revolution seemed to have led to a backlash by 1973 which once again strengthened the influence of professionals and the bureaucrats in the Ministry. The success of centralised coordina-tion in achieving its limited, but integrated policy goals seemed to have created in its wake imbalances and policy gaps which have weakened the thrust of the coordinated authority.

David Lampton who has studied the Chinese health policy during
and after the Cultural Revolution has made the following
prediction:[17]

While Cultural Revolution medical policy will undoubtedly
undergo change, the status quo ante is unlikely to be
restored. A corps of medical workers has been created,
a referral chain now exists, and China's peasants have had
their demands for medical care legitimated. This
represents a monumental achievement.

NOTES

1. K. Newell (ed.),Health by the People (Geneva : World
Health Organisation, 1975) pp.1-2.
2. D. Lampton, The Politics of Medicine in China (Boulder :
Westview Press, 1977), p.14.
3. Ibid.
4. V. Sidel and R. Sidel, "Health Care Services as part of
China's Revolution and Development", in N.Maxwell (ed.), China's
Road to Development (Oxford, 1979).
5. WHO, Organisation and Functioning of Health Services in
China, (Geneva, 1978). (Hereafter referred to as the WHO Report)
6. Most of the data presented here are drawn from the WHO
Report.
7. V. Sidel & R.Sidel, op.cit. p.158
8. Lampton, op.cit. Chapter 2
9. R.Sidel and V.Sidel, "Revolutionary Optimism : Models for
Commitment to Community from other Societies", Fifth Vermont
Conference on the Primary Prevention of Psychopathology, June, 1979.
10. The term "barefoot doctor" was first used in the communes in
the Shanghai area where farmers worked barefoot in their rice
fields. A barefoot doctor earns about as much as a farmer. There
are no additional economic incentives. He earns "workpoints" in
recognition of his services.
11. The individual contributes by participating in mass
movements and the cooperative medical system. Patients pay a
nominal cash fee. The communes meet part of the cost through the
funds raised by them.
12. Quoted in the WHO Report, p.60.
13. Each center had its own equipment to prepare medicaments from
the local medicinal herbs. The usual shortages of imported drugs
did not plague traditional medicine.
14. P.Willenski, The Delivery of Health Services in the People's
Republic of China, IDRC, 1977.
15. See Lampton, op.cit., Chapter 11.
16. The commune health programs were, for the most part, a self-
financing activity.
17. Lampton, op.cit. p.244. In spite of the changes in policy
since 1976, Lampton predicts that major changes in the mass health
programs are unlikely to take place.

7
Mexico's
Rural Education Program

We have forty children in our community school in this
village. I not only teach them, but also meet with the
elders in the community every week. At our meetings,
in addition to school matters, we also discuss community
problems and other matters in which adults have an
interest. The community committee takes a lot of
interest in the school. Their concern for education
has increased my motivation a great deal.

Since we have over 40 children, we have two separate
classes. There is a girl instructor who teaches one of
the classes. The women in the community feel more free
to talk to her. I think the community school can be used
not only for educating the young children, but also
adults. I once showed some of the men how to do minor
repairs on radios. I enjoy my work   a great deal. I
could have got other jobs too. But I find this greatly
satisfying.

Thus spoke Constantino, a young community instructor in a
remote village located about 150 miles east of Mexico City in the
State of Puebla about his experience with the Rural Education
Program in Mexico in November, 1980. Constantino was one of 19,000
instructors who belonged to Conafe, a public agency of the
Government of Mexico which had pioneered a major national program
for rural education in 1973. These instructors lived and worked
in nearly 19,000 remote rural communities which were located in
some of the most inaccessible areas of Mexico.

THE BACKGROUND

The Federal Ministry of Education in Mexico was responsible for
elementary education in the country. In many states, federal
schools co-existed with elementary schools run by the state governments. From time to time, the Federal Government had attempted to
extend education to the rural areas. But on the whole, these
efforts had very little impact and the education system continued to

retain its essentially urban character. A major problem was in finding teachers who were willing to go to the remote rural areas. Once teachers became part of the large federal bureaucracy with its security of tenure and transfer privileges, they were reluctant to serve in rural areas with the result the rural communities with a population of 500 or less usually had no educational facilities. In fact, most of these isolated communities received no public service whatsoever. The polarisation between the exploding urban centers and the poor rural areas had thus reached alarming proportions by the late sixties.

Most of the people living in rural areas were engaged in farming, although it was common for men, especially in the northern region, to migrate elsewhere for work, leaving their women and children behind. Climatic and cultural differences were significant among the regions of the country, reinforced by the extreme lack of communication and movement that prevailed in rural areas. Spanish was spoken and understood in most areas, though indigenous languages were the sole means of communication in some of the most remote and small rural communities in the hills. Poverty, illiteracy, and low levels of socio-economic development were common to all these rural communities which were left behind as the process of urbanisation gained momentum in Mexico.

Conafe (Council for the Promotion of Education) was established as a "public organisation" under the Ministry of Education by President Echeverria in 1971. Mexico had many such public organisations and parastatals which the government had set up for special purposes. It was customary for a new President, for example, to set up several such new public agencies and to dissolve others which may have been set up by his predecessors. Conafe was set up as a semi-autonomous public agency under a Presidential Decree which empowered the new organisation to formulate and implement policies and programs for the promotion of education in the country.

Establishment of Conafe

It was during the presidential election campaign of 1970 that Echeverria publicly acknowledged the urgent need to address the problem of rural education. During his visits to rural areas, he was struck by the extreme poverty and illiteracy that prevailed in the majority of the country's rural communities. He was convinced that conventional educational systems were incapable of meeting rural needs and that new approaches had to be invented to cope with the emerging situation. One of the persons to whom Echeverria turned for advice was Prudencio Lopez Martinez, a leading industrialist of Mexico who was known for his dynamism and deep interest in national affairs. It was in the course of a dialogue between these two men during the presidential campaign that the basic idea of Conafe was born. When Echeverria became President in 1970, he invited Lopez Martinez to plan and organise Conafe and to be its first Director General.[1] The latter accepted the invitation and stayed on as Director General for a period of six years.[2]

Prudencio Lopez Martinez believed that Conafe would achieve its mission only if three important conditions were met.

First, he wanted a high degree of autonomy for the new agency. He was certain that Conafe would not get very far if it had to follow the Education Ministry's practices and decision making processes. An important task he performed in the formative years was to negotiate with the President and Education Minister for the maximum autonomy of Conafe and to create an internal culture and willingness within the new organisation to make effective use of the autonomy given to it. As a result, both in financial and administrative matters, the Council was given considerable flexibility to frame its own regulations. The legal device of "public organisation" permitted such autonomy and the new Director General took full advantage of it.

Second, he was determined that Conafe should remain a small but creative organisation. Most ministries had grown so large and unwieldy that effective control over them was impossible. The key to the development of innovative programs, according to him, lay in the creation of a compact group of competent and well motivated professionals who could draw upon expertise from outside. He did not, for example, wish to hire on a permanent basis, experts whose services could be bought through contractual arrangements. Given the vast distances in the country and the widely scattered network of communities which required educational services, managing programs from head-quarters would have called for a very large bureaucracy. The Director General was anxious to search for new organisational devices to deliver the services.

Third, the focus of Conafe, according to Lopez Martinez, was to be on rural education. Though Conafe's mandate was broad, he felt that the initial thrust of its program had to be on the rural population. There was considerable interest in education in rural areas. Many parents were anxious that their children be educated so that their chances of economic advancement could be improved. As a matter of policy, federal and state schools did not operate in communities with a population below 500 or where a minimum of 30 children could not be registered. Thus children in small rural communities had no access to elementary education even if their parents were keen on educating them. The first priority of Conafe, under the guidance of Lopez Martinez, was to devise a program to deal with this important social problem. There was no competition in this area. It was like moving into a neglected, wide open space.

The core group that Lopez Martinez gathered around him consisted of young professionals with some experience and competence in education. The technical group was led by Enrique Garcia Arista who was named the Technical Director of Conafe. He had taught in schools and belonged to the Ministry of Education which he left to join Conafe. The initial design of the rural education program was done under the leadership of Garcia Arista.

Given its broad mandate, it was not surprising that the Ministry of Education called upon Conafe to perform certain services which were of a financial nature. For example, the Ministry authorised

Conafe to be its channel for subsidising selected institutions of higher education. Funds for the publication of books, especially for adult education, were also distributed through Conafe. But from the outset, there was no doubt that the primary focus of Conafe was on developing new rural education programs.

EXPERIMENTAL PROJECTS

One of the problems in designing new national programs for rural areas was that there was little experience available on this subject in Mexico. No one in Conafe had any clear idea as to the interventions which were likely to succeed in rural communities. They began, therefore, with experimental projects to test out different approaches in the field. Attempts to organise rural schools using federal teachers ended in failure. One concept which seemed to have generated positive community response in the course of experiments was what came to be known as the "community course". The idea was indeed a simple one, though it had no precedent in Mexico. In rural communities which agreed to participate in the pilot project, Conafe agreed to send one instructor each to organise a one room school. The construction of the one room tenement was the responsibility of the people in the community. They were also expected to provide boarding and lodging facilities for the instructor, who was to live in the community. In a way, a community's willingness to offer these facilities was a test of its interest in the education of its children. The instructors assigned to the community schools were young men and women who had completed secondary school education and were from rural background. Conafe gave them contract appointments for one year at a time, with the understanding that their period of service with Conafe could not ordinarily exceed four years. An instructor would receive an annual stipend of about $ 160 per year in addition to the resources provided by the community. Most of the young instructors used their period of service to prepare for technical or other higher examinations which could improve their career prospects.[3] The young people who joined the Conafe experimental program had thus no career interest in rural education. They were attracted by a sense of social service and the economic compensation and opportunities for further studies offered to them by the new scheme.

The nature of the experimental project changed considerably as it evolved. Initially, young instructors were assigned to teach in the communities in which they grew up. Soon this was found to be unsuitable and therefore certain modifications were introduced. Community response seemed to be better when instructors came from other places. But in all cases, instructors had a rural background and were familiar with the local customs and mores. Transactions with the community were conducted informally to begin with. As experience accumulated, communities were encouraged to elect small committees which negotiated with the instructor and Conafe on the terms and arrangements for setting up the school.

In the experimental project, Conafe's endeavour was to evolve the design of an elementary (primary) education program suited to the isolated, small rural communities of Mexico. Rural children in the age group of 6-14 formed the target group of the program. The intention was not merely to make these children literate, but also offer them an opportunity to join the mainstream of Mexican education. The rural primary education therefore had to be compatible with the rest of the country's primary school system. The quality of education had to be such that those who completed primary education in rural areas were able to go on to secondary schools, if they wanted to do so. A major concern of Conafe was to design a curriculum for the course that met national standards and yet was well adapted to the context of the remote rural communities. The manual for instructors that grew out of the experimental project reflected this concern adequately. It emphasised the learning of language, writing, and arithmetic in the early stages and added on natural science and social science based inputs towards the end of the course. Instructors were then given considerable flexibility to use local materials and examples to make the curriculum more relevant to specific situations. Instructors also played a part in planning the curriculum and preparing the manual.

Important Lessons

Garcia Arista and his colleagues learned a number of lessons from the experimental projects and incorporated them into the national program which was launched in 1972-73.

Since the children had no prior experience or preparation for education, the instructors determined the groups to be formed within the school. Within the one room school, the instructor would organise the children into smaller, more homogeneous groups for purposes of teaching. They became the basis for differentiating between different grades.[4] The readiness and progress of children in class rather than age became the dominant criterion for such differentiation. The same instructor attended to the different groups in the class and helped them along at their pace. He was given considerable flexibility to determine class schedules, timings, and assignments as warranted by his specific situation.

Experimental evidence led the Conafe officials to conclude that a six week training program was optimal for the selected instructors. Instead of giving extended training as was done in the federal school system, the emphasis here was on careful selection and intensive development. Conafe was anxious that the young people they recruited had a commitment to the new program. The stipend offered to the instructors was substantially below the salary and benefits received by the teachers in the federal system. The training program was used not only to create technical competence and commitment, but also to weed out those who did not appear suitable for the task ahead.

Once in the field, very little direct supervision of instructors could be organised from headquarters. Communities were often difficult to reach and means of communication were extremely limited. A system of "assessors" was established to visit the community schools periodically to assist the instructors in solving their

problems and answering their questions, if any.[5] The assessor was
also a young person who himself was an instructor for some time
and was usually made responsible for about 50 schools. He was
able to visit each school only twice or thrice in a year, but had
meetings with groups of instructors in different locations from
time to time. His reports to the state level offices of Conafe on
the basis of these visits and meetings constituted the basic
information system for Conafe. The instructors did not have any
administrative or reporting responsibility towards the state
offices.

Since monitoring the course and instructors from above was
indeed difficult and costly, Conafe concluded that it must depend
on the community itself to exercise effective control. The
concept of the community committee elected by members, sharing of
the costs of education and frequent meetings between the committee
and instructor to review the progress and resolve problems were
seen as elements that gave the community an active role and a sense
of responsibility in running the local school. It was based on
this experience that the community committee, instructor, and the
municipal president of the area were required to enter into a
written contract which stipulated the obligations and responsibilities of each party whenever a community school was established.
Conafe offices depended for the most part on the community
committees for feedback on how well the schools were doing. If a
committee was dissatisfied with an instructor it usually did not
take long for an assessor or the state office of Conafe to learn
about it.

The rural education program that evolved out of the experimental project was for the first time extended to 100 rural communities in the state of Guerrera in 1972-73. Further modifications
and improvements were introduced into the program in the light of
this experience, but the basic design remained the same. Soon
afterwards, Conafe made plans to extend the program to the 20,000
rural communities which it identified as the population to be
served. The program was called the "community course" and it soon
became the single major activity of Conafe. By 1980, community
courses were established in 19,000 rural communities in different
parts of the country, with a coverage of 3,50,000 children and
serving a rural population of approximately 1.5 million.

ORGANISATIONAL STRUCTURE

One of the early problems that Conafe faced had to do with the
organisation structure for the program. When only a few states
were involved, the head office could play an active role in terms
of planning and supervision. When the program spread to 31 states
and covered over 15,000 schools in 1976, the state offices had to
be systematically created and managed. In each state, there was
a committee appointed by the Governor to oversee Conafe's programs.
The Governor was the president of the state committee. Its vice
president was the state government's education officer and the
treasurer was a local banker. Other members were drawn from the

government as well as private business. The Conafe officer in the
state (delegate) was made the secretary of the committee and was
the link between the state and Conafe headquarters. Conafe's
budget for the state plans of activities, and allocations were to
be approved by the state committee. Conafe met 75 per cent of the
budget whereas the remaining 25 per cent was contributed by the
state government.

Conafe maintained an office in each state with a small staff
headed by the delegate who was also secretary of the state Conafe
committee. Under him were officials concerned with the programs
in the state as well as financial and administrative services. The
assessors of the community courses in the state were supervised by
the state office. The salaries of instructors were paid from the
Conafe state budget. In the state of Puebla, for example, there
are over 1,100 community schools and instructors. A state office
employee visits four different locations in the state where the
instructors assemble every month to collect their salaries. Many
of them work in remote areas and would find it difficult to visit
the state capital for this purpose.

The field staff of Conafe was indeed large. This was in sharp
contrast to the limited staff in the head office and state offices.
The field staff consisted of instructors and assessors, totalling
nearly 20,000 young people. The drop out rate of this category
was 15-20 per cent per year. These rates varied from region to
region. With the oil boom in the south, it was becoming more
difficult to find young people to stay on the job in adequate
numbers.

Autonomy has been an important aspect of Conafe. According to
the Director General,

A part of it was given to us and a part has been created by
our own performance. The council which is presided over by
the Minister of Education is authorised to make decisions on
Conafe's policies, programs and budget. The council
consists of important officials from ministries as well as
leaders from other walks of life. But basically, we are
part of the Education Ministry. Once the council has made
the policy decisions, there is no need for us to go back to
the Ministry for approval. In part, mutual trust and confidence reinforce autonomous behaviour. For example, I can and
I do write a check for a million dollars without going through
the cumbersome procedures of the Ministry. No senior official
of the Ministry can do that. We formulate our own purchase
policies and guidelines for hiring and firing. We are not
obliged to follow the government's administrative regulations.
The auditors come and verify our expenditure. But they do
not question the propriety of our decisions or actions. It
is true, of course, that even when government grants some
autonomy, some people may not wish to use it !

We started as a very small organisation. A lot of decisions
were taken through internal group discussions, and highly
personalised relationships characterised our style of working.

Not that we have not systematised our operations through
manuals and guidelines for different subjects. But on
the whole, we have shied away from too much structuring
and building of organisational walls. The time has come
for us to look at ourselves and see whether some restructuring is in order. The structure should, of course,
be related to the growth of our activities. Changes will
hurt some. That is inevitable. But the question is
whether the changes facilitate our new tasks.

Decentralisation

When only a few states were involved, the head office could do
a great deal of centralised planning and decision making. With
growth, the role of the state offices and state delegates evolved
over the years. Decentralisation did not happen overnight.
Evolving the core curriculum, selection and training of instructors,
and allocation of funds were the key functions. But increasingly,
state officers proposed activities and managed their programs.
First, headquarters used to give them directives and targets as
part of a top-down process. As they gained experience, they
proposed action plans, raised resources and the head office's role
was to strengthen their ability to plan and implement. This was
clearly a move towards effective decentralisation. The management
of the program at the community level was highly decentralised.
The community committee and the instructor were virtually in
control of the operation.
The Director General pointed out how the role of the state
committee and state delegate evolved over the years.

Decentralisation cannot be put into action mechanically.
When the state offices were first opened, headquarters
did give them directives and targets. This would seem
like a top-down process. But the fact of the matter is
that our state offices were new and small and needed
strong direction from us. As they gained experience, we
have let them propose ideas and plans to us. Today, they
are in a better position to explore on their own, propose
action plans to us and seek resources for the programs
they wish to expand. Our job is to respond to their
initiatives and strengthen their ability to plan and
implement on their own. That,in my view, is a move
towards effective decentralisation.

Eduardo, the state delegate of Puebla, gave his side of the
story:

I have been in this office only for two years. We manage
a very large program here with 1,100 community courses. We
have some other urban activities also, in addition. The
state committee is quite active in planning our activities.
One of my major functions is to keep close contact with

members of my committee who are key officials in the state
ministries whose support is essential to us. For example,
the state education officer can tell me about the remote
communities which need the community courses. We jointly
work out the number and locations of the new community
courses. If the state education department which has a
much wider network than mine did not cooperate with me,
I will be in trouble. We then take our expansion plans
to the committee. From there, we negotiate with Conafe
head office over the resources and other support we require
for our expansion. Generally, they respond positively.
Sometimes, when Conafe head office asks us to mount new
programs or experiments, we tell them that we are not
ready. They see our point of view. I don't feel that the
Conafe head office is pushing down its plans on us. Don't
forget that we raise part of our resources in the state.
Even our municipal presidents and local political leaders
play a role in suggesting where we should expand.

In the northern state of Baja California, the state office of
Conafe had initiated some activities through community instructors
which were not done elsewhere. Rosa Maria, who had worked in that
office, said:

When we found that we could provide some limited health
services, we took the initiative. We organised sports
for the children. We even organised some dental education
and check ups for the children because we felt that this
was a serious problem. Our instructors are given rudimen-
tary first aid training when they are first inducted into
Conafe. The point is that the head office never stood in
the way of our doing these things. There has been a case
when the state committee asked for funds for a technical
institute in the state, Conafe head office was unable to
support the idea. But they never scuttled our initiative
or objected to our proposing such ideas.

POSITIVE FEATURES

Selection and induction of instructors received considerable
attention in Conafe. As a senior official put it:

We advertise our requirements of instructors widely. We
encourage young school teachers to visit our state offices
and get acquainted with our work. Our state officials
regard this promotional work as an important part of their
job. We conduct periodic general tests for those applying
for the instructors' posts. Out of these, we select a
large number who are then given another specialised test
based on our community course manual. This is really to
test their interest in teaching and understanding of the
subject. Those who pass this test are called upon to parti-

cipate in our training courses. There, we are able to
observe them at close range. Some people are rejected
at the end of these courses. Thus our selection
process is an elaborate and expensive one. But for the
job to be done, nothing less would do.

We are now planning a new package to attract young people.
We will ask them to work for two years for us. During
these years, we will arrange with technical schools to
give them special coaching during the summer at our expense
when they are free. In the third year, these technical
institutions will offer them full time training at our
cost. Thus, they would have acquired valuable qualifica-
tions which will hopefully improve their career prospects
by the time their service with Conafe is over.

An important feature of Conafe was the organisational cohesive-
ness and commitment of its staff. Its small size clearly was an
advantage. But, according to the Director General, there was more
to it than that.

I would stress three factors in this connection. First of
all, our work is not like steel making or mass assembly.
The staff are involved with people. They can see the
impact of their work on the children. There is professional
satisfaction in what they are able to achieve. We are
probably attracting people who have a liking for this kind
of service. They have a sense of pride in the success of
the community course and the response to their program
throughout the country.

Second, the autonomy they enjoy at work is a source of motivation. Look at our instructors and how they are left free
to improvise. Our state offices are increasingly able to
plan and act on their own. The feedback they get when they
act is quick. This is true in the head office too. When
new ideas are generated, they don't get buried in files.
They get discussed. The response they get makes them feel
that they can influence action. So they will think on
their own and take initiative. Third, we provide our regular
staff pretty good economic compensation. They are certainly
better paid than the ministry officials. They have better
fringe benefits. They may not be as well off as those in
private industry. But they are not far behind. All these
factors should be taken together to understand the motivation processes at work. One can assert categorically that
the mere use of authority could not have achieved the level
of commitment you will find in Conafe.

Even after five years of work, Conafe was not widely known
within Mexico. In 1978, a study sponsored by the Ford Foundation
established for the first time that the quality and level of

attainment of the children in Conafe's community courses were about
as good as those of the children in the federal system.[6] After six
years of schooling, the first batch of children from the community
courses took their national elementary school test in 1979-80
Five thousand of these children received their certificates in
1980. The general consensus in educational circles in Mexico
appears to be that the Conafe Program compares favorably with the
national urban oriented elementary education program in spite of
its newness and severe handicaps. In terms of costs, the program
claims to be much cheaper than the federal program since both staff
and establishment costs are significantly lower.[7]

Mexico with a population of 70 million has over 15 million
children of school going age. Of these, 12 million are in urban
areas. Of the 3 million rural children, the Conafe program accounts
for 3,50,000 or roughly 12 per cent. According to observers,
Conafe is catering to the bottom 12 per cent of Mexican children.
However, it has not reached the children of extremely small and
remote communities with four or five families. If this most remote
rural segment is kept aside, Conafe has come close to reaching the
poorest segments of Mexican rural society as far as elementary
education is concerned.

NOTES

1. The director general is the chief executive officer of
Conafe. The Council was presided over by the Minister of
Education whose involvement was at the policy making level and on
a part time basis.

2. He was replaced by a new director general when Echeverria's
term ended and a new President took over. Presidential appointees
in such key positions tend to be replaced whenever a new president
comes into power.

3. In Mexico, the educational system permitted students to
study privately and appear for higher level examinations without
having to attend classes in a regular manner.

4. The primary school system in Mexico had six grades. In
the community schools, progression in terms of grades was done
using the judgement of the instructor.

5. This feature was introduced only when the program was
launched across the country.

6. Based on a national sample of schools selected for the
study.

7. A federal teacher on the average costs over $1500 per year
whereas the Conafe teacher costs about a fifth (including subsidies).
Establishment costs are clearly lower and for the most part borne
by the community.

8
Strategic Management:
The Orchestration of Congruence

In Chapter 1, we briefly defined "strategic management" as the set of top management interventions which influence the design and orchestration of the strategy, organisational structure and processes of a program in relation to its environment. The analytical framework we shall develop in this chapter is based on the well known thesis that the performance of an organisation depends on the joint influence of these four interacting variables, namely, the organisation's environment, its strategy, structure, and processes. In the public context, strategic management may be defined as the ongoing process by which those who manage development programs continually appraise and influence these variables and maximise their positive interaction effects or "synergy" in order to achieve the desired program outcomes.

THE KEY VARIABLES

By "environment" we mean those forces external to a development program which creates opportunities and constraints for its survival and expansion. The political, economic, and social forces in the country, the characteristics and attitudes of beneficiary groups, and key actors external to the program are part of the environment. The mix of these forces may turn out to be favorable or unfavorable in a specific situation. "Strategy" refers to the longer term choices concerning a program's goals, design of service, policies, and action plans which seldom get spelt out in the national development plan. Strategic choices are usually formulated and negotiated between the program leadership, and the supervising body (Ministry or Department) in the government. Whether a program will focus on a single goal or multiple goals, and how it proposes to adapt its services to diverse beneficiary groups, for example, are questions of strategy. "Structure" may be defined as the durable organisational arrangements, the distribution of authority, and reporting relationships within the program. These arrangements are likely to vary depending upon a program's strategy and certain features of its environment. Organisational purpose is achieved through "processes" which influence the behavior of program staff and beneficiaries. A process entails the application and sharing of work, information, influence, and power by a program manager to direct their energies toward desired common goals. Participation of staff and beneficiaries in decision making and action, monitoring and feedback of performance, and use of incentives and authority reflect organisational processes.

Empirical Evidence

During the past two decades, a great deal of empirical evidence has been generated on how these variables influence the performance of large organisations. Most of the studies have been on enterprises although the experiences of non-profit organisations are also beginning to be investigated. In general, these studies support the hypothesis that there is a positive relationship between organisational performance and "congruence" among the variables defined above.[1] Their major finding is that the management interventions which influence each of the variables as well as their mutual "fit" contribute to improved performance. The argument is that the positive interaction effects or synergy resulting from the congruence among these variables cause performance to improve. By the same token, when the management interventions designed to influence these variables are poorly planned and incompatible with one another, the evidence is that performance suffers.

Diagram 8.1

The Basic Variables and their Interaction

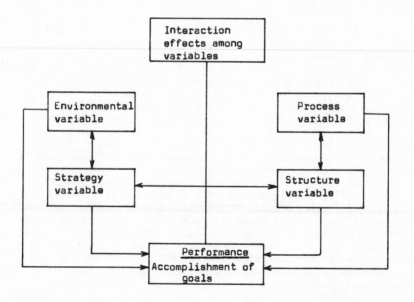

Diagram 8.1 presents a simplified view of the adapted model of strategic management. The four variables shown in the diagram and their interrelationships will be discussed in detail in the following sections. The interaction effects among the four variables are indicated as a separate influence on program performance in order to highlight the importance of congruence. The arrows to and from the different boxes symbolise the interactive nature of the basic variables. There are many examples of such interaction effects in science and technology. For instance, the simultaneous application of a congruent combination of fertilisers, water, high yielding seeds, and other inputs in agriculture causes the crop output to increase to levels which cannot be explained by the individual contributions of the different inputs alone. The interaction effects implicit in the crop production function are comparable to those of the four variables depicted in diagram 8.1.

We believe that the performance of development programs is influenced by the same set of variables though their scope and content might vary from those observed in the enterprise context. Public and private organisations differ not in the relevance of these variables, but in the degree to which those managing them have the ability and will to control or influence them. It is highly probable that governments and program leaders recognise the importance of each of these variables, but do not either understand or attempt to orchestrate them in order to achieve congruence.

Insights from Earlier Studies

Most authors who have examined the managerial and institutional factors critical to program performance have tended to take a rather partial view of this problem. Some scholars have investigated in depth selected organisational aspects and managerial processes of development programs. A good example is Montgomery's study of the relationship between the outcomes of a sample of land reform programs in poor countries and the degree of decentralisation associated with their implementation.[2] Similarly an inter-country analysis by Uphoff and Esman has brought out the importance of local organisation in rural development programs.[3] Studies by Korten have emphasised the role of innovative organisational structures and client participation in development programs.[4] In the light of a study of World Bank financed projects, Smith has concluded that the management problems highlighted in the project reviews were in fact problems of organisation design.[5] Some others have proposed new concepts of "community participation" and "integrated project planning and management cycle" as aids to improving project management.[6] Grindle and her coauthors have reviewed a number of development projects with a view to explaining their outcomes in terms of the context and content of the project.[7] Ickis has examined several rural development programs in Latin America and concluded that their problems were related to weaknesses in the design and maintenance of organisational structures and related processes.[8] Ickis bases his work on the concepts of business policy which we shall also draw upon in evolving our framework. These, therefore, offer important insights and provide some useful building blocks for developing a more comprehensive framework.

While we propose to build on the insights generated by these authors, it is necessary to draw attention to their relative neglect of the interrelationships among the relevant variables and the possibility that there might be varying combinations of the variables influencing performance and which are appropriate under different conditions. Attempts to redefine the concept to suit the public context have been relatively rare. As a first step, therefore, we propose to adapt the concept of strategic management in order to provide a framework for analysing the management interventions of development programs. We shall define the basic variables and the meaning of congruence keeping in view the special features of development programs. It is within this adapted framework that the management interventions of the six programs will be analysed in the following chapters.

THE ENVIRONMENTAL VARIABLE

In development planning, it is customary to examine the national economy in terms of its past trends, growth potential, and resource availability as a prelude to the formulation of the plan, its goals, and policies. In effect, this represents an attempt at dovetailing the development plan to the national environment. A plan that ignores the realities of the environment tends to create severe problems of implementation. Terms such as "unrealistic" and "overambitious" are used to characterise plans which, among other things, failed to match their environments. The point is that the goals and policies of a development plan must be consistent with the potentials and limits of the environment in which it is to be implemented.

The same logic applies to the design of development programs. An understanding and analysis of the environment of the program is a pre-requisite for designing its strategy and organisational structure. In the life cycle of a program, environmental assessment, formal or informal, is critical at three stages. First, when the service or product of the program is being designed and tested (through pilot projects or other efforts), knowledge about the environment is being generated and used which provides inputs for designing the services. Second, an understanding of the relevant segments of the environment becomes critical when the program strategy for replicating the service is being formulated. At that point, an analysis of the forces and actors in the environment (national or regional) capable of influencing the demand for and supply of the service will be useful in evolving program strategies and organisational structures which are most adaptive to the emerging opportunities and constraints in the environment. Third, once implementation has begun, program performance will depend a great deal on the mutual adaptation between design and implementation necessitated by environmental as well as other changes. Environmental assessment is a critical element in facilitating this process.

The conventional view of environmental analysis focuses on the economic, political, social, technological and related segments of the relevant environment. The segmentation process is an aid to the identification of opportunities and constraints underlying the environment. Industrial enterprises introduce new products and processes designed to meet the emerging needs in the market environment.[9] In development programs, the nature of opportunities are not always economic or market oriented. In an agricultural program, the role of economic gains tends to be strong whereas in a health or educational program, the presence of other motivating factors in the environment may have to be sought. In agricultural and industrial programs, the focus of analysis tends to be on the economic and technological segments of the environment. As one moves towards social programs, on the other hand, the political and socio-cultural segments of the environment may assume greater relative significance than the purely economic or technological segment. The thrust of environmental analysis must, therefore, reflect the nature of the program under consideration. In all cases, however, the specification of factors such as the beneficiaries to be served, their potential demand for the service, the strategy for service design and delivery, and the key actors who are likely to influence the program will be facilitated by a careful analysis of the environment.

Important Dimensions

There is another way of viewing the environment which complements the segmentation approach outlined above. The environment of a program may be analysed in terms of its properties. Organisation theorists, for example, have identified several environmental dimensions which they believe to be relevant to the design of organisational structures.[10] We shall argue here that there are certain dimensions of the environment which are relevant to the design of management interventions. These dimensions may be examined under three categories, namely, scope, diversity, and uncertainty. Program environments tend to vary along each of these dimensions.

Scope: All programs and projects are not national in their coverage. Pilot projects and programs servicing limited areas do not have to cope with the total national environment.[11] When a program deals with only one sector of the economy, the scope of the environment it interacts with is more limited than that of a multi-sectoral program. The size of a program thus is not an adequate index of the scope of the environment facing it. The scope of the environment that a large integrated multi-sectoral rural development program, for example, has to interact with is broader than that facing a single sector program, even if both cover the entire country.

The dimension of scope has important implications for the design of both strategy and structure. As the scope of the environment increases, the strategic aspects of sequencing the program in space and time assume greater importance. Mobilising demand for the

program's services and planning the supply of service also are
aspects of strategy which will be influenced by the scope of the
environment. Similarly, as scope expands, the use of conventional
organisational structures may break down and new forms may have to
be created to achieve program goals. For example, hierarchical
control over some parts of the structure may become increasingly
infeasible. The new structure may then take the form of a network
of institutions over which the program managers may have only
indirect control.

Diversity: The environment of a program may not necessarily be
homogeneous in terms of physical-geographical features, cultural,
socio-economic, and political characteristics. The diversity of the
environment in these aspects tends to create heterogeneity among
key actors such as the beneficiaries of the program. When diverse
beneficiary groups have to be served, it becomes necessary to adapt
the service to their different needs. An agricultural program
serving different groups of farmers, for example, must tailor its
services to the diverse settings in which the farmers operate. A
strategy which focuses on a uniform service or input combination
will be inappropriate in this context. Problems of mobilising the
demand for and supply of services also become more complex as
diversity increases. Equally important is the impact of diversity
in the environment on the design of organisational structure. The
manner in which program tasks are differentiated and grouped together
must reflect the degree of diversity present in the environment.
Decentralised structures are in part a response to the problems of
managing diversity.

Uncertainty: Conditions underlying the environment are seldom
stable in any country. Environments vary in the degree of
uncertainty facing the beneficiaries and their socio-economic,
political, and even physical conditions. When changes in these
conditions are frequent and difficult to predict, the program
strategy has to be designed with greater flexibility to facilitate
adaptation to unforeseen contingencies. The design of the organisational structure should take into account the problems of
information processing and decision making at different levels
caused by increasing uncertainty. Decentralisation, in some cases,
is a response to the problem of uncertainty in the environment.
Participation of beneficiaries in the design and delivery of
services, and increased autonomy of operation to functionaries at
the bottom of the implementation ladder, may also be interpreted
as an adaptation to environmental uncertainty.

These three dimensions do not necessarily move together in a
given environment. The scope dimension may increase without a
proportionate increase in diversity. Environmental uncertainty may
be high even when diversity is low or scope in terms of scale is
limited. A program, however, has a highly complex environment to
deal with when all the three dimensions assume high values. An
environment which is national in scope and is characterised by the
presence of highly diverse actors and forces, operating under

severely uncertain conditions, will be more difficult to cope with than a regional or local environment with considerable homogeneity among its actors and reasonable stability in terms of underlying conditions. As the complexity of the environment increases, the management of the program becomes more difficult. The environmental variable, however, is not the sole determinant of a program's performance. This is because a program's strategy, structure, and processes can respond to and compensate to some extent for the effects of environmental complexity. Even when the degree of complexity is low, a program may fail to perform if its strategic, structural and process responses do not match that level of environmental complexity.

There are many ways in which a program seeks to achieve a "fit" with its environment. Pilot projects are a way of testing the level of complexity and working out strategic interventions which are more appropriate to a given setting. When diversity is high, pilot projects or experiments may be tried out in different areas or for different beneficiary groups. On the other hand, when strategies are adopted without the benefit of such field testing, performance tends to be sub-optimal. Another example is the use of studies and sample surveys of the national environment to assess likely responses of diverse beneficiary groups to the proposed program "service". This approach is popular especially with programs involving economic activities, e.g. programs for crop development, small industry development, etc. When there is a great deal of uncertainty about public response and the logistics of supply, strategic interventions to maintain high levels of inventories may be an appropriate means of achieving a fit with the environment. Strategic interventions by top managers are often based on their assessment of the environment through both formal and informal means. In brief, the influence of the environmental variable on program performance is felt not only through the dimension of its intrinsic complexity, but also through its interaction with the management variables which are more within the control of the program leaders. Successful managers will not only assess the degree of environmental complexity, but also intervene to induce support for their programs from the forces and actors in the environment, aided by an assessment of its segments and dimensions. The different examples of the environmental assessment given above illustrate how such interactions between a program and its environment could be used to improve performance through their influence on (1) the demand for the program's services, (2) the supply of its services, and (3) the key actors in the environment who may be relevant to both demand and supply. To the extent these interactive responses are compensatory in nature, they help neutralise the negative impact of environmental complexity. Since environmental conditions tend to change over time, monitoring them and generating adaptive responses which fit the changing conditions become an important responsibility of program managers.

THE STRATEGY VARIABLE

Strategic decisions **are relatively long term decisions
specifying the operating goals**, policies and courses of action of a
development program. A goal **defines** in concrete terms a "future
state" to be achieved by the program.[12] The term "design" borrowed
from the world of technology is often used in development literature
interchangeably with strategy. The degree of freedom a program
manager has in formulating strategy is influenced by the manner in
which the government initiates his program. No development plan
nor government can possibly spell out the design or strategy of
every program in detail. The degree of freedom that program managers
enjoy in strategy formulation does vary from case to case. Government objectives for development programs are sometimes stated in
terms of vague expected outcomes such as improved quality of life,
and sometimes in terms of quantitative growth or output targets.
Even when measurable targets are given, goal-means relationships
and the trade offs involved are seldom specified. Under these
conditions, program managers may have room to initiate and influence
the formulation of strategy. The point to note is that even when
broad and multiple objectives are given to development programs,
their managers may have some flexibility to position their
strategies within the "space" available to them. If the space is so
restricted that the public manager has no role in decision making
of a strategic nature or perceives no such role, he will remain
a mere implementor.

The strategy of a development program is influenced by two
factors. One is the objectives laid down by the government for the
program and the resources allocated to it. The other is the
environment in which the program has to be implemented. The
objectives lay down the framework within which operational goals
have to be specified. As we have seen, some situations yield
greater flexibility to the program manager to choose, interpret,
and sequence operating goals. The complexity of the environment
is the other factor that influences the choice of operating goals
and action plans of the program. The greater the complexity of
the environment, the more difficult and challenging will be the
tasks of managing a program. Similarly, the more complex the goals
of the program, in terms of diversity and measurability of outputs,
the more difficult will be the program's management because of
increased problems of information processing, conflict over
resources, and control of performance. The top management will
get over-loaded as decisions are passed up unless the organisational
structure is drastically redesigned. There are limits to the
extent to which such structural reorganisation can be attempted in
the public context. Furthermore, competing goals lead to conflicts
over the distribution of scarce resources. Top management may not
always have the competence to evaluate the performance of groups
dealing with services based on different technologies. The tendency
of program managers under these conditions will be to adapt to
their environment by limiting the operating goals of the program.[13]
Even when multiple objectives are given, they are likely to search

for a dominant goal as the kingpin of the program strategy. This is
a "complexity reducing" approach in the absence of which performance
would have suffered. The pursuit of highly diverse goals would have
meant the management of diverse outputs leading to severe system
overloads. The program's multiple objectives are therefore likely
to be achieved through a strategy of <u>sequential diversification</u> of
goals and outputs as the organisation learns and gains credibility
in the environment. The major implication of this argument is that
simultaneous diversification of goals and services will be resisted
in a complex environment for fear of hurting program performance.

Strategy : Symbiotic Components

The strategy of a development program may be disaggregated into
two basic components which have a symbiotic relationship to each
other. We shall call the first component "the service-beneficiary-
sequence" (SBS) strategy and the second "the demand-supply-resource"
(DSR) strategy. The SBS is concerned with the specification of
<u>goals</u> and DSR with the specification of <u>tasks</u>. The interdependence
between the two makes it necessary to plan the two components
together.

The <u>Service-Beneficiary-Sequence Strategy</u>: SBS seeks to answer
three questions: <u>What</u> is the service or output of the program? <u>For</u>
<u>whom</u> it is designed? <u>When</u> is it to be provided? What, for whom,
and when are the key dimensions of operating goals. These are
questions which must be addressed within the "objectives-environment
space" facing the program. The service of the program is the output
it makes available to its beneficiaries, consistent with the
objectives laid down by the government. Pilot projects, for example,
may be viewed as instruments for testing out services which are then
replicated nationally or regionally. An integrated rural development program designs its service to achieve the goals of raising the
income levels and quality of life of its target groups simultaneously. Its service may be defined as the total and inter-related set
of activities for delivering the inputs for economic and social
services needed by the rural community. The apparent product or
physical outputs that beneficiaries deal with may not necessarily
constitute the service of a program, since services can only be
instrumental in generating those outputs or outcomes. In a dairy
development program, for example, the service cannot be defined
as the output of milk or increased incomes, but as the set of
integrated activities of extension, procurement, processing, and
marketing of milk which have been instrumental in augmenting the
supply of milk and hence incomes of farmers.

A useful way of analysing strategies is by categorising them by
the major dimensions of the underlying services. First of all, the
service of a program may be <u>single</u> or <u>multiple</u>. The focus here is
on the dimension of <u>diversity</u> at the output end of the program.
When a program offers differing sets of services to different crops
or multiple sectors, its services are multiple in nature.[14] On the
other hand, when a program caters to a single crop or activity which

does not call for diversity at the output end, we have a case of single service, even if at the input end there is considerable diversity. In other words, a single output-multiple input situation can be described as a single service case.

The diversity dimension of service may well be a matter of degree. A second dimension to explore, therefore, is the degree of integration or relatedness of the multiple services referred to above. Multiple services may be closely inter-related either for technological production reasons or reasons relating to utilisation by beneficiaries. Two crops with common production characteristics or complementarity in market terms or client needs may permit a degree of integration within a program comparable to what obtains in a single crop program. On the other hand, a program that deals with crops which do not have such complementarity either in production or consumption may have to live with an extreme case of service diversity. Unrelated services thus add to the degree of diversity facing the program.

A third dimension of service relates to the measurability of the service and its outcome. Generally speaking, development programs with an economic orientation provide services and outcomes which are, on the whole, measurable. The degree of measurability declines as programs move into the realm of social services and activities which attempt to bring about behavioral changes in beneficiary groups. In some cases, inputs of services lend themselves to measurement, but not their outcomes.

These three dimensions have important implications not only for the strategy variable, but also for the structural and process variables which in turn influence program performance. How a program positions itself in terms of these dimensions may provide useful clues for planning its sequencing decisions and its organisational structure. It is also possible that the problems in making structural adjustments within the governmental setting may lead managers to limit the scope of operating goals and hence of program "service" along the dimensions discussed above.

The specification of the beneficiaries to be served is implied in the definition of service, but deserves to be treated seperately. The objectives-environment space provides a basis for the specification of the program's beneficiaries. The diversity of clientele in the environment may make it necessary even for a single service program to differentiate its services so as to adapt to the varying needs of its beneficiary groups. As a program moves from its pilot project or experimental stage to the replication phase, a major task it faces is to work out a pattern of differentiation in its services that matches its beneficiary diversity. This may call for the design of varying combinations of inputs, each combination matching the needs of a specific beneficiary group. A standardised service and a uniform combination of inputs may be inappropriate when the program has to cater to beneficiaries who differ in terms of income, assets, location, and cultural and social characteristics.

Once a basic concept of service has been designed, it is important to test its suitability by reference to the relevant beneficiary groups. The range of variation needed may be such as to call for considerable differentiation in the program service or alternatively, a deliberate limitation on the groups to be served if such differentiation is infeasible or highly uneconomical. A high degree of differentiation may also make it necessary to examine the costs and benefits of designing separate progrms for different population segments, eg. separate regional programs, programs for small farmers, etc.

The complexity of the environment and service-beneficiary diversity have a direct bearing on strategic decisions concerning the phasing of the program in time and space. Though national programs sometimes cover the entire country all at once, it is not uncommon to find a sequential approach to implementation in many cases. A major reason for phased coverage is paucity of financial resources. Our argument is that environmental complexity and service-beneficiary diversity are important reasons for building sequential moves into the program strategy itself. Failure to do so could impose serious management problems on the program and adversely affect its perfor- mance. Programs which take several years to build up their full range of services and extend the same to an entire region or county are essentially matching their sequencing strategy to their service- beneficiary diversity and environmental complexity. If strong inter- dependence among services exists in a multi-service program, the strategy is likely to favor sequential phasing in space(e.g., implementing the multiple services in one defined area first and then moving on to others). If the interdependence among the services does not call for their simultaneous supply, the strategy may focus on the promotion of one service followed by others, thus pursuing a process of sequential diversification over time.

Strategic choices in terms of sequencing moves, therefore, may be viewed as responses to the limits of management rather than to resource constraints in the conventional sense. Abundance of funds does not necessarily eliminate managerial problems and the need to cope with these constraints through an organisational learning process. The experience of large integrated rural development projects in many countries bears eloquent testimony to this proposition.

The Demand-Supply-Resource Strategy: While SBS focuses on the operating goals of a program, DSR calls attention to the identifi- cation of the key tasks and functions the program organisation must perform in order to achieve its goals. The two together provide the basis for designing the action plans of the program. Even when the specification of goals has been sensibly done, a program may fail because the tasks relevant to the goals were not properly identified.

Three basic tasks which are relevant to most development programs are (1) public response to or demand for the service, (2) supply or delivery of service, and (3) mobilisation of resources for the program from key actors in the environment. The mix of tasks to be performed and the relative importance to be given to each in a program will vary with its goal and the complexity of its environment. Irrespective of the goals chosen, many programs have been managed as supply systems with an exclusive focus on production

and delivery.[15] Under conditions of shortage or excess demand for
services, this approach might be adequate, e.g., in economic sectors
such as industry operating in protected markets. But in programs
which attempt to induce social or behavioral changes and which do
not provide immediate and direct economic benefits to the beneficiaries, public response or demand in the classical sense may surface
as a constraint. Mobilising demand then becomes a key task of the
program. Programs for population control or preventive health, for
example, do not generate the kind of response from the public that
an agricultural program might attract from farmers. Deliberate
strategies may have to be formulated to create demand for the
services of such social programs.

Both ability and willingness on the part of beneficiaries play
a role in their response to a public program. If the constraint on
response is likely to be a lack of willingness and not a lack of
ability, the tasks to be emphasised will be of two types. Where
free standardised services are involved, the answer lies in the
dissemination of information and advice.[16] Where a great deal of
local adaptation of services and mobilisation of local resources
is called for, and prior design is difficult due to environmental
uncertainty, the answer lies in the participation beneficiaries in
the design and production of the outputs.[17] Beneficiary participation is of value in and of itself and is rightly treated as a
goal in many programs. Our argument, however, is that it has an
important role in demand mobilisation. A good example is adult
education in rural areas which generates a great deal of response
when designed locally and with the participation of the people.
The same program when offered as a top-down, standardised activity
usually tends to fail. Participation makes the services more
relevant to the local needs and this in turn increases the
motivation of beneficiaries to respond to the program. But if
ability to respond is a problem, neither information nor participation will provide the answer. If the costs of services, (actual
or opportunity costs) limit the ability to respond, income
generation will be a prerequisite for mobilising demand. As long
as incomes do not rise, beneficiaries may be unable and unwilling
to demand the program services.[18] This explains the poor response
to primary education in some countries. If, on the other hand,
major institutional reforms are needed before response to the
program can occur, the use of power to bring about the reforms
through government or peoples' organisations will be the answer to
the problem of program response (e.g. land reform implementation
as a prerequisite for agricultural programs).[19] Dealing with the
problem of ability is thus a more difficult task and calls for
interventions which address the problem directly. Effective land
reform improves the income earning power of the small farmer and
motivates him to adopt better practices. Improved income levels
motivate people to pay greater attention to their children's
education. In both cases, ability is the variable being influenced.

The second component of DSR, namely, supply is a task the
nature and scope of which is derived from the requirements of the
demand for the program. The planning of the supply of service
without reference to demand has been a serious problem for many

development programs. There are three strategic considerations which should govern the organisation of the supply task. First, the degree of service-beneficiary diversity may indicate the extent to which service differentiation has to be planned as part of the supply task. This is further complicated when a service in turn is based on the integration of diverse inputs. The mix of inputs to be integrated may vary when the needs of beneficiary groups differ. In fact, the nature and type of integration of inputs should take into account the extent of inability of beneficiary groups to integrate inputs on their own. Second, the strategic decisions on the sequencing of the program may provide important guidelines for the planning of the supply task. Third, every effort has to be made to avoid the shortage syndrome which characterises the supply side of programs in many developing countries. Vested interests thrive on the perpetuation of shortages. Hence the need to give special attention to the logistics of the supply of program services.

Irrigation programs and projects in developing countries provide illuminating examples of the pitfalls in planning supply without paying attention to the nature of demand. Engineers have planned and built grandiose irrigation dams only to find that the utilisation of water by farmers fell far below their expectations. Evaluation studies have shown that poor utilisation was a major problem in cases where the differing needs of the diverse farmer segments were not taken into account in organising the supply of water. From an engineer's point of view, water is a homogeneous commodity that all farmers must want. Yet the timing and other conditions of the supply of water were important considerations governing farmers' response to the scheme.

The mobilisation of resources for the program from the key actors in the environment is a task whose importance increases with the relative strengths of the individuals and interest groups influencing the supply of and demand for the program's services. Key actors comprise political and administrative leaders, opinion leaders, and others who can provide support to a program. The program implementation process tends to entail coordination with several other agencies whose support and active cooperation become critical to the success of the program. External linkage building may turn out to be a key function of the top management of a multi-sectoral program which has to deal with diverse beneficiary groups and several departments in the government whose resources, both political and financial, are important for the program. Even if sound strategic plans are made, negelct of this function and the consequent failure to mobilise the support of key actors in the relevant environmental segments may result in poor performance of the program.

The thrust of the strategic interventions that a program adopts will influence the mix of managerial functions/tasks that gets emphasis in a specific situation. People's participation tends to receive greater attention when energising demand is seen as high priority though participation may be treated as a goal in some programs by virtue of its contribution to self reliance. In resource intensive infrastructural programs such as highways, power development or income generating programs involving industry, careful planning of supply may become the leading function with much less emphasis on beneficiary participation. In a multi-sectoral program influenced by a great deal of diversity in the political environment, a critical function of program management may turn out to be the mobilisation of key actor support and active external linkage building. The mix of management functions accorded high priority in a program will thus reflect the critical areas for complexity reduction chosen by the program leader.

To sum up, it is through the choice and adaptation of operating goals (SBS), and tasks (DSR) that program leaders make strategic interventions. SBS seeks to answer the questions of _what_ service will be provided and for _whom_ and _when_. DSR addresses the question of _how_ the service will be provided. That there is a symbiotic relationship between the two may not be self evident. Most observers will readily agree that DSR is derived from SBS. However, the complexity and magnitude of DSR tasks may well lead to a modification of the SBS strategy. The decision to pursue a strategy of sequential diversification may, for example, be a response to the feedback from DSR to SBS. Since managers formulate SBS and DSR strategy components within the context of the program environment and given objectives, the process tends to proceed in an iterative fashion. The SBS-DSR dichotomy should therefore be viewed as an analytical device for disaggregating the strategy variable. The six elements which constitute the SBS-DSR components are amenable to managerial intervention and provide the framework for planning the program's organisational structure, processes, and operating decisions.

THE STRUCTURE VARIABLE

Organisational structure affects program performance through the implementation process. The design of structure for a national program cannot be derived from the experience of a pilot project or limited area experiment. A pilot project is of considerable assistance in defining certain dimensions of strategy. But the scaling up of a program in its replication phase would render the pilot project structure irrelevant for adoption in most cases.

The tendency of most governments will be to encourage their program organisations to adopt centralised structures similar to those of their ministries and departments. The difference between the structural requirements of the central systems and the field oriented program agencies, however, can be significant. To the extent that the environment, goals, and tasks of a development program differ from those of its sponsoring ministry, there is a case for designing the program's organisational structure along lines which differ from the bureaucratic mode. There are two features of the bureaucratic mode in the DCs which could pose severe constraints on the organisational structures of programs.

First, a ministry or department is usually structured along _functional_ lines, based on a definition of its major tasks. The Agriculture Ministry, for example, may be organised on the basis of functions such as extension, research, evaluation, and general

administration. These functions are believed to be relevant to all
sub-sectors and crops with which the Ministry is concerned. New
programs with a different definition of the problem and a set of
tasks which cut across different ministries and even external
organisations may not perform well when structured along the same
functional lines. Second, ministries usually have highly
centralised structures which are inappropriate for the performance
of tasks which require a high degree of local adaptation. Local
adaptation is necessary when considerable diversity exists in the
environment (beneficiaries with different needs) and prompt
decision making at lower levels is required because of environmental
uncertainty. Imposition of the centralised structure on a program
whose task requirements call for a decentralised structure will be
dysfunctional.

The appropriateness of a structure, however, can be judged only
in relation to the program's strategy and environment. A functional
structure may be optimal for a single service program whereas a
multiple service program may require a structure differentiated by
service. A limited area program may find a centralised structure
appropriate whereas a large, national program may call for a
decentralised structure. There is thus no unique structure that
fits the requirements of all programs.[20] We discuss below three
dimensions of the structure variable which are relevant to development programs.

Structural Forms : Differentiation and Integration

The SBS-DSR components of strategy provide the basis for differentiating the tasks within the program organisation. All tasks
need not be performed directly by the program agency. The normal
tendency within government, however, is to increase differentiation
of functions, reinforced by the specialist orientation of officials.
Unfortunately complex differentiation calls for strong mechanisms
for integration; but governments' ability to integrate tasks tend
to be limited in most developing countries. The problem could have
been mitigated by the beneficiaries or markets performing a part of
the integrative role. These alternatives do not always appeal to
the governments concerned for bureaucratic or ideological reasons.

Problems of differentiation and integration of tasks can,
however, be dealt with satisfactorily within the conventional
structures of government in some cases. Thus where a program is
small in size, production processes are standardised, routinised
procedures exist, technology is simple, and information processing
is relatively easy, it could well be handled as part of the
centralised structure of government (e.g., regulatory or infrastructural service programs).

The nature and scope of differentiation and integration and the
degree of decentralisation are key factors which tend to influence
the structural forms of development programs. Organisational
theory has a rich literature over a wide variety of structural
forms. The three structural forms described below, namely, the
functional structure, the matrix structure, and the network

structure, are perhaps among the most relevant for development programs.[21] It is important to note the conditions under which each of them becomes relevant to a program. In reality, structures do not necessarily follow these pure forms. Mixed forms also exist, as our case studies have shown.

A functional structure is appropriate when a single service program operates in a limited area. Its organisation can be structured by reference to the major functions underlying the program service. The divisions within the program agency are responsible for planning and performing the different functions. The work of these divisions is then integrated by the chief executive (top program manager). A functional structure will perform well only when a single service or output is involved. If the environment of a program is relatively stable and homogeneous, a program with a single service can be managed through a functional structure though it does not necessarily have to be a centralised structure.

A matrix structure will fit two categories of programs. Single service programs which must cover diverse geographical regions will need structures which permit a dual focus on regions and functions. Multiple service programs will need structures which permit dual control over services and functions. In both cases, the assumption is that better decisions will be made when authority is delegated to the regional and service levels where the integration of the relevant functions/tasks are taking place. Management control is effected not through the use of centralised authority, but through a decentralised structure that permits problem solving at levels where competence and involvement of implementors are presumed to exist. In the matrix structure, the final control still rests with the top management of the program agency. Its uniqueness lies in pushing decision making in certain areas down to organisational levels where managers are required to exercise joint control.

Large national programs of a single or multiple service type, facing considerable environmental complexity, may adopt network structures. In the network structure, there is no single organisation with full control over the program. The national program agency works in coordination with a network of organisations or institutions which jointly provide the components of the program service. The network concept permits a high degree of decentralisation which in turn is a response to the existence of extreme environmental complexity. When considerable regional diversity exists, it becomes necessary for the program agency to involve the regional or local governments in the program operations. When there is uncertainty about beneficiary response, the program agency may find the participation of beneficiaries in the design and delivery of service an effective means for mobilising demand. It is paradoxical that the more complex a program and its environment, the greater the programs' need to depend for its performance on interorganisational cooperation rather than on the use of authority. Inter-organisational cooperation becomes imperative because no organisation has under its control all the inputs or elements needed to generate the desired outputs. A structural intervention that seeks control is justified when the close interdependence among certain inputs makes it too risky to leave their integration to voluntary coordination. In a large and complex program, however, such control may be physically impossible to achieve even if the interdependence condition is met. The operation of the network structure, however, violates the unity of command concept so deeply entrenched in government.

When a program has to be implemented through a network structure which consists of several organisations with specified roles and none of which is directly under the control of another, new structural devices have to be devised to ensure program performance. Structural interventions within the program organisation cannot be the remedy when there is no authority structure behind binding the relevant organisations together. The focus must shift to devices which can make the inter-organisational coordination effective through some form of <u>reciprocal interdependence</u>.[22] The program organisation within the network structure must depend for its task performance on a variety of lateral influences. The role of authority, as the primary source of power decreases while <u>sources of lateral influence</u> such as the use of funds, joint planning, political support, mobilisation of demand among beneficiaries, and participation of beneficiaries in program operations assume greater significance.

Decentralisation

The pattern of authority sharing in an organisation is reflected by the degree of decentralisation in its structure. A structural form does not necessarily imply a predetermined degree of centralisation or decentralisation. It is therefore useful to consider this structural feature separately. Given the same structural form, the mix of functions decentralised may vary depending on the nature of the program service and the environment.

When the nature of program tasks calls for flexibility at the lower levels of the organisation, a centralised structure will simply get overloaded and perform unsatisfactorily. Decentralised structures become far more appropriate when (a) a diverse client environment calls for considerable local adaptation; (b) demand or responsiveness of the public to program outputs depends on speedy program responses; (c) relevant information is generated at delivery points and central information processing is either infeasible or likely to cause delays or distortions in decision making; and (d) responsible participation of field level officials and beneficiaries in program planning and implementation is conducive to good performance.

Decentralisation can be sometimes accomplished without departing from conventional government structures. What is required is greater delegation of authority for which there are many precedents in government. Officials at lower and more relevant levels could be empowered to make decisions which are more appropriately made at these levels, but without changing other organisational processes that government structures are used to. It should be noted, however, that decentralisation has its costs in terms of the increased complexity of management control and development of better trained decision makers at lower levels.

Organisational Autonomy

When task requirements call for structures and processes different from those of the government, program organisations with some degree of independence from government may have to be set up. This form of intervention leads to the creation of <u>semi-autonomous</u> structures within the government. The processes of decision making, evaluation, control, and compensation traditionally used in government are often inappropriate in development programs. Where more adaptive and innovative activities are to be performed, and technology and the motivation of staff require different organisational processes, program agencies may require greater autonomy from government.

The degree of autonomy that an organisation requires can be determined only by reference to the areas of decision making in which it needs freedom of action. Generally speaking, a program within government could be defined as autonomous when its supervising body retains "strategic" control, leaving operational control in its hands. Strategic control may involve goal setting, control over the budget, and key appointments and review of performance. For autonomy to be meaningful, there should be an agreed upon division of areas of discretion between the autonomous body and its supervisory authority. Furthermore, for autonomy to be effective, government should have the capacity and the will to monitor and control program performance. When program tasks and services are difficult to measure, and the monitoring and control task becomes problematical, participation of beneficiaries in program management may offer a preferred means of control.

In the literature, organisational autonomy is often described and analysed in terms of the legal forms and structures of organisations. Legal structures are important insofar as they de ne in formal terms the extent to which an organisation can depart from the norms and practices (in financial, personnel, and decision making processes) of its parent or autonomy giving body (**nominal** autonomy). However, the <u>effective</u> autonomy an organisation enjoys may well exceed or fall below what is permitted legally. Organisations in the public as well as private sectors often derive what may be termed <u>induced</u> autonomy when those who have power over them permit them to exceed their nominal autonomy. Thus the trust and support of political leaders and other decision makers who have authority over the organisation may result in effective autonomy that exceeds the nominal limits. Induced autonomy becomes possible because of the discretionary powers those in authority **over** organisations can deploy in order to augment their effective autonomy. On the other hand, those managing an organisation may not wish to fully utilise the autonomy formally available to them either due to commitment to government norms, inertia, or risk aversion. In this case, their effective autonomy may fall below their nominal autonomy. Effective autonomy thus is the sum of nominal autonomy and induced autonomy.

The tendency to seek autonomy when program complexity (caused by environmental factors and program strategy) increases is clear from the tendency of many international donor agencies to set up projects outside of the framework of governments. However, this is a different approach from the structural intervention we have outlined above which seeks organisational autonomy within the government framework. Hirschman's observation that eventually autonomy seems to wither away merely reinforces the argument that the pre-conditions referred to above must exist for semi-autonomous structures to operate within government.[23] Organisational autonomy for the sake of insulating an agency from politics or corruption is not an adequate basis for sustaining this structural intervention.

To conclude, the choice of structural forms, pattern of authority sharing and autonomy are the media through which the structural variable influences program performance. Through the specification of these dimensions, the structure variable seeks to respond to the complexity of the environment and the requirements of the program strategy. Our analysis shows that in the more complex programs and environments, structures may tend to operate as networks which seek to achieve results through inter-organisational cooperation rather than through the use of authority. Among the sources of influence deployed by the program agency to achieve inter-organisational cooperation are control over the allocation of resources, joint planning, political support, mobilisation of demand at the grassroots, and the participation of beneficiaries in program activities.

THE PROCESS VARIABLE

Organisational processes are the influences on human behavior leading to decisions and actions. The focus is not on the substance of the outcomes, but on **how** the outcomes are reached. This is an important consideration in the management of development programs which are bound to be influenced by the organisational processes of the government which spawns them. Governmental processes share several common features. First, they are dominated by the concept of hierarchical authority in decision making and gaining compliance. Second, as a corollary, the focus of the processes generally tends to be on the observance of procedures rather than on the achievement of results. Third, the processes are usually operated in an inflexible manner with little room for variation to suit the requirements of changing tasks. It is not surprising that the carryover of these features into the organisational processes of development programs whose tasks and environments are substantially different from those of the central systems of government leads to serious problems of performance. For example, if a program set up with a decentralised structure puts in motion a top down planning process, dysfunctionalities are bound to surface in the program's management.

We shall examine the organisational processes of development programs with reference to four critical areas of decision making and action : (1) participation, (2) monitoring, (3) human resource development, and (4) motivation. While many other processes also

exist, these four exemplify the key areas which tend to make a significant difference to the accomplishment of organisational purpose.

The Participative Process

A development program may use the participative process to formulate action plans, sequence its activities, and allocate
resources. The process is concerned with the role of participation
of beneficiaries and staff in the planning and implementation of
the program. The nature of the process chosen will depend on the
knowledge required for planning and the commitment of various actors
required for planning and implementation. A centralised, top-down
process might limit the scope of issues for discussion with other
levels and therefore include very few actors in decision making
because the top group has the required knowledge. This may be
contrasted with a process that encourages participation from below,
negotiates on key issues, and responds to the ideas and problems
raised by the relevant actors. The Japanese practice of negotiation and consensus building is a good example of a process that
involves prolonged deliberations among interest groups, but leads
to speedy action and implementation aided by the commitment created
by the process itself. The process generates the knowledge to plan
and allocate, and the commitment to implement the plan. A process
that encourages the participation of people at different levels, and
gives employees the internal autonomy to plan their tasks, may yield
not only better plans by generating ideas which the top management
on its own cannot do, but also impart greater motivation and commitment to the participants for action.

The Monitoring Process

Most organisations, including government bureaucracies, have
information and reporting systems. Yet the control process in
government tends to rely more on the observance of procedures and
rules governing the processes of decision making, budgetary
control, etc., than on performance. Development programs which have
complex development goals are likely to shift the focus of the
control process from procedures to performance. The design and use
of the monitoring process plays a key role in this shift. There are
three dimensions of the monitoring process which are relevant to
program performance. First, the question who is concerned about the
information is critical. When information is of direct concern to
the top management, it gives strong signals to other members of the
organisation. In government where procedures receive priority over
performance, the signal given leads to a greater emphasis on the
former. Second, what the information conveys is an important matter.
When key information inputs directly relevant to program goals are
monitored, they clearly convey what managers expect of their people.
When a simple information system is used and a fast feedback is
given to the staff   at different levels, it conveys a sense of
urgency that motivates people to respond promptly. Third, how the
the information is used   also makes a big difference. When the

feedback is timely and used for problem solving and mid-course corrections at different levels, monitoring becomes a live process, perceived by members as functional. Information of a post-mortem type that does not get fed back into the decision making channels of the organisation is likely to be seen as less relevant. For this reason, the monitoring process ought to emphasise its direct relevance to program management by virtue of the information it provides on the course of performance.

The monitoring process may work through both formal and informal routes. For development programs which operate in uncertain environments, field visits by supervisors and informal gathering and sharing of information could be as important as formal information systems. As programs and environments become more complex, the role of the monitoring process as an integrative communication device assumes greater importance. Under these conditions, the monitoring process becomes a tool for raising the level of motivation and commitment of the members of the organisation. When monitoring is weak in terms of the three dimensions mentioned above, prompt responses to adapt to the environment and steer the course of performance in desired directions cannot be made. In other words, the managerial functions of integration and control will not be performed effectively.

The Human Resource Development Process

The identification and development of program staff are a major challenges for development managers who are called upon to perform new and complex developmental tasks. The routinised processes of government for the recruitment, development, and compensation of personnel run counter to the more flexible processes programs need to identify, select, and develop their personnel. As a result, the match between people and program tasks becomes a problem. The task requirements of a program call for departures from the normal conventions of government in these matters. Part of the reason for granting some measure of autonomy to program agencies is to facilitate modest departures from these norms and to enable them to evolve more suitable processes to recruit and train their staff. Where conventional tasks are involved, neglect of these processes may not cost the organisation much, at least in the short run. In programs whose strategies are sensitive to human skills and motivation and whose structures call for adaptive abilities on the part of the employees, the adoption of selection and development processes which differ from those of government may be essential.

The Motivation Process

The problem of motivation is an extremely complex and controversial subject. In government, compliance is seen as a function of the use of authority. On the other hand, experience of business enterprises lends support to the role of utilitarian or economic motivation as the driving force.[23] The use of economic incentives to motivate beneficiaries and program staff may be appropriate in development programs whose services are economic in nature. On the other hand, in programs which offer no direct economic benefits, the use of economic incentives could be dysfunctional. Non-economic incentives including commitment to an ideology may be more appropriate in the change oriented social programs. This is not to rule out the value of economic incentives, but to say that the role of non-economic motivating factors may have to be larger in the "mix" of incentives. There is a wide spectrum of incentives available to programs for motivating compliance. Monetary incentives, status and recognition, participation, ideology, authority, and coercion constitute the key elements in the spectrum.[24] Varying combinations of these elements could be used by program managers to motivate their employees and beneficiaries.

The motivation process should distinguish between the needs of program employees and beneficiaries. In an agricultural program, motivation of beneficiaries could be achieved through the use of economic incentives. A similar use of economic incentives, however, may not be feasible with respect to the program staff. For them, it will be in order to use other elements like status, recognition and participation, bearing in mind the problems in linking their performance to economic rewards. In brief the argument is that different actors and types of programs will need different combinations of incentives to motivate commitment and that the combinations must be linked to the nature and strategies of the programs.

Diagram 8.2 presents the different dimensions of the four variables which have been discussed above. We have already noted the interdependence among the dimensions of each variable. The diagram also focuses on the interdependence among the variables through these dimensions and their joint influence on performance. Strategic and structural interventions, as noted earlier, will be dysfunctional when environmental features are not properly taken into account. The effectiveness of the interventions will be further limited when they cease to be supported by flexible organisational processes. Effective autonomy permits program managers to move along the wide spectrum in which the four processes could potentially operate. Viewed thus, there is a mutually interdependent relationship among strategic, structural, and process interventions. Structures are intended to differentiate and integrate the tasks of organisations in a manner that is consistent with their strategy and environment. They need to be reinforced by organisational processes which give signals and influence the behavior of members so that the integration being sought is facilitated. Complex programs, with difficult to measure outputs and change oriented goals, may find certain organisational processes more functional than others. Structures may then be found that permit these processes to operate more effectively. Structures created for research and development or educational programs may for this reason differ from those of a manufacturing unit or government department by inducting processes that facilitate innovation and creativity rather than the use of routines and precedents.

Diagram 8.2

The Key Variables and Performance

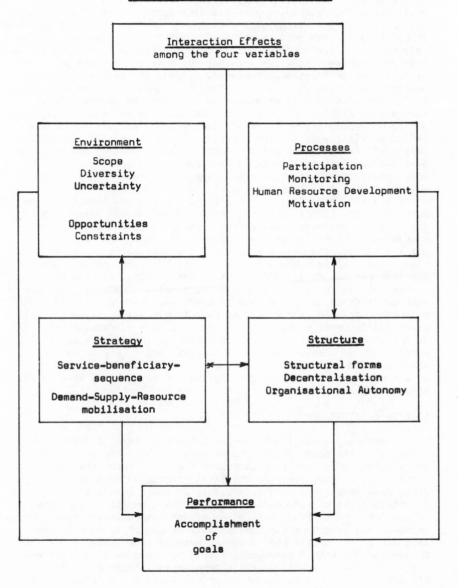

CONGRUENT COMBINATIONS AND INTERACTION EFFECTS

Having examined the four variables in some detail, we are now ready to explore their inter-relationships and the meaning of congruence. It is evident that each of the variables has a direct influence on the performance of development programs. An adverse environment for example, may have a disastrous impact on the outcome of a program. A strategy with a strong technology behind it may lead to positive program performance even if other variables are relatively weak. On the other hand, if the variables do not reinforce one another, even an innovative strategy may fail to make its potential contribution to program performance. Except in the case of the environmental variable, it is difficult to apply a unique criterion of "goodness" to the other variables. They can be termed good or bad only in relation to their fit with each other. A strategy turns out to be appropriate because it has responded well to the environmental complexity facing the program. Performance will be optimal only when the variables are congruent with one another and generate positive interaction effects in the process. Since the relationships among these variables are interactive, their planning and operation cannot be treated in isolation.

Since the dimensions of the different variables tend to change over time, the fit or congruence achieved during one period may not hold good in another. Environmental variations, for example, may necessitate changes in strategy, structure, and processes. In the private sector, the necessary adaptations tend to follow without much delay. Under competitive conditions, delayed action may spell disaster for the firm. In the public sector, such adaptations generally tend to be cumbersome and difficult. The lack of a market test tends to cover up the cost of inaction. Maintaining the state of congruence among the variables over time should receive special attention in development programs, as there are no natural external or internal pressures which will quickly set in motion a self-correcting mechanism. Successful programs are likely to be characterised by the effective creation and continued maintenance of a high level of congruence among their environments, strategies, structures, and processes.

Four Types of Programs

In general, a congruent combination may be said to exist when a change in the state of any one or more of the dimensions in the combination causes positive interaction effects among the variables to decline, thereby lowering the level of program performance.[25] Since development programs vary widely in their nature and scope, it is difficult to specify generally applicable conditions of congruence in precise terms. The specific set of management interventions which represents a congruent combination will be unique to each program. In order to facilitate the design of such interventions, we propose to examine the set of strategic, structural, and process interventions which approximate congruent combinations in four distinctly different types of development programs. Diagrams 8.3, 8.4 and 8.5

127

Diagram 8.3

Strategic Interventions

Objectives / Environment	Complexity of Program Objectives	
	Single Economic Goal	Multiple Social Goals
Low	Standardised single service Focus on homogeneous beneficiary group Limited attention to demand mobilisation I	Multiple social services Focus on homogeneous beneficiary group Moderate attention to demand mobilisation III
Complexity of Environment Scope Uncertainty Diversity High	Single service-differentiated Moderately varying combinations of inputs (integration to match needs of heterogeneous beneficiary groups) Moderate attention to demand mobilisation Matching emphasis on logistics of supply. II	Multiple differentiated social services Diverse combinations of inputs to match needs of heterogeneous beneficiary groups Strong focus on demand mobilisation Matching emphasis on supply logistics. IV

Diagram 8.4

Structural Interventions

Objectives	Complexity of Program Objectives	
Environment	Single Economic Goal	Multiple Social Goals
Low	Functional form Limited Decentralisation Limited organisational autonomy I	Matrix form – simultaneous focus on service and function Limited use of network Increased decentralisation Use of authority cum lateral influence for integration Moderate organisational autonomy III
Complexity of Environment Scope Uncertainty Diversity **High**	Matrix form – simultaneous focus on region and function Moderate use of network Increased decentralisation Integration more through lateral influences than authority Moderate organisational autonomy II	Matrix form – simultaneous focus on region, service and function Extensive use of network High degree of decentralisation Integration chiefly through lateral influences High degree of organisational autonomy IV

Diagram 8.5

Process Interventions

129

Objectives Environment	Complexity of Program Objectives	
	Single Economic Goal	Multiple Social Goals
Low	Limited beneficiary participation Moderate attention to selection and training Informal, subjective monitoring Motivation through use of authority and economic incentives. I	Increasing beneficiary participation and internal autonomy for staff Mix of formal and informal information for monitoring Increasing emphasis on selection and training Motivation chiefly through non-economic incentives III
Complexity of Environment Scope Uncertainty Diversity High	II Increasing beneficiary participation and internal autonomy for staff Mix of formal and informal information for monitoring Increasing emphasis on selection and training Motivation through a mix of economic and non-economic incentives	IV Dominant role of beneficiary participation Considerable internal autonomy for staff Formal information as main basis of monitoring Considerable emphasis on selection and training Motivation chiefly through non-economic incentives.

summarise the critical interventions which seem to vary from one type
of program to another. The set of strategic, structural, and process
interventions given against each type of program in the three
diagrams constitutes a congruent combination of the basic variables.
Congruence requires that the management interventions in a
program are consistent with its environment and the objectives of
the government for the program. In the three diagrams, therefore,
programs are classified by the complexity of the program environment
and objectives. The environment increases in complexity in proportion to the importance of scope, uncertainty, and diversity. The
complexity of objectives given by the government is regarded as low
when a program has pursue a single economic goal, and high when
it is asked to achieve multiple social goals. Needless to add that
these are rather over-simplified assumptions. In reality, the
three dimensions of the program environment need not increase or
decrease together. An environment may be high on uncertainty, but
low on diversity. There is no doubt, however, that the most complex
combinations is the one with high values for all the three dimensions.
Similarly, there are many combinations of objectives other than
those indicated which exist in reality. A program may have a single
social goal, multiple economic goals, or mixed economic and social
goals. The multiple goals may be related or unrelated and the
latter clearly will add more complexity to a program. Again we
should emphasise that for the sake of simplicity, we have treated
"complexity" as a continuum and have marked only their extreme
points. Many intermediate combinations are possible and the trade
off between two combinations can be made only in the light of
considerable situational knowledge. The programs which fall into
the four quadrants of the diagrams thus signify four distinctly
different types: (1) programs which are low on both environmental
complexity and complexity of objectives, (2) programs which are low
on complexity of objectives, but high on environmental complexity,
(3) programs which are low on environmental complexity, but high on
the complexity of objectives, and (4) programs which are high on
both dimensions. We shall refer to these four categories as
Types I, II, III, and IV. It is obvious that all development
programs cannot be fitted into these four types. However, the
nature and scope of management interventions could be interpolated
for other intermediate combinations on the basis of the insights
offered by these diagrams. Each quadrant of the Diagram 8.3 spells
out the nature and scope of the strategic interventions appropriate
to the distinct type of program it represents. Each quadrant of
Diagrams 8.4 and 8.5 does the same in respect of structural and
process interventions respectively. When the interventions given
against a specific program type in the three diagrams are put
together, we have a congruent combination for that type of program.
To keep the exposition simple, only the most critical dimensions of
management interventions have been presented in the diagrams.

The interpretation of these three diagrams should be relatively easy as the interventions entered against each program type are drawn from the discussion of the four variables in the preceding sections. Thus against Type I in Diagram 8.3, "standardised single service" is given as a strategic intervention. This is compatible with an environment that is low in diversity and uncertainty and meets the mandate to pursue a single economic goal. Focus on a homogeneous beneficiary group is appropriate when diversity and scope of the environment are low. Demand mobilisation does not call for a great deal of effort as dissemination of information in a limited (spatially) and homogeneous environment is relatively easy and private economic gain has a direct appeal to beneficiaries. The strategic interventions thus hang together. The strategic interventions, however, get increasingly complex as one moves to the other program types. Thus in Type IV, a strong focus on demand mobilisation, possibly involving beneficiary participation is called for as the multiplicity and social nature of services render public response increasingly difficult. Since beneficiaries do not see any immediate gain, their normal response will be poor unless a deliberate strategy is evolved to mobilise demand. Again, Type IV requires a strategy to match the needs of its heterogeneous beneficiary groups by creating diverse combinations of inputs for its multiple, differentiated services. Not only are different services (eg. health, education, nutrition, etc.,) required but also tailoring them to the needs of diverse population segments (eg. regional, social, and cultural diversity of beneficiaries) becomes necessary. This is the rationale of differentiated services. The structural and process interventions shown against the different types of programs could be interpreted along similar lines. In each case, it will be evident that any departure from the consistent set of interventions given against a program type will mean a decline in performance.

An Interpretation of Congruence

These diagrams are useful not only to demonstrate the variations among different types of programs in respect of management interventions, but also to highlight the significance of congruence among their strategic, structural, and process interventions. An examination of the three types of interventions in the diagrams against each program type will show that together they represent a congruent combination. Let us start with Type I programs which may be treated as relatively small programs with limited, measurable outputs in relatively stable and homogeneous environments. We have already commented on the strategic interventions of Type I. Diagram 8.4 tells us that an organisational structure that differentiates and integrates by function is adequate for Type I. Given the small size of the program and the standardised nature of its service, a relatively centralised structure will perform satisfactorily. Since routinisation of practices will be relatively easy and the need for local adaptation is limited, the role of organisational autonomy will be minimal. For the same reasons, the role of participation

will be limited in Type I (Diagram 8.5). When direct economic
gains from the program are perceived by beneficiaries, they are
likely to respond to the program even if the participative process
is weak. The program leadership is able to supervise the program
directly and could therefore do with an informal monitoring process.
The focus on selection and training of staff is moderate in view of
the prevalence of central decision making and limited local adaptation. Given the small size and economic nature of the program, the
use of authority and economic rather than non-economic incentives
for motivation is dominant. Thus the major dimensions of the
structural and process interventions discribed above are compatible
with the strategic interventions indicated for Type I in Diagram
8.3.

Let us now turn to Types II and III. The management of Type II
is more difficult than that of Type I because of the increased
environmental complexity of the former. The management of Type III
is also more difficult because of the increased complexity of
program objectives. Consequently, their strategic interventions
have become more complex. Type II offers basically the same
service as Type I but is differentiated to cope with the diversity
among beneficiaries. Different combinations of inputs are integrated to yield differentiated services. The larger size of the
program (possibly national in scope) and heterogeneity of beneficiaries calls for increased emphasis on demand mobilisation. Supply
logistics which was not a problem in Type I now assumes increased
importance. Type III differs from Type I in its focus on multiple
social services and increased attention to demand mobilisation
arising from the fact that information alone does not bring about
public response to programs which have no immediate economic appeal.

Diagrams 8.4 and 8.5 show that the structural and process
interventions corresponding to Types II and III differ significantly
from those of Type I. From the functional form of Type I, Types II
and III move towards the matrix form of structure for the program
agencies. They seek inter-organisational cooperation through the
creation of networks. Structures get more decentralised, autonomous
and depend less on authority and more on lateral influences for
integration. A significant difference between the structures of
Types II and III is that matrix form in the former focuses on region
and function while the latter focuses on service and function.
This is clearly an adaptation to the nature of the diversity faced
by the two types. The complexity of the environment in Type I and
the multiplicity of services and need for local adaptation in
Type II require them to link up with other organisations as all
the needed inputs are not within the control of the program
agencies. The operation of such networks in turn is facilitated by
increased decentralisation, autonomy and use of lateral influences.

The processes which reinforce these strategic and structural
interventions in Types II and III are indicated in the diagrams.
First of all, the participative process becomes stronger than in
Type I as beneficiary participation assumes greater importance and
program staff are given greater internal autonomy. Both are a
recognition of the increasing need for local adaptation, the limits
to central information processing and the compulsions of demand

mobilisation. The growing complexity of tasks and more autonomous roles performed by the network lead to a greater emphasis on staff selection and training which are processes for matching people and tasks. Second, the monitoring and motivation processes continue to be important, but undergo a shift in their focus. Monitoring becomes a more formal process than in Type I reflecting the increasing complexity of information and the need for more systematic and fast feedback. In respect of motivation, the limits of economic incentives and authority become more evident and increasing use is made of non-economic incentives. Again the directional changes observed in the structural and process interventions seem to be consistent with the strategic interventions and environmental complexity of Types II and III.

Type IV programs are characterised by a high degree of both environmental complexity and complexity of program objectives. This is clear from their strategy of offering multiple social services differentiated to cope with the diversity among beneficiaries. Their diversity of input combinations to match the needs of different beneficiary groups is much greater than those of Types II and III. Similarly, given the increased uncertainty in the environment, their focus on demand mobilisation is much stronger and the logistics of supply receive increased attention.

The structural and process responses of Type IV to these strategic dimensions consist of an intensification of the directional changes we have already observed in Types II and III. Moves in any other direction would have led to sub-optimal performance. The extensive use of network structures, the dominance of the participative process, primary reliance on non-economic motivation and the high degree of organisational autonomy deserve special attention. All these are interventions which are consistent with the complexity of Type IV environment and the nature of program objectives. The contrast between Types I and IV is not merely in the external forces operating on them, but in the entire set of management interventions relevant to them.

Two important insights seem to emerge from the foregoing analysis of the three diagrams. First, when development programs differ significantly in their environmental complexity and nature of objectives, strategic management calls for different types of interventions. Any attempt to standardise management interventions across a wide spectrum of programs will only lead to sub-optimal performance. The political and bureaucratic tendencies to seek uniformity without any reference to environmental and goal differences adversely affect the practice of strategic management. Second, while the conditions of congruence cannot be spelt out for all types of programs, the directional changes to be effected in order to achieve congruent combinations of strategic, structural, and process interventions are indicated by our diagrams. Response in terms of any one type of intervention alone may not be adequate. A combination of interventions which moves in the directions indicated in the diagrams, on the other hand, tends to have a synergistic effect on performance. In the real world, no program

perhaps will succeed in achieving and orchestrating a congruent
combination fully. Many programs learn and evolve through a process
of trial and error. The role of program leadership lies in facilitating the directional changes which approximate the conditions of
congruence.

NOTES

1. A. Chandler, _Strategy and Structure_ (Cambridge:MIT Press,
1962); P. Lawrence and J. Lorsch, _The Organisation and the
Environment_ (Boston : Harvard Business School, 1967); J.Galbraith
and D.Nathanson, _Strategy Implementation : The Role of Structure and
Process_ (St.Paul : West, 1978); P. Khandwala, "Mass Output Orientation of Operations Technology and Organisation Structure",
Administrative Science Quarterly, March, 1974; pp.74-77; T. Burus
and A.M. Stalker, _The Management of Innovation_ (London : Tavistock,
1961);
2. J.D. Montgomery, "The Allocation of Authority in Land
Reform Programs : A Comparative Study of Administrative Process and
Outputs," _Administrative Science Quarterly_, March, 1972.
3. Uphoff and Esman, _Local Organisation for Rural Development :
Analysis of Asian Experience_, RDC Monograph No.19, (Cornell,1974).
4. D.C. Korten, "Community Organisation and Rural Development:
A Learning Process Approach," _Public Administration Review_,
September-October, 1980. See also Korten's paper in Stifel, et.al.,
op.cit.
5. Smith, et. al., _The Design of Organisations for Rural
Development Projects - A Progress Report_, World Bank Staff Working
Paper No.375, March 1980.
6. Uphoff, Cohen & Goldsmith, _Feasibility and Application of
Rural Development Participation_, RDC Monograph Series, (Cornell,
1979); D.A. Rondinelli, "Why Development Projects Fail : Problem
of Project Management in Development Countries," _Project Management
Quarterly_, March 1976.
7. M.S. Grindle (Ed.), _Politics and Policy Implementation in
the Third World_ (Princeton: Princeton University Press, 1980).
8. J. Ickis, _Strategy and Structure in Rural Development_
Doctoral Dissertation, (Boston : Harvard Business School, 1978).
9. Market segmentation is a popular concept in enterprise
management. The application of this concept in the context of
public programs has been rare.
10. Khandwala, P.N., _The Design of Organisations_ (New York :
Harcourt Brace, 1977); Thompson, J.D., _Organizations in Action_
(New York : McGraw Hill, 1967); Galbraith, J., _Organization Design_
(Reading : Addison-Wesley, 1977).
11. These examples illustrate the relative nature of scope. The
emphasis here is on the spatial dimension of the environment.
12. See Etzioni, A., _A Comparative Analysis of Complex
Organization_ (Chicago : Free Press, 1975).
13. Simon, H.A. and March, J., Organisations(New York:Wiley,1958);
Cyert, R., and March, J., _The Behavioral Theory of the Firm_ (New

York:Prentice Hall, 1973).

14. When diverse crops have to be attended to, there is a multiplicity of services even though all of them come under a single sector, namely, agriculture. The problem of multiplicity cannot be gauged simply by counting the number of services involved. The "relatedness" of the services clearly has a bearing on the problem of multiplicity.

15. Governments are used to clients seeking services. This is a familiar feature of regulatory programs, e.g., industrial licensing, rationing systems.

16. For instance, advertising, promotion campaigns, personal contacts, educational activities, etc.

17. The literature on participation has hardly noted the demand mobilisation aspect.

18. The failure of social service programs in many cases might be attributed to this problem.

19. The examples of Korea, Taiwan and Japan show that major land reforms preceded the significant breakthrough in their agricultural productivity.

20. Lawrence and Lorsch, op.cit. The literature on the contingency theory of organisation, and Business Policy has thrown up impressive evidence in support of this view.

21. Organisation theoreists have devoted a great deal of attention to structures, the focus of their work has been in industrial enterprises. See, for example, Galbraith, op.cit.; Thompson, op.cit

22. Litwak, E. and Hylton, L.F., "Interorganisational Analysis," Administrative Science Quarterly, 6, 1962; Benson, J., "The Interorganisational Network as a Political Economy," Administrative Science Quarterly, July, 1975; D.F.Berry,L.Metcalfe and W.McQuillan, "Neddy - An Organisational Metamorphosis", Journal of Management Studies, February, 1974, pp.1-20.

23. Hirschman, A.O., Development Projects Observed (Washington D.C: Brookings Institution,1967)

24. See Ilchman, W., and Uphoff, N., The Political Economy of Change (Berkeley: Univ. of California Press,1974), chapter 3 for a discussion of "political resources" as means of compliance.

25. Though the concept of congruence has been used in the literature on industrial organisations, it has no generally accepted definition that facilitates empirical testing of the phenomenon. For a review of studies which have attempted the test of congruence in the industrial context, see Galbraith and Nathanson, op.cit.

9
Strategies:
Matching the Environments

How did our six development programs match their strategies and environments? Did their strategic interventions have anything in common? We shall explore these questions in this chapter and present detailed evidence on the two interdependent components of strategy, viz., service-beneficiary-sequence, and demand-supply-resource, and their compatability with the environment with respect to each program. A summary statement of the major environmental factors underlying the program and the strategic interventions adopted in response to them is presented at the end of each section.

An analysis of the strategic interventions of the six programs brings to light several common features. In brief they are:

- The focus of most programs on a single service to begin with;

- Sequential diversification of program services;

- Integration of program inputs to match the beneficiary's inability to integrate them on his own;

- A high degree of demand mobilisation;

- Strong linkages between pilot projects and national programs;

- Deliberate phasing of program implementation.

The common themes underlying the strategies and a set of propositions which brings them into sharp focus are discussed in the concluding section.

INDIA'S DAIRY DEVELOPMENT PROGRAM

It is clear from the case study that promotion of dairy development was the primary objective laid down by the Government of India (GOI) for the newly established National Dairy Development Board (NDDB). No guidelines were given by GOI to NDDB on how this

objective was to be established. The circumstances in which NDDB
was created and the Prime Minister's commendation of the "Anand
Pattern" pointed to the direction in which dairy development was
expected to move. Broadly speaking, NDDB was to promote dairying
as an aid to rural development. Operation Flood was the strategy
eventually formulated by NDDB in response to its mandate. NDDB's
early attempt to offer technical assistance to state governments to
set up dairy plants and producer cooperatives brought forth a
rather lukewarm response, in spite of the explicit support of the
Prime Minister to the new agency. Clearly, NDDB had failed to
understand its environment and come up with a strategy to exploit
the underlying opportunities in its early years.

Positive Features

NDDB's leaders identified four positive trends in the Indian
environment as they began their search for a new strategy:
First, rural milk producers definitely had a comparative cost
advantage over the urban milk producers. Increasing congestion and
the high cost of cattle feed and maintenance in cities had tilted
the economics of milk production in favour of the lower cost rural
areas. From a national point of view, it made more sense to keep
the cattle in rural areas and transport the milk to urban markets.
Second, transport bottlenecks and storage problems which in the
past had encouraged cattle colonies in the cities seemed capable of
being resolved as new technological developments began to take
place. Expansion of the railway system, introduction of long
distance haulage using refrigerated rail cars, milk powder production, and chilling and feeder balancing plants for milk made it
easier to collect milk from rural areas, store, and transport it
to the cities.
Third, the long term demand for milk in urban areas seemed
likely to grow fast, given the expansion of cities and the relatively income elastic demand for milk. Milk was always in short
supply in the cities and the urban dairies, most of them publicly
owned, were unable to procure adequate supplies and consequently
had considerable idle capacity.
Fourth, most small farmers in different parts of India were
used to keeping cattle even if commercial sale of milk was not well
organised in the villages. Familiarity with dairying was a
positive feature of the environment. Family labour and farm residue
were the main inputs provided by the farmer who found keeping a
couple of buffaloes or cows a useful subsidiary occupation. As a
result, small farmers and the landless together accounted for over
50 per cent of the milk production in rural areas.

Problems of Uncertainty and Diversity

Despite these positive features, there existed four major
problems in the environment which NDDB leaders took into account
in formulating the strategy of Operation Flood. They also
reflected the degree of uncertainty and diversity present in NDDB's

environment.

First, small farmers could not be counted on to increase the production and supply of milk, given the market uncertainty facing them. The seasonal nature of milk production and price fluctuations, irregularity in payments by milk traders, and the unorganised nature of farmers added to the uncertainties faced by dairy farmers in relation to the market.[1] When returns were seen as inadequate and unstable, farmers tended to treat dairying as a risky venture.

Second, farmers faced considerable uncertainty on the production front. Veterinary care, extension, fodder and other essential inputs needed to improve milk production were not adequately available in most villages. Neither private nor public delivery of these services existed in an integrated fashion.[2] Small farmers could hardly be expected to augment milk production and maintain regularity of supply when their access to these basic inputs and services was limited.

Third, while the Amul experience (popularly known as the "Anand Pattern") had led to a viable strategy for coping with these market and production uncertainties, it was not certain that all state governments would respond to NDDB's initiative positively. Political and bureaucratic leadership in several states were known to be lukewarm or even hostile towards the adoption of the Anand Pattern. There was thus some measure of uncertainty about the prospects for implementing any national program NDDB might eventually promote.

Fourth, the import of milk powder and other dairy commodities had worked against the interests of small farmers through their depressing effect on milk prices. The emerging (in the late sixties) international surplus in dairy commodities was expected to exacerbate the situation. If the EEC countries were to export the surplus as part of their aid to India, there was likely to be increased pressure on GOI to distribute it to the urban dairies at subsidised prices. Uncertainty as to how the aid might be utilised was yet another problem in the environment.

Uncertainty with respect to the market, production, and aid meant that farmers' ability and willingness to respond to any national program by NDDB would be limited. Uncertainty with respect to implementation meant that NDDB could not count on the cooperation of the state governments which were responsible for action in the field.[3] These were all factors which would have limited the demand for NDDB's program. An analysis of the environment made it clear to NDDB that it must formulate a strategy to effectively cope with these uncertainties.

The Anand Pattern evolved out of the experience of one district in the country. The diversity of India with its 19 states and numerous districts was an aspect of the environment NDDB had to consider while promoting the Anand Pattern. The local conditions of farmers, and their preferences and problems varied from one region to another. The institutional setting, attitudes, and interests of the state governments were not identical. In several states, the existing departments of dairying, animal husbandry, and cooperatives were well established and did not look with favor upon a move to hand over dairy development to an independent cooperative institution. The administrative and leadership resources and experience with the cooperative structure also varied considerably among the states. It was clear that a straight forward and rigid replication of the Anand Pattern would not be appropriate under these circumstances. Though NDDB's focus was on a single commodity, namely milk, the national scope of its operations and the different sources of uncertainty and diversity it faced made its environment an extremely complex one.

Service-Beneficiary-Sequence Strategy

Operation Flood's concept of service, which was a response to these environmental factors, consisted of three parts : (a) the functional integration of the inputs required for milk production at the farm level through the village cooperative society, (b) the vertical integration of milk collection, processing, and marketing at the district level, and (c) provision of financial and technical assistance to the state level implementing authority. This definition of service was unique in that it integrated a number of interdependent elements which the small farmer would not have been able to do on his own. In the process it also reduced his market and production uncertainties. The cooperative form of organisation was the instrument promoted by NDDB to achieve the proposed integration.

The validity and relevance of the first two components had been adequately tested and demonstrated by Amul. In fact, they were at the core of the Anand Pattern. The Anand District Cooperative Union had entered into contracts to supply milk to the Bombay Dairy. It had set up its own processing plants and worked out a viable scheme to provide the inputs needed for milk production to the members of the village cooperatives. The third component, however, was not derived from the Amul experience. Financial and technical assistance from NDDB and its affiliate IDC were the means by which the first two components and their integration could be facilitated in the states in which Operation Flood was to be implemented. The three parts of the service that NDDB offered could be interpreted as a strategic move to minimise the uncertainties in relation to the market, production, and implementation and increase the responsiveness of farmers and state governments to its new program. Underlying this definition of service was NDDB's perception that by linking the production and supply of rural milk to the growing urban milk markets, a viable approach to rural development could be generated.

Implicit in this approach was the concept of the small farmer as the beneficiary. The strategy of integrated service was most relevant to the small farmer family which owned a couple of buffaloes. The large commercial farmer could have achieved much of this integration on his own. The choice of dairy development as the "entry point" to improve the lot of small farmer groups gave NDDB a strong, single focus around which a program could be built.

While the farmer was NDDB's primary beneficiary, the state government was the medium through which the services for the farmer were to be channelled. In a number of states, NDDB agreed to the creation of dairy development corporations to be the implementing agencies instead of district cooperative unions which the states could not easily create at the outset.[4] This was not the case in some states such as Gujarat where NDDB could deal directly with district cooperative unions. Here is an example of the adaptation of the strategy to the diversity in the environment, bearing in mind the need to satisfy an important category of clients.

Though the mandate of NDDB was national in scope, Operation Flood did not cover the entire country to begin with. The program was designed to cover 18 rural milk sheds in the states and four urban metropolitan areas in its first phase. Operation Flood Phase II which is currently in progress is to be extended to an additional 150 milk-sheds (districts) and 150 towns. During Phase II NDDB has also diversified its operations by entering the oilseeds sector where a similar strategy of creating and linking up farmer coopera- tives, processing facilities, and large scale marketing is being attempted. This is a very recent move and little evidence is available as to its outcome. In Phase I, Operation Flood began with four metropolitan areas whose needs were most urgent and where the chances of success seemed reasonably bright. The limited financial, technical, and managerial resources of NDDB were therefore applied to an important segment and not to the entire country. The complexity of the integration required was such that a wider coverage might have hurt the program. Expansion was therefore gradual and there was a strategy for learning from experience and building on the lessons of the past into the designs for the future.

Demand-Supply-Resource Strategy

There is considerable evidence in the case study to show that creation of "demand" for Operation Flood was built into its strategy. The early experience of NDDB with its rather passive approach to technical assistance seems to have reinforced the need to take beneficiary response to the program seriously. There were four elements in the strategy which were designed to energise demand.

First, the emphasis on paying a good and stable price to the farmer for his milk (quality tested) on a daily basis was meant to attract him to the program. Amul experience had demonstrated the viability of this approach. Credit was not part of the package provided to the farmer. If he receives cash payment for his milk daily, the need for credit was to a large extent obviated. As a result, NDDB did not have a loan component in its program. Second, the functional and vertical integration of inputs for the service which have been discussed above made it easier for the small farmer to respond to the program. Linkages with the market, processing, and collection of milk and the simultaneous provision of inputs through the cooperative reduced his uncertainties and assured him a return on his investment which no alternative system could match.

Third, in states where farmers were unfamiliar with the program and skeptical of its benefits, the intervention of "spearhead teams" had a "demonstration effect". These teams of young veterinary doctors, fodder specialists, and extension experts, through their work in the villages, literally mobilised demand for the program. Their deployment in the districts by NDDB and their training of the "counterpart teams" deputed by the states helped prepare and win over thousands of farmers to participate in the program. Fourth, the response of the state governments and urban dairies to the program was greatly influenced by the innovative use of the aid received by GOI in the form of dairy commodities. By routing these through IDC and using the aid proceeds to finance Operation Flood schemes in the states, GOI and NDDB transformed a potential threat into an opportunity for rural development. The financial and technical assistance offered by IDC and NDDB now appeared attractive to the states even if the Anand Pattern which was also part of the package seemed at first unpalatable. A demand strategy which focused on the farmer, but ignored the state governments would have had little chance of success.

On the supply side, NDDB had a great advantage in that the Anand Pattern had perfected a supply system for the delivery of the functionally and vertically integrated services at the village and district levels. The basic strategy was to replicate this system in each of the milksheds. In the light of local circumstances some variations in the basic system were permitted. For example, where daily payment for milk was not favored, the system was altered to pay on a weekly or fortnightly basis. Some flexibility was given to the spearhead teams to work out local adaptations. This was a response on the supply side to environmental diversity.

There were other elements in the supply strategy which deserve to be noted. Design and standardisation of dairy plants taking advantage of the economies of scale made possible by the size of the program, and collaboration with the Indian Railways and equipment manufacturers for improving the technologies for transport and storage are examples of other supply tasks on which NDDB took strategic action. Actions on the supply side were planned and integrated by the lead agency NDDB which also played the major role in mobilising demand.

In terms of resource mobilisation, the single most strategic intervention by NDDB was in generating funds for Operation Flood through the import of dairy commodities under the World Food Program. This development not only provided massive funds for the new program, but also paved the way for NDDB's relative autonomy of operation.[5] The key actors which NDDB's leaders had to influence in this were GOI officials (political leaders and bureaucrats) and officials of international aid agencies.

Equally important was the mobilisation of support from actors who had the most to do with the success of the program on the ground. Influencing farmers was an important part of NDDB's strategy as is clear from the innovative use of spearhead teams and the careful attention given to the training of village society

Exhibit 9.1

Operation Flood

Environmental Factor → **Strategic Intervention**

Unstable returns and high risk in dairying ──→ Stable prices and regular, daily payment to farmers for milk purchased.

Large numbers of small farmers engaged in the subsidiary occupation of dairying, but unable to obtain and integrate needed inputs.

Market domination by private traders and middlemen.

Comparative cost advantage of rural milk.

Underutilisation of capacity of urban dairies alongside shortage of milk in cities.

Potential high growth of urban demand for milk.

Ready availability of dairy technology.

Technological changes in long distance rail transport, refrigeration and storage, good prospects for international dairy aid.

Varying attitudes of state governments towards Anand pattern.

Large size and cultural and physical diversity of the country.

Demand mobilisation in rural areas.

Small rural farmer as client.

Functional and vertical integration of service to rural milk producers with linkages to major urban dairies.

Appropriate mix of technologies (milk production on small scale, milk processing and marketing on a large scale).

Large investment and technical assistance programs.

Mobilisation of key actors.

Adaptation of Anand Pattern.

Use of spearhead teams.

Phasing of program.

Sequential diversification of services.

secretaries. State level leadership (political and bureaucratic)
was another target group whose commitment and attitudes NDDB tried
to influence through frequent visits to state capitals and the
involvement of their representatives in the decision making
processes of the organisation. The creation of State Dairy
Development Corporations to manage the program initially was a
product of this mobilisation strategy.

Thus the strategy of Operation Flood was firmly rooted in the
objectives of NDDB and well adapted to the Indian environment. The
focus of the program was on the small farmer. It was his inability
to integrate the inputs and linkages needed for dairying which led
NDDB to undertake the task of integration, both functional and
vertical, as part of the program strategy. The complexity of
integration was such that a geographical phasing of the program was
built into the strategy by NDDB. The single minded focus on milk
was a characteristic of the strategy until the program matured. By
offering an integrated service, the program increased the farmer
responsiveness and reinforced it by the innovative use of spearhead teams. Dairy commodity aid which emerged as a potential threat
to the cause of the farmer was turned into an asset that strengthened
the program and made the state governments more responsive to the new
strategy. The supply system which evolved out of the Anand Pattern
was at the core of the integrated delivery system at the district
and village levels, supported by a strategy to create the large
scale processing and transport facilities required by a gigantic
national program.

MASAGANA - 99

Masagana-99 was organised by the National Food and Agriculture
Council (NFAC) in response to a national emergency faced by the
Philippines. NFAC was given a very clear objective by the President
to attain national self-sufficiency in rice in the shortest
possible time. The new program was planned with considerable
political support and commitment behind it.

Apart from strong political support, there were other favorable
environmental factors which NFAC took into account in planning
Masagana-99. First of all, a highly productive new rice technology
was available in the Philippines. As the case study shows, the new
high yielding technology was widely adopted by farmers though the
productivity per hectare had not moved up significantly.[6] Second,
the spread of irrigation over the years had increased. Over one
third of the land under rice cultivation had access to irrigation.
Third, there was a good network of 420 rural banks in the country,
though they were not engaged in lending to small rice farmers.
They financed commercial farmers for the most part, but the credit
infrastructure was in place. In addition, the introduction of
martial law improved the law and order situation in the country
somewhat though the individual responses of thousands of farmers
could not have been controlled through this process.

NFAC's environmental analysis highlighted a number of factors
which had important implications for the demand and supply aspects

of the new program. The following were the key findings relevant
to demand. First, the uncertain returns from rice weakened the
farmers' incentive to increase his investment in the crop.
Uncertain weather conditions and the consequent price fluctuations
in the market made it unattractive for him to respond to the new
practices and inputs promoted by extension agents. Second, a
number of different inputs were required simultaneously by the
farmer to raise the level of his rice output. Seeds, water,
fertiliser, pesticides, and improved practices were required in
specified combinations or sequences. On their own, most farmers
were unable to obtain these inputs in time, given the severe market
imperfections and access problems that plagued the rural sector.
The small farmer's inability to obtain and integrate the necessary
inputs had to be overcome if he was to respond to the new program.
Third, the implementation of land reform in the country brought in
its wake a disruption in the credit arrangements that existed
between landlords and tenants. Uncertainty with respect to credit
was thus seen as an emerging problem in the environment.

There were several developments in the environment which had
implications for the supply side of the program. (1) While a
majority of rice farmers had adopted the modern rice varieties,
problems regarding timely supply of the different inputs needed
by the farmers (including credit) were severe. Given the strong
interdependence among these inputs, failure to supply any one of
them brought about a considerable drop in productivity. Different
agencies of the government as well as private companies were
involved in these operations. Achieving coordinated action through
these diverse agencies was by no means certain in this complex
environment. (2) The task of supplying and integrating the inputs
had become an even more difficult operation given the time
constraints involved and the uncertainty in weather conditions.
(3) Uncertainty was a characteristic of the rice economy of the
Philippines. The diversity of farming conditions aggravated the
problem. Unirrigated or dry land farms which accounted for two
thirds of the rice area were more risky in terms of output even if
inputs were supplied to them. (4) The Bulacan project which was
in the nature of a pilot experiment had yielded very valuable
lessons in organising a supply system to deliver the inputs needed
by rice farmers. It demonstrated that an efficient, integrated
delivery system could be created in the villages to make up for
the farmer's inability to obtain and integrate the needed inputs
on his own.

Service - Beneficiary - Sequence Strategy

In launching Masagana-99, NFAC's strategy was to augment rice
output through the integrated delivery of all the inputs needed by
the farmer. The concept of 'integration' was the main feature of
the service with credit as the binding element in the package. The
physical inputs of seeds, water, fertiliser, and extension were the
major components of the service. The demand for these inputs was
sought to be energised through three other program elements

(a) credit, (b) price support, and (c) communication. Agricultural
loans provided through the network of rural banks and other
institutions were designed to mobilise the farmers' response to the
program and create demand for the farm inputs. Price support through
the National Grains Authority was meant to assure the farmer stable
returns from rice. A major communication campaign was mounted to
educate the farmer on the program and its benefits and the steps
he should take to raise his rice output and earn higher income.

The concept of service reflected both functional and vertical
integration. There was a strong interdependence among the inputs
required for rice production. Procurement, storage, and price
support by the National Grains Authority were among elements in the
program which followed rice production and created vertical linkages
to ensure the farmer's motivation to produce. NFAC's approach was
to incorporate all elements into the service which the farmer was
unable to integrate on his own. This was an important adaptation
to the Philippine environment, especially since the inputs to be
integrated functionally were within the purview of different
ministries or agencies.

The focus of the program was on the farmer with irrigated land.
This definition of the beneficiary reflected an attempt to minimise
the impact of the uncertainty arising out of a diversity in
clientele. Farmers of unirrigated lands were less likely to increase
rice production in the short run and the integration task would have
been more complex with respect to dry lands when the need of the
hour was to maximise output. The sharp focus on the small rice
farmer was reinforced by NFAC's decision to concentrate on rice,
giving lower priority to the other crops for which also it was
responsible. It was only after Masagana-99 had achieved self
sufficiency in rice that NFAC began to pay increased attention to
the corn program.

Masagana-99 was extended to all provinces which had rice farming.
But in each province, priority was given to irrigated lands.
Attention to unirrigated lands was given only in the second phase
when research and extension services to deal with their special
problems were developed. Thus, there is some evidence of an
attempt to phase the program consistent with its objective of achieving self sufficiency in rice in the shortest possible time.

Demand - Supply - Resource Strategy

The demand component of the strategy consisted of four elements
which were built into the integrated service : (1) the communication
campaign which disseminated information on Masagana-99 was aimed at
persuading farmers to join the program. The messages were tailored
to the needs of farmers in different regions and delivered through
the media most accessible to them. (2) The price support scheme
was meant to instil confidence in farmers about the stability of
returns from rice cultivation. Their confidence, it was hoped,
would make them respond positively to the program. (3) Credit
without collateral, perhaps, was the most influential element in the
package as far as farmers were concerned. Resources for cultivation

Exhibit 9.2

Masagana-99

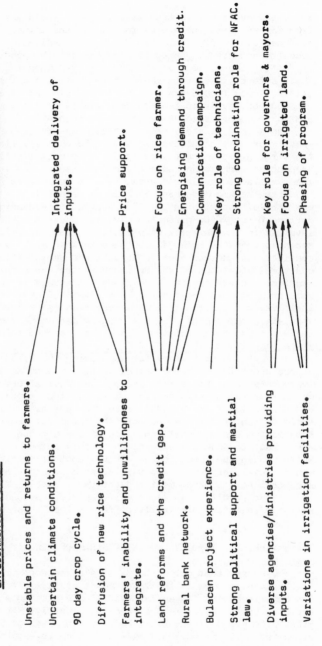

Environmental Factor

Unstable prices and returns to farmers.

Uncertain climate conditions.

90 day crop cycle.

Diffusion of new rice technology.

Farmers' inability and unwillingness to integrate.

Land reforms and the credit gap.

Rural bank network.

Bulacan project experience.

Strong political support and martial law.

Diverse agencies/ministries providing inputs.

Variations in irrigation facilities.

Strategic Intervention

Integrated delivery of inputs.

Price support.

Focus on rice farmer.

Energising demand through credit.

Communication campaign.

Key role of technicians.

Strong coordinating role for NFAC.

Key role for governors & mayors.

Focus on irrigated land.

Phasing of program.

were made available to them at low risk. There was strong motivation for farmers, therefore, to utilise the integrated service
provided by the program. (4) If the communication campaign, price
support, and credit pushed farmers towards the program, the
production technicians in the field pulled them towards the program.
Their efforts to canvass the farmers locally and assist them in
getting loans from banks were meant to help the beneficiaries
respond positively to the program. These elements were well integrated into the demand strategy of Masagana-99.

The supply strategy of the program was derived from the
experience of the Bulacan project. The most important aspects of
the strategy were the following: (1) The participating banks and
production technicians were given important roles and special
inducements at the local level. (2) A deliberate attempt to
transfer the knowledge and experience gained in the pilot project
was part of the strategy.[7] (3) A strong coordinating role was
envisaged for NFAC, given the diverse inputs and agencies/ministries
involved in the integration process. Production technicians were
seconded from the Extension Bureaus to NFAC which exercised
considerable control over their work and performance. (4) Increased
political power behind the delivery system was considered essential.
Provincial governors and local mayors (leaders of local governments)
were brought into the program as chairman of program committees in
their respective areas and made responsible for performance.[8] Their
initiative and support for the program were thus tapped to ensure
the smooth operation of the delivery system and resolve conflicts
at the local level.

The program's strategy for mobilising the resources and key
actors consisted of three parts. First, having made credit the
lynchpin of the integration process, a major effort was mounted to
mobilise rural bankers to participate in the program and to get an
adequate allocation of credit from the Central Bank. Second, the
mobilisation of farmers who were the potential beneficiaries of
the program was a significant part of the strategy; the strategic
moves made to ensure the response of this set of key actors have
already been spelt out above. Third, another critical group of
actors, viz., governors and mayors, were brought into the program to
decentralise its management and get their local influence and power
to achieve results. In all these respects, Masagana-99 adopted a
strategy which was distinctly different from those of the preceding
programs.

THE SMALLHOLDER TEA DEVELOPMENT PROGRAM OF KENYA

The decree that set up SCDA, KTDA's predecessor, had specified
its basic objective as the development of five different crops for
the benefit of the Kenyan farmer. KTDA's emergence followed a
decision by the Government of Kenya to restrict the objectives of
SCDA. The new decree established KTDA in place of SCDA and
empowered it to promote tea as a cash crop to augment the income of
the small farmer and help diversify his cropping pattern. The
single commodity focus given to KTDA reflected the new government's

awareness of the complexity of managing programs for diverse crops simultaneously through the same organisation.

There were several positive features in the Kenyan environment which favored a smallholder tea development program. First, the international demand for quality tea was growing and Kenyan private tea estates had already got a firm footing in the international market. Second, climatic and soil conditions in the Rift Valley of Kenya were well suited for tea cultivation. The stability of weather conditions meant that cultivation practices could be standa-rdised and farmers trained in the necessary routines. Third, the pilot projects undertaken by the government had demonstrated the viability of small farm cultivation of tea in different areas. The African farmer was basically a subsistence farmer who had little familiarity with cash crops. Some of them had worked as laborers on large private tea estates, but had no experience in operating tea farms as owners. The pilot projects demonstrated to the African farmers the potential of the new crop and tested out the support services needed to elicit sustained response from them.

The major problems in the environment which had implications for the demand and supply dimensions of the new program were several. The relative unfamiliarity of African farmers with tea cultivation created considerable uncertainty as to how well they would respond when the model based on the pilot projects was replicated on a large scale. Yet another problem was that tea cultivation required multiple inputs such as stumps, fertiliser, appropriate cultural practices, and credit. Regular arrangements for leaf collection and linkages with factories and markets had to be integrated with tea growing. Small farmers had no access to these inputs and facilities. No private agency existed which could perform these developmental roles. These interdependent inputs and processes could not possibly have been integrated by unskilled farmers on their own.

Finally, ensuring quality control in tea plucking could be a serious problem when thousands of small and inexperienced farmers were involved. The international tea market was extremely sensitive to quality.

Service - Beneficiary - Sequence Strategy

Though the small farmer was not defined in precise terms, KTDA's policy of subsidising the sale of only 3000 stumps reflected its intention to promote tea growing only on one acre holdings.

KTDA's concept of service was an adaptation to the unique envi-ronmental setting of Kenya. That farmers were unable to integrate the required inputs on their own seemed to have influenced the design of the service as its different dimensions testify.

(1) In the initial years, the focus of KTDA was on the promo-tion of tea cultivation through the provision of the relevant inputs to farmers. Standard practices were evolved which the field staff disseminated to the farmers. (2) Farmers' response was elicited through the declaration of profitable and stable prices and regular monthly payments against leaf collection. Payments were

linked to quality which was strictly enforced at the leaf collection stage. (3) Tea processing and marketing were left to
private tea factories which existed in Kenya. The emphasis to
begin with was on functional and not vertical integration. As KTDA
gained experience, it set up its own factories and took over
marketing. Thus in a phased manner, both functional and vertical
integration were achieved. (4) To plan and implement functional
integration, the program utilised the extension staff of the
Ministry of Agriculture who were seconded to KTDA. Their salaries
were paid by KTDA which exercised full control over their performance. (5) Consultation with representatives of farmer-members at
different levels (division, district, province, and nation) was
built into the strategy. Views and feedback of farmers were thus
available to KTDA though the former were not a part of the decision
making process.[9]

As explained above, the program strategy was to start with the
most critical part of its service, namely, functional integration.
The phasing of the program was partly in spatial terms, but more
importantly, in terms of the tasks or functions to be performed.
Eventually, all tasks relevant to integration, both functional and
vertical, were performed by KTDA.

Demand - Supply - Resource - Strategy

Elements of the strategy designed to energise farmer response
to the program were (1) announcement of a stable and profitable
price for tea to be paid to farmers on a regular basis, (2) credit
provided to the farmer through the sale of stumps, (3) promotion of
the program and its services through the extension staff, and
(4) the role of advisory committees in mobilising the support of
farmers at large. Assured economic returns and credit appealed to
the economic motivation of farmers. Field staff and advisory
committees mobilised demand through communication and the creation
of personal relationships.

The supply strategy of KTDA focused on the integrated provision
of inputs to farmers. Cultivation practices were standardised
based on the results of adaptive field trials. Given the unfamiliarity of farmers with tea cultivation and the strong interdependence
among inputs KTDA exercised direct control over the delivery system
and the field staff. KTDA was also responsible for payments to
farmers though processing and marketing were left to private
factories in the initial years. Monetary incentives paid to the
field staff were again part of the supply strategy. The concept of
quality control was reinforced at two stages, viz., extension and
leaf collection, and was critical to forging the vertical integration linkages (processing and marketing) which took advantage of
the economies of scale in these operations.

Financial resources for KTDA were raised chiefly through the
Commonwealth Development Corporation (CDC) and the International
Development Association (IDA) of the World Bank. The decision to
set up KTDA as a self financing public agency without dependence
on annual budget allocations from the government was a strategic
move to ensure a fair measure of autonomy to the new organisation

Exhibit 9.3

KTDA : The Smallholder Tea Program

Environmental Factor	Strategic Intervention
Large number of small farmers.	Focus on small farmer
Farmers' unfamiliarity with tea cultivation	Integration of inputs and processes - horizontal and vertical
Farmers' inability to integrate inputs	Stable price - regular payments
Farmers' uncertainty about returns from tea.	Strict quality control
Growing international demand for quality tea	Mobilisation of farmer demand through field staff, credit
Standard technology in the cultivation of tea	Standardisation of practices and service routines
Favourable and stable weather and soil conditions	
Suitability of Rift Valley	Regional focus of program
Experience with tea processing and marketing available in the country	Focus on tea cultivation and extension in first phase - processing and marketing integrated later.
Existence of large private tea estates	

and to instil a sense of accountability in its management. In terms of key actors, KTDA's mobilisation efforts were aimed at international development agencies, local farmer-leaders who were influential in the village and private tea companies which provided the early linkages to processing and marketing.

THE INDONESIAN POPULATION PROGRAM

The primary objective of the Indonesian Population Program was fertility control though this term was not explicitly used in the initial years when the environment was considered rather hostile. Both rural and urban population were covered by the program though most of the attention and resources were received by the rural areas where the vast majority of the population lived.

Key Environmental Features

The strong political support for population control that emerged in Indonesia towards the late sixties, the availability of modern technologies for fertility control, increased availability of resources for population control through international aid and the concentration of Indonesia's population in two islands were positive factors which were conducive to mounting an effective population program in the country. There were, however, several other features of the environment which might have had a negative impact on the program. These features were taken into account by BKKBN in planning the demand and supply strategies of the new program.

First of all, while political support was strong, there was considerable hostility among Islamic leaders against family planning. Since Indonesia was a predominantly Muslim country, their opposition could have brought about poor public response to the program. Second, Islamic opinion was vehemently against certain family planning methods. Lack of sensitivity to such feelings in designing the program could have meant reduced response to the program. Third, while traditional (indigenous) methods of birth control were used in the country, the population was by and large unfamiliar with modern methods. The UN-World Bank Mission had reported that integration of the diverse program inputs such as information, education and training, and supplies required the coordination of several ministries. The task of eliciting and integrating these inputs was beyond the capacity of the largely rural and illiterate population. Unless some one performed this task, public response was likely to be most uncertain. Neither the market nor any other private institution seemed capable of playing this role. Fourth, Indonesia's rural communities were well organised with village organisations responsible for a variety of social and welfare matters. Village opinion and cooperation were typically mobilised through these organisations, a potentially powerful asset for any social development program, but hardly ever exploited for this purpose. Fifth, the population distribution among the islands and urban rural differentials added to the diversity in the environment. The concentration of people in Java and Bali with their unique village structures was quite different from the sparsely populated Outer Islands where close knit communities did not exist. A standardised supply or delivery, however, was unlikely to succeed given this degree of diversity. Finally, the Health Ministry's network of clinics did not go below the sub-district level. As a result, there was no delivery base in the village. There was thus an important gap on the supply side.

Service - Beneficiary - Sequence Strategy

That population control and family planning were not exclusively health matters was the starting point in defining the concept of service in the program. Though the primary clients of the program were 'eligible couples', it was recognised that influencing all adults, leaders, and even children in schools was important for the program's success. Dissemination of information, education through the school system, use of religious teachers, service through health clinics, involvement of the local governments, and at a later stage participation of village community groups were considered the major inputs necessary to make the program effective. These were inter-dependent inputs and hence their delivery had to be integrated carefully. There were three dominant elements in the service strategy.

First, the service consisted of a set of interrelated inputs which were integrated through the medium of the program. This concept was based on the assumption that neither the individual beneficiary nor any single ministry by itself could perform the task of integration. It was customary for social programs of this kind to focus only on some aspects of the supply or delivery of service and ignore public response. A number of inputs from diverse ministries integrated by the Indonesian program (eg., information, religion, and education) were explicitly designed to energise demand. These were important responses to the uncertainty present in the environment.

Second, matching the supply of family planning services to the demand being generated was another important element. Given the religious restrictions on the methods which could be used, the program had no option but to rely on the use of oral pills and condoms whose regular resupply was crucial to the program's success. A strategy for keeping adequate stocks of these items using the flexible funding procedure devised by a major donor was built into the program to facilitate the supply task. The willing-ness to vary the family planning methods was an adaptation to the diversity in the environment and the stocking policy was a response to the prevailing uncertainty.

Third, the use of field workers, local government and community groups in service delivery, and the mobilisation of demand were important responses to the limitations of the clinic network. Community participation was introduced when demand for the program seemed to taper off. Unlike in agricultural programs, there was no external market linkage in this case to create a strong economic

motivation in the client. Instead, the community's participation
and interest in the program were used to elicit improved public
response.10

The program's phasing was geographical in nature. It took
advantage of the population concentration in Java and Bali to
confine its operations to these islands in Phase I. Subsequently,
the program was extended to the Outer Islands in two phases. Given
the size and diversity of the country, this approach to phasing
helped to keep the scope of the program environment within reasonable
limits. The diversification of the program into the nutrition field
in 1978 took place after the population program had attained some
measure of maturity.

Demand - Supply - Resource Strategy

A number of elements in the demand strategy have been commented
upon in the section on 'service'. Many strategic moves were made to
mobilise demand for the program. (1) There was a persistent campaign
to influence the thinking of Islamic leaders in favour of the
program. (2) Integration of inputs from the different ministries
through BKKBN was done to facilitate the response of the target
group and widen the clientele for the program (3) While different
ministries provided their inputs which were then coordinated by
BKKBN, two inputs directly controlled by the latter were the field
workers and contraceptives supplies. Field workers were not only
agents for service delivery, but also mobilisers of demand for the
program. (4) Similarly community groups and volunteers were used
to promote the program at negligible cost (5) An important source
of ideas on demand mobilisation and service delivery was the
frequent use of 'pilot experiments' which tested out ideas against
the local environment.

Integration of diverse inputs usually is a difficult task to
accomplish. The supply strategy of BKKBN which addressed this
problem, was unique in several ways (1) BKKBN had control over the
funds to be allocated to the different ministries which were
responsible for the inputs to be integrated. (2) It had control
over the import and distribution of the contraceptive supplies for
the program. The flexible funding procedures developed to expedite
decision making facilitated adequate stocking of supplies, thus
avoiding the shortage syndrome so common in other programs.
(3) Pilot experiments were used by BKKBN to introduce appropriate
variations in the supply system of different regions. The practices
adopted varied even between East Java and West Java. This was an
important adaptation to the diversity in the environment.
(4) Community participation and decentralised decision making
involving local government reduced the costs of the program and made
the delivery system more responsive to local needs.

BKKBN had a strategy for influencing the key actors relevant to
the program. The deliberate efforts to win the support of Islamic
leaders have already been referred to. Heads of the local governments, provincial governors and community leaders were other actors
whom BKKBN tried to actively involve in the program. Responsibility

Exhibit 9.4

Indonesian Population Program

Environmental Factor	Strategic Intervention

Environmental Factor

Islamic leaders' opposition.

Cultural restrictions on certain family planning methods.

The beneficiary's inability to integrate inputs

Large rural population and strong rural community structures

Limited network of clinics

Diverse community structures and logistical problems at local level.

Population concentration in Java and Bali

Large size of the country.

Strategic Intervention

Deliberate efforts to win support of opponents and influential leaders

Avoidance of unpopular methods

Integrated service through BKKBN

Community participation in program planning and implementation

Use of field workers, volunteers

Flexible funding procedure

Encouragement to regional BKKBN office to initiate

Pilot experiments to meet local needs

Adequate stock levels of supplies

Phasing of program on geographic basis.

for the program at the regional level was vested in the Governor who was given credit for the program's accomplishments. BKKBN's office at the provincial and local levels liaised closely with the heads of the governments in the respective territories.

In brief, while the strong political support enjoyed by BKKBN was a favorable factor, the program's strategy shows considerable evidence of the deliberate steps taken to integrate its service, mobilise demand for the program, and to match the supply or delivery side to meet the new demand. The basic strategy did evolve over time, adapting to changes perceived in the environment and regional diversities. The special efforts made by the program leadership to influence key actors in the environment, especially religious and local leaders, and mobilise community participation are also evidences of a dynamic strategy.

THE CHINESE PUBLIC HEALTH PROGRAM

The strategic guidelines for organising public health services in post-Liberation China were evolved by the Communist Party and its leadership. When the Communist Party gained power in China, it declared health as a human right and recognised its key role in increasing the productivity of the people. A detailed strategy for achieving 'health for the people' was to be formulated, keeping in view the four guidelines given by the Party in 1950. The strategic directions and key tasks of the public health program were thus set by the Party for implementation by the government and the people. The considerable experience party leaders such as Chairman Mao had in finding answers to public health problems during the period of the struggle played the role of pilot projects and clearly influenced the new strategy.

The strategic guidelines underlying the Chinese Program called for the delivery of two distinctly different but related services, viz., preventive and curative. They may be perceived as seperate and yet related outputs which required different sets of inputs including skills. Though complementary at the consumption stage, they differ in their demand characteristics and the types of organisation and personnel needed to deliver them. There are very few developing countries where these two services or outputs have been well integrated. The general tendency is to give more priority to the curative service than to preventive care. The Chinese strategy is therefore of considerable significance.

Environmental Features

The Chinese environment and the country's political and social institutions had a tremendous influence on the new guidelines and the national health strategy that emerged in the Fifties. Three sets of environmental factors deserve to be noted.

First, the large size of the country, its diversity, and its predominantly poor and rural population scattered over vast distances posed serious problems to the centralised health services delivery of the kind found concentrated in urban areas. Many of

the diseases in the country side had to do with problems in the
environment and hygiene (eg. communicable diseases, water borne,
or parasitic diseases). The availability of trained western
style doctors in the country was limited. Rural health services
manned by such doctors did not exist, nor could they be provided
for in view of the country's resource constraints. Practitioners
of traditional Chinese medicine were the main sources of services
in the rural areas.

Second, the Ministry of Health was dominated by western style
doctors who, in spite of the new political setting, attached top
priority to research and curative practices of high standards
commonly accepted by the profession. This was reinforced by the
influence of Soviet style health policies and practices. Whether
the bureaucracy would play the roles required by the party
guidelines was not entirely clear in the Fifties.

Third, even after Liberation, the traditional organisations of
the urban and rural communities continued to function in China. In
fact, the Party used these structures to mobilise the masses for
various purposes. Agriculture and other economic and social
activities were being organised through communes, brigades, neighborhoods, etc., which provided much scope for local initiative and
participation. The political influence on these organisations was
decisive and facilitated public compliance in spite of the diversity in the environment.

Service - Beneficiary - Sequence Strategy

The public health program that emerged in the Fifties responded
to these environmental factors in rather innovative ways. First of
all, from the conventional concept of serving the public through an
urban oriented curative approach, there was a marked shift towards
the provision of preventive care for the masses.[11] The strategy was
to mount mass campaigns all over the country for immunisation,
cleaning up the environment, and improving general sanitation.
Education and mobilisation of large masses of people were the
instruments used to achieve the goal of prevention. Second, elementary preventive and curative services were provided in rural and
urban areas through a network of para-medical personnel drawn from
workers and farmers and trained over short periods. A minimum
level of health services was thus available to all even in small
rural communities through their own local organisations. Traditional medicines and traditional practitioners were thus used to
augment these services in rural areas. Third, treatment for serious
ailments was provided through a network of hospitals located in
different centers. Paramedical staff (barefoot doctors) would refer
patients to hospitals if they could not treat them.

This three part strategy was in sharp contrast to the urban
oriented curative focus of the health bureaucracy of the government. The new strategy, however, was consistent with the
government's objectives and more in tune with the problems,
constraints, and opportunities in the environment. Preventive
campaigns used the most readily available and relevant resources,

namely, people. Elementary health services were delivered through
relatively unskilled people through existing community organisations. Traditional practitioners, who were a readily available
resource, augmented an extremely scarce pool of skills. The
opportunities and strengths in the environment were thus used to
achieve objectives which at first sight, seemed difficult. The
new strategy redefined the service and identified its components
in a manner distinctly different from what the medical experts
had traditionally advocated. Both in the identification and
integration of the components, the Party, local organisations, and
the government played a role that matched the needs of beneficiaries.
     The conflict between the Party leaders and the health bureau-
cracy arose partly due to different perceptions as to who the
beneficiary was. As part of an effort to redress the imbalances
in society, the Party wanted the focus to shift to the rural scene.
The bureaucracy with its elitist and urban bias found this too
radical a shift. But health for the people did warrant increased
attention to the problems of the rural population. The strategic
moves of the new program were thus consistent with this definition
of the beneficiary.

Demand - Supply - Resource Strategy

     Health services, it is generally presumed, do not face a demand
problem. While this is largely true of curative services, it is by
no means self-evident in respect of prevention. It was significant,
therefore, that the preventive component of the Chinese Program
relied heavily on education and mobilisation of the masses. The
participation of the Party cadres,   communes,and other peoples'
organisations was designed to create greater commitment and
enthusiasm among the people for preventive work. Dissemination of
information and the mounting of periodical campaigns were the
means by which public interest in this component was kept up.
     A second aspect of the demand strategy related to the decentra-
lised nature of health delivery. The location of responsibility
for primary services within the community using people who belonged
to the same groups could be expected to create more public satisfaction than a centralised system, operating through remote control.
The staff and facilities would under these circumstances be more
responsive to local needs. Public response to the program appeared
to have been strengthened by the decentralised nature of its
management.
     The supply strategy of the program represented an interesting
adaptation to the environment and the nature of health delivery.
First, while broad policy making was done by the Party and the
government, only a few tasks relevant to supply were centralised.
These were the training of doctors and paramedical staff, drug
manufacture, and control over hospitals and their staff. In
managing the network of barefoot doctors and their stations, and
mass preventive campaigns, communes and local organisations played
a more active role. The second feature of the supply strategy
was the active participation of the people in the design and

delivery of the services.[12] The bureaucracy's role in this area
was considerably reduced over the years and was a source of
tension between the medical establishment in the Ministry and the
Party leadership. The integration of health services with the
commune structure along with agriculture and other activities was
tantamount to taking advantage of an organisational resource that
existed and had the capacity to integrate the new function on its
own.

A third feature was the cost sharing arrangement of the
program. The local organisations had their own budgets of which
health was a part. They received only partial support from the
central government. Commune funds and individual contributions by
members ensured a considerable measure of autonomy to the local
health delivery systems with implications for responsiveness to
local needs. Finally, the supply task was considerably eased by
involving traditional practitioners of Chinese medicine in the
delivery of health services. This innovation certainly augmented
the manpower needed especially in rural areas and supplemented
the scarce medical personnel in the country. At the core of the
supply strategy was the distinction between the key functions which
had to be standardised and managed centrally, and those which were
to be managed by the beneficiaries. This division of labour, it
was felt, would let the program adapt to local needs more
effectively.[13] The basic elements of the strategy were inspired by
the experience of the Liberation struggle period when many of
these ideas were tried and adapted especially in North West China.
Thus, the program benefited from the considerable experimentation
that had occurred in the preceding period though this was not
planned as a pilot project.

The remarkable feature of the mobilisation strategy of the
program was its focus on the people and local organisations. Both
in preventive and curative work, considerable emphasis was placed
on involving the people and traditional institutions. The mobilisation of the traditional practitioners of medicine stood out as
another example of utilising local resources. Surprisingly, one
influential group which could not adequately mobilised was the
health bureaucracy of the government!

The Chinese Public Health Program is a case in which strategic
directions were clearly given from the top. The program strategy
did undergo changes and sometimes swings which represented attempts
by the leadership to correct the deviations from the declared
objectives as perceived by the political leadership. The basic
strategy and its underlying concept of service were consistent with
the environment and geared to utilising the opportunities and
resources available in that environment. The emphasis on prevention using mass campaigns, the integration of preventive and
curative services at the grassroots through local organisations,
induction of traditional practitioners to supplement barefoot
doctors who played the key role in health services delivery were
mutually compatible, intensive in the use of readily available
local resources and institutions, and hence cost effective.

Exhibit 9.5

Chinese Public Health Program

Environmental Factor

- Large population - major part living in scattered rural communities
- Ignorance and low standards of living, poverty and diseases due to environmental and hygienic factors - general paucity of qualified doctors.
- Domination of western oriented doctors in Health Ministry - prevalence of conservative and curative oriented attitudes
- Constraint on resources for health and other social services
- Experience of leaders during the Liberation struggle in public health experiments
- Organisation of agriculture and other economic activities through communes
- Existence of traditional community structures in urban and rural areas

Strategic Intervention

- Preventive campaigns through mobilisation of the masses
- Popular participation to energise public response.
- Deployment of barefoot doctors to deliver preventive and curative services
- Integration of traditional medical practitioners with the system
- Reduced role for the Ministry
- Large hospitals used for referral
- Sharing of costs by beneficiaries
- Health services integrated into the communes structure
- Decentralised management using peoples' organisations

THE MEXICAN RURAL EDUCATION PROGRAM

Conafe was set up as a decentralised public organisation to promote education in Mexico. It was the context of the Presidential election in 1970 and the Mexican environment that persuaded the first Director General to focus on rural education as its first priority. No guidelines on the nature of programs to be offered or on implementation were given to Conafe by the Government of Mexico. Considerable flexibility was therefore available to Conafe to plan and manage its activities.

Environmental Features

Programs for rural education in Mexico had failed in the past in spite of the efforts of the Federal Ministry of Education to organise primary schools in rural areas. The Ministry found it difficult to retain teachers in rural communities and concluded that the environment was too inhospitable for an educational program. Conafe, on the other hand, saw the environment somewhat differently. While there were negative features in the environment, its leaders saw some opportunities too and evolved a strategy to exploit them. The critical environmental features they took into account were the following:

First, pilot experiments showed that latent demand for education in rural areas was strong. Parents were interested in their children going to school and joining the mainstream of life in the country. But people living in remote communities could not take advantage of schools away from their villages partly because of logistical problems. Their urge to educate the children was not strong enough to overcome these problems.

Second, a significant proportion of the rural population lived as small communities in isolated, mountainous regions without access to motorable roads and other modern means of communication. Differences in local dialects and customs existed among these communities. The number of children (aged 5 years or more) in a community varied between 30 and 40 on the average. The costs of delivering conventional educational services, given the problems of logistics, small size, and diversity were perceived as prohibitive.

Third, the federal system of primary education was rigid in its curricula, teaching practices, and procedures. Its standardised systems could not match the diverse needs and resource constraints of the poor and isolated rural communities. The reluctance of teachers to go and teach in these remote places added another serious obstacle to service delivery.

Fourth, on the other hand, in the absence of any educational infrastructure, the rural environment had considerable 'free space' for trying out new approaches to education. There were no vested interests or competition to be fought. If, for example, the federal school system was entrenched in the rural areas, it would have been more difficult for a new agency to operate in that environment.

Fifth, the political support of the new President and his
government was a positive feature of the environment. Both in
mobilising the needed resources and influencing key actors in the
environment, presidential support was bound to be invaluable.

In light of this analysis, Conafe concluded that the supply
side of the program needed greater attention than demand. The
key problem was defined as organising a delivery system to match
the diversity and resource constraints of the rural environment,
taking advantage of the potential demand for education that already
existed or could be mobilised if the supply system was well
conceived.

Service - Beneficiary - Sequence Strategy

The concept of service underlying the new rural education
program (community course) was built around five elements: (1) A
core curriculum to give rural children an understanding of the
basic strengths needed to complete primary education; (2) Sufficient
flexibility in the curriculum to adapt to local conditions;
(3) Young teachers selected from rural areas who were given a short
period of training and orientation; (4) Supervision of the program
at the village level through the local community and its committees
to which the teacher was responsible; and (5) Sharing of costs by
the community providing modest school facilities and meeting the
local costs of the instructor. The identification of these elements
and their integration was the service offered by Conafe.

The service was a strategic adaptation to the environment not
only in its educational technology, but also in the processes and
actions which were incorporated into it. Developing a strategy for
the integration of the technology, people, and actions was Conafe's
responsibility. The community actively participated in implementing
the program at the local level, and in local planning and generation of resources.

Though the primary school age children in rural areas were the
beneficiaries of the program, in a real sense, the community was
the client. While the children were learning in the classroom, the
community through its participation was also involved in a learning
process. The instructor, by living in the community and interacting
with its members also contributed to this process. The concept of
service evolved by Conafe focused attention on children with the
active participation of the community.

When pilot experiments were satisfactorily completed, the
program was inaugurated with 100 community schools in one state.
The program was subsequently expanded to cover all the 31 states,
but only after experience was gained by scaling up the pilot idea
in one state.

Demand - Supply - Resource Strategy

Demand mobilisation took a different turn in this program. As
already noted, there was some latent demand for education, even in
remote rural areas. The main strategy appeared to have been to
ensure genuine demand for the program by getting the community to

Exhibit 9.6

The Mexican Rural Education Program

Environmental Factor

Remote, small rural communities with low literacy.

Inability of federal system to penetrate rural areas.

Diversity in local conditions.

Uncertainty in environment due to poor logistics, lack of communication.

High costs of operating conventional schools in rural areas.

Latent demand for primary education in the rural environment.

No competing agencies in rural areas.

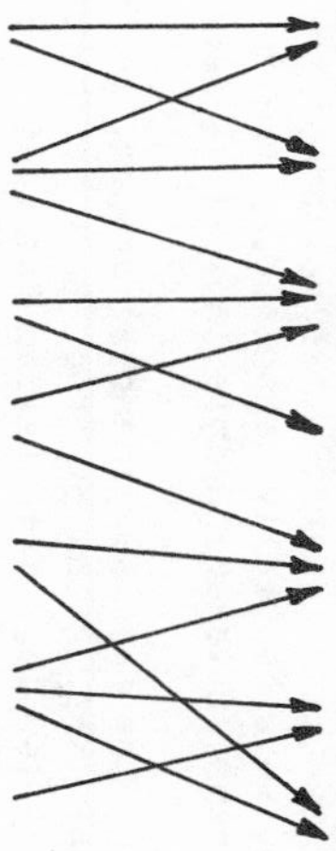

Strategic Intervention

Special curriculum with flexibility for adaptation.

Use of young instructors selected from rural areas.

Community participation in managing programs.

Planning of integration of inputs through Conafe's decentralised structure.

Invitation to communities to share in program costs.

Mobilisation of resources of states for the program.

Influencing young people to become instructors; public leaders in states mobilised to support program.

meet part of the program costs. One consequence of this policy was
that some rural communities which had genuine interest, but limited
capacity to raise resources were left out of the program. This
anomaly was corrected subsequently by providing subsidies to
deserving communities.

A second evidence of demand mobilisation was found at the state
level where Conafe worked out a sharing arrangement in respect of
program costs. Local bankers, businessmen, and other public leaders
were brought into the state level committees of Conafe as part of an
effort to promote the program and raise resources.

It was on the supply side that the strategic interventions of
Conafe were the strongest. The major components of the supply
strategy were (1) the development of a special curriculum and manual
for instructors in the preparation of which instructors participated, (2) the selection, training, and induction of instructors from
rural areas, (3) organisation of communities to contribute
resources and participate in operating and monitoring the program,
(4) a major role in the program for the state level offices, local
community committees, and the network of assessors.

Essentially, the supply strategy was to centralise the delivery
of certain inputs which required special knowledge and skills and
some measure of uniformity. Thus, the planning of curriculum and
production of teaching materials, selection of instructors, and
their training were centrally organised. Creation of local facilities, supervision of teaching, grading, etc., were done at the
local level.

Even though the federal financial support to Conafe was considerable, it was part of the strategy to mobilise resources at the
state and local levels. This called for special efforts to
influence leaders in the states and local communities. Of even
greater strategic importance was the approach adopted to attract
qualified young people from rural areas to join the program as
instructors for specified periods. This strategic innovation
marked a major departure from the conventional approach to rural
education. The strategy was also marked by a definite shift towards
the use of local resources.

STRATEGIC INTERVENTIONS : SOME COMMON THEMES

In this section, we propose to explore the common themes that
emerge from a comparative analysis of the strategies of the six
development programs. The content of their strategies and the
manner in which they responded to their national environments are
by no means identical. Though three of the programs are agriculture based, their commodities and underlying technologies are
different. The same is true of the three social development
programs whose services or outputs are not comparable. It is not
surprising, therefore, that there is considerable diversity in the
substance of their strategies and the specific interventions they
adopted to cope with their environments.

On the other hand, it appears that there are common managerial
features behind these diverse strategies. That these programs are
high performers is a feature common to all of them. None of the

cases, however, lends support to the hypothesis that success is due to a favorable or benign environment. While there were favorable factors, the environment in all cases had also negative features and problems caused by uncertainty, diversity, and hostility. An analysis of the program strategies to cope with these problems and exploit environmental opportunities reveals some significant features. A summary of these features is given in Table 9.1 at the end of this section.

Five out of the six programs were characterised by a single service. The exception was the Chinese program which had two interrelated services. Four of the six programs followed a strategy of sequential diversification. The Kenyan Program which was envisaged to be a multi-crop program narrowed its scope to tea only and did not diversify at all. The Chinese Program did not go for further diversification after a mix of preventive and curative services was adopted. The integration of multiple inputs to produce and deliver services was an important dimension of all program strategies. Demand mobilisation was high in all cases except the Mexican Program. Pilot projects were used by all programs in designing the program service and as an aid to the replication process. All programs were implemented in a phased manner, either on a geographic or a functional basis.

The dominance of the "single service" as the key strategic intervention in most of these programs is certainly a significant one. There is no doubt that the movement towards a single service was not the result of a grand design, but rather an intuitive adaptation by the program leadership to a difficult environment. While a program strategy is seldom planned in toto or at one point in time, the lessons of these programs can be useful aids to program leaders and designers in focusing sharply on a set of strategic issues relevant to many development programs. We present below a set of propositions on strategy based on the evidence from the preceding sections.

Choice of Goals

The management of a development program with scarce techno-managerial resources operating in a complex environment is facilitated by a single goal/service strategy. If multiple goals/services are desired, such diversification tends to yield better results when attempted sequentially and in related goals/services.

(Proposition 9.1)

An important strategic intervention concerns the choice of goals and the program's services or outputs. The proposition refers to goals as well as services to emphasise the fact that moving from a single goal to multiple goals or a single service to multiple services both entail increased complexity. This is not to imply that goals and services are substitutes. It is recognised that services are derived from goals and that a single goal may sometimes be consistent with multiple services. When a program has a dominant goal, with other goals being subsidiary, it could be regarded as falling between a single goal and multiple goals.

Even where program agencies started off with multiple goals, both governments and the program leaders involved seemed to have opted for the pursuit of a single or dominant goal to begin with. The Indian Dairy Program's focus on milk, Indonesian Program's focus on fertility control, and the Mexican Program's focus on rural primary education illustrate this point. The program leader leaders limited the diversification of their services in the early stages. Legally, there was nothing to prevent NDDB, NFAC, CONAFE, OR KTDA from pursing multiple goals and providing multiple services simultaneously. Yet their approach was to look for a single "entry point" which gave them an achievable goal to begin with. This single goal/service strategy appears to have been an important adaptation to their environments. First of all, their environments were characterised by a high degree of uncertainty in relation to markets or public response. A fair measure of diversity was present in most of these environments. In relative terms, the diversity factor appeared to have been less intense in the KTDA case as tea cultivation was confined to a region with relatively stable climatic and homogeneous soil conditions. The scope factor also was the least problematic in the Kenyan case. Even so, the integrated service delivery required under these environments meant that multiple services were considered unmanageable in the initial stages. The program managers had to give concentrated attention to both the demand and supply sides of these services. Simultaneous attention to the diverse and conflicting requirements of unrelated multiple services would simply have taxed their limits in the early stages.

Second, in most developing countries, technical and managerial skills are in relative short supply. Instead of spreading them thinly, these scarce resources are applied to the development of the basic service which is perceived to be critical to the program's success. The single or dominant goal/service approach is in part an adaptation to this constraint. Third, as experience is gained and the single service matures, diversification may not pose excessive managerial burdens. It could also be that a program organisation which has performed well in the delivery of one service is perceived as an efficient vehicle to "piggy back" other related services. BKKBN which did exceedingly well in family planning was encouraged by the government to move into the nutrition field also. But BKKBN diversified into other population activities and NDDB into oilseeds only after their initial services had stabilised. Sequential diversification thus fits the environment and helps the program gain strength through gradual organisational learning. The initial focus on a single service found in our programs therefore represents a conscious positioning strategy by their leaders in their objectives-environment space. It reflects an effective approach to reducing complexity in a program's initial phase.

The Chinese case could be interpreted as a move towards sequential diversification. Urban oriented, curative services were the focus of public health in China until the Communists took over. The new regime's strategy was to shift the focus to preventive and rural oriented services. Curative services, however, were not dismantled. The addition of preventive services thus led to a sequential diversification of goals.

In his pioneering study of development projects nearly 15 years ago, Albert Hirschman who investigated several projects in Asia, Africa, and Latin America observed that a good strategy for an organisation was to first achieve competence in the pursuit of one purpose and then proceed to become multipurpose.[14] Though his terminology is different from ours, his argument is essentially in support of sequential diversification.

Integration of Inputs

Beneficiary response to a program is improved by a strategy which identifies and integrates the interdependent or sequential inputs/elements required to produce and deliver a service when beneficiaries are unable to achieve such integration on their own.

(Proposition 9.2)

A common feature of the strategies of the six development programs was the nature and scope of integration underlying their concept of service. It appears that an important contribution of the programs has been in integrating a set of interdependent or sequentially dependent inputs or components to create a service which the beneficiaries could not have done through the market mechanism. Public response to a program goes up when a 'felt need' is thus met. The inability of a beneficiary to identify and integrate inputs may be due to four types of barriers:
(i) Technological barriers: The beneficiary may not have the technical skills and infrastructure to attempt integration on his own. (ii) Access barriers: He may be prevented from getting the required inputs because of institutional handicaps, caste or social handicaps, remote location, administrative hurdles, and distrust of existing institutions which inhibits him from seeking access. (iii) Economic barriers: The size, cost, and riskiness of investment and market imperfections may limit his ability to respond. (iv) Organisational barriers: The beneficiary may be incapable of getting organised as part of a group to demand and share the benefits. The skills and leadership may simply not exist. A program's service delivery will succeed only when all the relevant barriers faced by the beneficiaries in a given situation are effectively overcome. The degree of integration required of a program will be directly related to the severity of the beneficiary's inability to integrate the relevant inputs on his own.

168

In the three agricultural development programs, the integration entailed the whole gamut of inputs from the production stage to market linkages. Without the market linkage, the beneficiary response to the programs would not have been as positive. In the Philippines, earlier rice development programs which attempted partial integration by focusing only on the diffusion of technology and extension services did not make the desired impact because certain critical barriers had not been removed. Masagana-99 succeeded only when it integrated the neglected inputs along with new rice technology and extension. Similarly the intensive cattle development program (ICDP) which preceded Operation Flood in India focused on the supply of improved breeds of cattle and extension to farmers, but failed to pay adequate attention to other critical inputs and linkages they needed. The superiority of Operation Flood's strategy lay in identifying and integrating a range of elements only some of which had been taken into account by ICDP.

The strategic concept of functional and vertical integration is reflected in social development programs too. In the Indonesian Program, for example, the functional inputs from the different ministries had to be combined with the support services from the provincial and district governments which were closer to the delivery scene. In these programs, market linkages were obviously not relevant. Instead, community participation, along with other inputs was integrated into the concept of service as a device for response mobilisation. Social development programs in countries which have taken a partial or inappropriate view of integration have not been very effective. Family planning programs which followed a purely clinical approach, for example, have performed poorly. Similarly, integrated rural development programs which attempt to integrate multiple services whose inter-dependence is dubious have also run into problems. It is the complexity of this integration process which makes the seemingly simple single goal/service strategy a managerially demanding endeavor. On the whole, the evidence from the six programs and what we know of some of the less sucessful ones confirm the importance of strategies which compensate for the beneficiary's inability to integrate the required inputs of the service in question.

Learning from Pilot Projects

Replication of program services on a national scale is facilitated when pilot projects/experiments are integrated into national programs as part of a deliberate strategy.

(Proposition 9.3)

An important means by which the six programs tested their environments is through 'pilot projects'. Only four of them had pilot projects designed systematically as a learning or research and development (R&D) device. But both NDDB and the Chinese Program had the benefit of past experiences which played the role of pilot projects in relation to their strategy formulation. The scope and

design of the integration of service were calibrated through these
experiments and their appropriateness to beneficiary needs was thus
tested under real life conditions. The replication of a service in
a complex national environment without benefit of such R&D work is
an error committed by many programs. The experience of the
Indonesian Population Program demonstrates the value of such experiments in coping with the uncertainty and diversity in the environment. This approach not only led to the formulation of more
realistic strategies, but also brought forth a set of people with
experience, skills, and knowledge of the environment who were
extremely useful at the replication stage.

It is significant that those who managed the programs had an
active role in the pilot project planning and operations. Pilot
projects were not viewed as a separate activity to be left to
researchers. The interaction between the people engaged in pilot
projects and the national programs was very strong. The managers
and implementors were thus able to internalise the lessons
effectively and were motivated to use them in their strategic
planning. Where the pilot experience preceded the program as
in NDDB's case, the same results were achieved by getting those
who participated in this experience to plan and manage the new
program.

Demand Mobilisation

Successful programs tend to pursue demand mobilisation and
credibility building as an integral part of their strategy.
Market linkages and economic incentives play a key role in
the demand mobilisation strategy of economic programs
whereas community participation or involvement plays a
similar role in social programs.

(Proposition 9.4)

Many development programs see themselves as delivery systems
and pay scant attention to the demand side. The programs we have
examined are unique in that demand mobilisation (energising public
demand or response) was an important aspect of their strategies.
NDDB's use of financial and technical assistance, its deployment of
spearhead teams to the districts, NFAC's use of credit without
collateral and an elaborate communications campaign, BKKBN's
involvement of village community organisations and their leaders
in the program and the Chinese Program's extensive use of mass
preventive campaigns are examples of strategic interventions to
energise public demand or response. Supply strategies were then
tailored to match the demand being created. Thus in the Indonesian
case, liberal stocks of contraceptive supplies were kept at local
levels to meet the demand being generated through community
mobilisation. If demand mobilisation had not taken place, the
supply strategy would have been unproductive. An important aspect
of the demand and supply components of the strategy was the
deliberate manner in which the program leaders sought the support

of the key actors in the environment. The Indonesian Program's
mobilisation of Islamic leaders and community leaders illustrate
this point.

The Mexican Rural Education Program was the only case where the
primary focus was on the supply strategy. The existence of
latent demand for the program in rural communities permitted the
program leadership to concentrate on the supply function. The
functions or tasks which get special emphasis in the successful
program are thus influenced by what a careful analysis of the
environment reveals.

Phasing of Programs

Phasing of development programs in spatial or functional
terms is an adaptation to the uncertainty, diversity, and
scope of the environment and paucity of techno-managerial
resources, and a means by which programs can successfully
build on experience.

(Proposition 9.5)

Phasing in terms of geographical coverage or degree of integration has been a feature of the strategies of the programs we have
examined. Eventhough the program was national in scope, the
strategy was to extend the service across the country in a phased
manner. Operation Flood is being implemented in two phases.
Masagana-99 started with irrigated lands. BKKBN covered the country
in three phases. In KTDA, the strategy was to phase by first
attempting functional integration and moving towards vertical
integration in subsequent stages. CONAFE in Mexico started with
100 communities in one state and then expanded gradually. The
Chinese Program shifted the focus to preventive campaigns to begin
with. A simultaneous replication of the service all over the
country was avoided in all cases.

The phasing strategy seems to have been influenced by two
considerations. One is the paucity of technical and managerial
manpower resources which makes it difficult to cover vast areas
all at once. A judgement is being made as to what is manageable
given the country's environment and the program's resources. A
second consideration is the need to start with segments of a
program or a region where the chances of success seem most favourable. For a new program that is getting off the ground, this is an
important factor both for making the most of its resources and
gaining confidence. That the development programs we have reviewed
were careful about their phasing strategy is a factor that seems to
have contributed to their successful performance.

The foregoing analysis demonstrates the importance of strategic
interventions in the management of development programs. While the
political support behind a program and the adequacy of its resources
are important factors, it appears that leaders of successful
programs build   on these strengths by evolving strategies which
match their operating environments. The evidence we have presented
on the six cases shows that a broad policy decision to initiate a

new program does not necessarily provide adequate guidelines or a
framework for its implementation. It is from the strategy of the
program that these guidelines are derived.

The common themes and approaches which have emerged from the
preceding analysis of the six program strategies are a modest
addition to our understanding of how successful development programs
are managed. Strategies, however, are only a part of the story.
In the next two chapters, we turn to an examination of the
experience of the six development programs in respect of structural
and process interventions.

NOTES

1. Market control by a few traders and other market imperfections were major problems for farmers who did not have any
organisation of their own to counter these tendencies.

2. Private firms might have found this a high cost operation
as they could not have reaped the benefits of economies of scale
from these services in widely scattered villages. Public delivery
might have been possible, but there were serious doubts about how
efficiently service delivery could be organised.

3. In the federal structure of India, agriculture and dairying
were among the subjects or activities left to the state governments.

4. This is partly a problem of the organisational structure
of the program. For further discussion of this point, See Chapter
10.

5. The question of autonomy is discussed in greater detail in
Chapter 10.

6. It was reported that 56 per cent of farmers had already
adopted the new rice varieties.

7. The processes used to translate these strategic interventions
are discussed in Chapter 11.

8. See Chapter 10 for a detailed discussion of these structural
innovations.

9. The structural arrangements involved are discussed in
Chapter 10.

10. It is conceded that participation is of value even without
its demand mobilisation dimension. It is interesting to note that
participation was not brought into the program as a goal.

11. It should be noted that in China a strategy and structure
for delivering curative services was already in existence even if
it was urban oriented. The dominant goal of the Ministry was to
provide urban oriented curative services. The public health program
in the post-Liberation era did not ignore it, but tried to diversify
program goals by assigning preventive care greater priority.

12. A detailed discussion of the processes involved is found in
Chapter 11.

13. The structural aspects of this division of labour are
discussed in Chapter 10.

14. Hirschman, A.O., Development Projects Observed (Washington,
DC : The Brookings Institution, 1967) p.51.

Table 9.1

Key Strategic Interventions

Interventions	Indian Program	Philippine Program	Kenyan Program	Indonesian Program	Mexican Program	Chinese Program
Goal/Service	Single	Single	Single	Single	Single	Multiple£ related
Diversification	Sequential	Sequential	*	Sequential	Sequential	*
Integration of multiple inputs to provide service	Strong	Strong	Strong	Strong	Strong	Strong
Demand mobilisation	High	High	High	High	Moderate	High
Use of pilot projects as a learning device	Significant+	Significant	Significant	Significant	Significant	Significant+
Phasing of program	Geographic	Geographic	Functional@	Geographic	Geographic	Functional@

£ Though preventive care became dominant, curative services were also being provided. Thus there were twin goals closely related and complementary to each other.

* The Kenyan Program did not diversify at all. The Chinese Program did not go beyond its twin goals.

+ In the Indian and Chinese Programs, earlier experiences played the role of pilot projects but not by design. Smaller pilot experiments were conducted after the programs got underway.

@ KTDA expanded by vertically integrating in phases. The Chinese started with a shift to preventive care and in the next phase integrated preventive and curative services through communes.

10
Structural Interventions

The case studies presented in Chapters 2 - 7 describe in some detail the evolution of the organisational structures of the six development programs. In this chapter, we shall examine these experiences in order to understand the nature of the underlying structural interventions and their interrelationships with the program environments and strategies. In Chapter 8, three important dimensions of structural interventions, namely, structural forms, organisational autonomy, and decentralisation were identified.[1] We propose to analyse the structures of the six programs in terms of each of these dimensions. The highlights of the structural interventions analysed in this chapter are the following:

- a mutual adaptation of the program strategies and structures over time;

- considerable reliance of interorganisational cooperation through network structures rather than on hierarchical control through vertical program structures;

- significant use of multiple sources of lateral influence to make networks effective since direct control is infeasible;

- reduction in the costs of coordination through the use of diverse integrative mechanisms;

- degree of decentralisation that matched the program strategy and the complexity of the environment; and

- moderate level of organisational autonomy that facilitated the orchestration of planning and implementation.

At the end of each section of this chapter, we summarise the propositions which seem warranted by the evidence presented.

STRUCTURAL FORMS AND INTEGRATIVE MECHANISMS

Organisational structures evolved in different ways in the six programs under review : Let us examine the evidence on the organisational structure of NDDB. In 1970, NDDB had a functional structure with only two major divisions, viz., the engineering and technical division, and the management and manpower development division. By 1974, further differentiation of functions had taken place and a new and critical functional division called "farmer organisations and animal husbandry" (FO & AH) was added to the formal structure. Over the years, these major functions were further differentiated and in 1979 a separate division for "oilseeds and vegetable oil" was added with its chief also reporting to the secretary of NDDB.[2] We see here the beginning of a shift from the purely functional to a service based structure.

Emergence of the Network

The differentiation of functions within NDDB gives only a partial picture of the differentiation of tasks relevant to "Operation Flood". For example, the Indian Dairy Corporation (IDC) was set up in 1969 to perform the investment and finance functions of the program. The state level dairy development corporations were set up to implement the program in their respective areas. These in turn were expected to promote farmers' cooperative unions in the milkshed districts. Thus most of the functions of NDDB were to be jointly carried out with the IDC, the state dairy development corporation (SDDC) and the district cooperative unions (DCU). Even though the program agency had a functional structure, it operated with a network of organisations.

One is inclined to assume that the integration of these functions in a single service program such as Operation Flood was relatively simple. However the nature of differentiation of tasks described above was such that a variety of integrative devices had to be used.

First, the Dairy Board itself was the supreme integrative mechanism. As the lead agency which had representatives of the Government of India and state governments and dairy experts on its board, its primary task was to plan, promote, and monitor Operation Flood. Second, the practice of having a common Chairman and several common board members for NDDB and IDC was another device to facilitate coordination. Third, the creation of dairy development corporations by the participating states was motivated by the need to integrate the functions of the cooperative, dairying, and veterinary departments at the state level. The implementation of the program would have suffered if it had to interface with these diverse and independent agencies in each state. Fourth, as NDDB expanded, it set up regional offices in an attempt to facilitate the coordination of the program on a decentralised basis. Each regional director was empowered to coordinate the activities relating to the program in the participating states in his/her region with specialised staff

under the dual control of the functional divisions in headquarters
as well as the regional office. Fifth, within each district where
village cooperative societies were to be set up, the spearhead
team performed an integrative role at the grassroots. The interdisciplinary nature of the team and its responsibilities in
relation to the diverse tasks at the district level including
working with a counterpart team from the state called for
specialised skills as well as the ability to integrate the diverse
tasks in the district. The district cooperative union was to
perform this role eventually.

There was thus no single organisation which had complete
authority for the integration of functions in Operation Flood.
Instead, there was a network, the coordination of which required
the use of multiple integrative mechanisms. This reflected the
complexity of the network structure which had developed as the
program moved forward. Meanwhile, NDDB had evolved from a
functional into a matrix form of organisation. Though it had no
hierarchical authority to control the entire network, NDDB acted
as the coordinator of the linked organisations.

The Philippine Experience

In the Philippine Rice Program (Masagana-99), the differentiation of functions was considerable. As several of these functions
were within the purview of agencies outside the Ministry of
Agriculture, NFAC had the unenviable task of getting as many as 31
agencies together to contribute their inputs and services to make
Masagana-99 a success. The two additional subtasks or functions
taken over by Masagana-99 were the provision of credit and communication. Within NFAC, three divisions were created to plan,
administer, and control the performance of the programs. The
extension staff (production technicians) and their supervisors were
drawn from the Extension Bureaus of the Ministry. Though deputed
to NFAC, they were still under the technical control of the Bureaus.
NFAC thus operated as a matrix form of organisation.

A further addition of several inputs under Masagana-99 (in
comparison to earlier rice programs) may seem marginal. However,
the inputs of credit and communication were regarded as critical to
the program. These inputs again could not have been provided
directly by the Agriculture Ministry. The highly differentiated
functions involved and the Ministry's lack of direct control over
them made the task of integration at once urgent and complex. The
following integrative mechanisms deserve to be noted.

First, NFAC which was given the responsibility for Masagana-99
played the central role in integrating the numerous functions
relevant to the program. The 31 agencies concerned with these
functions were members of the Council which coordinated their
inputs primarily through a joint planning and allocation process.
The Council was the forum in which commitments were created from
the member agencies at the highest level. The Program's management
committee under NFAC played the more detailed role of integrating
operations in the field. (See Exhibits 10.1 and 10.2 at the end of

of this chapter).

Second, the naming of the Agriculture Secretary as an "Action Officer" for the Program by the President was designed to give him a status above other secretaries. This was presumably to augment his power and ability to command and coordinate resources outside his Ministry.[3]

Third, an important innovation introduced under the new program was to make the provincial governors and municipal mayors (district heads) chairmen of the Program in their respective areas. Coordination of functions at the local level was thus done through officials who had considerable political clout in their jurisdiction. Since numerous public and private agencies were involved, the integration of inputs and resolution of conflicts facilitated by these officials were important contributions.[4]

Fourth, in the village, the production technician played an important integrative role. He was concerned not only with extension, but also helping the farmer in getting all other inputs including credit.[5] This role enabled him to have an overview of the farmers' problems and act as an effective integrator at the grassroots. This is in sharp contrast to the limited specialist role the field staff played in earlier rice programs.

Fifth, two critical functions, credit and research (technology) involved very powerful agencies outside the Agriculture Ministry. The Central Bank which controlled credit and the network of rural banks and other financial institutions were beyond the Ministry's purview. Similarly, the agricultural research system including the universities and IRRI was quite independent of the Ministry. Special committees on credit and research were set up involving these agencies and the Ministry of Agriculture in order to facilitate coordination and link them more closely to the program. This was an example of lateral integration designed to reinforce NFAC's own coordinating efforts.

The Functional Form in KTDA

In Kenya's Smallholder Tea Development Program (KTDA), the differentiation of functions involved was more limited in scope compared to those of Operation Flood and Masagana-99. The program in its initial phase focused on promoting tea cultivation among the small African farmers. Distribution of stumps, extension, leaf collection, and payment to farmers were the main subtasks. The organisation of KTDA was therefore divided into three departments: technical services, finance, and administration. Subsequently, when KTDA got into tea processing by setting up its own factories and marketing, two new divisions to look after factory management and marketing were created. As the program expanded, leaf collection was separated from the technical department and put under a new assistant general manager. Thus KTDA retained a functional form of organisation.

The case study shows that integration of these differentiated functions took place primarily at the level of the head office. Operationally, all functions were controlled by the heads of the

different departments, who in turn were coordinated by the General
Manager. All tea officers, leaf collection officers, and factory
managers reported directly to their heads of departments.[6] There
was no single authority in the field who performed an integrative
role as they brought together the farmer representatives and the
officers in a given area. But then, it should be noted that these
committees were advisory in nature and did not operate as an
integral part of the decision making structure. The formal field
structure thus did not provide for any integrative mechanism. It
is reasonable to conclude therefore that the integration of tasks
was done primarily through the general manager and heads of
departments in the head office, and the KTDA board which met
periodically. The board had representatives of the Government of
Kenya, farmer members, and financial institutions.

Differentiation and Integration in Indonesia

The Indonesian Population Program (BKKBN) went through two
distinct phases in its differentiation of tasks and functions.
First, when family planning was the only service provided by BKKBN,
the differentiation was based on the subtasks or functions relevant
to family planning. Training, research, information and motivation,
contraceptive services, logistics, and reporting were the functions
organised under seperate bureaus. The first three were under one
deputy chairman and the rest under a second deputy chairman. These
functions were more or less fully represented at the provincial
level where the BKKBN offices were more directly responsible for
implementation. Second, when BKKBN took on additional population
activities such as nutrition, the basis of differentiation shifted
from function to service. There were now four deputy chairmen, two
of whom were responsible for the "family planning", and "population
activities" respectively and the other two were in charge of general
administration, and field supervision and controls. Under each of
these heads, the functions relevant to each service were further
differentiated. BKKBN thus evolved from a purely functional
organisation into a product or service based organisation over time.
(See Exhibits 10.3 and 10.4).

While the board consisted of the chairman, and deputy chairmen,
there was a Presidential Advisory Council on Population Affairs
which consisted of the Chairman of BKKBN, the ministers in charge
of the cooperating ministries and the Chairman of the National
Planning Agency. This body which advised the President was an
organisational forum in which those responsible for the diverse
inputs required by the program were represented. Like NFAC which
had to liaise with 31 different agencies, BKKBN had to coordinate
inputs from five different ministries.

The integrative mechanisms available to the program were four-
fold: (1) The key integrative mechanism was the top management
(chairman and deputy chairman) of the board of BKKBN. In the first
phase, the board had to integrate the functions relevant to family
planning only. Since 1978, the focus shifted to the integration of
two different services, viz., family planning and population

activities (eg. nutrition). (2) The Presidential Advisory Council
on Population reinforced the integrative function at the highest
level in terms of policy and facilitated the coordination of the
different ministries involved in the program. (3) At the regional
and local levels, the governors and district heads assisted by the
BKKBN representatives in their areas performed an integrative role.
(4) At the village level, the field workers coordinated several
activities. He motivated the client groups in his area, provided
contraceptive supplies to the village volunteers, and assisted the
latter in maintaining a list of current users. Furthermore, he
liaised with the community groups, volunteers, the clinic, and the
BKKBN office. The field worker thus was not a narrow specialist
concerned with only a limited aspect of the service such as
motivation or contraceptive supply.

Shifts in the Chinese Strategy and Structure

The Chinese Public Health Program went through some radical
shifts in terms of the differentiation and integration of functions.
In the mid-Fifties, health related subtasks were grouped into three
categories each of which was the responsibility of different
entities in the network of organisations concerned with public
health. The three categories are: (i) medical education and
research, hospital services, and drug production and distribution;
(ii) preventive services and mass campaigns; and (iii) rural health
services. The bureaucracy (Ministry of Health and its affiliates)
was organisationally responsible for the first set of functions.
The Party sub-committee (political) was responsible for the second
set of functions. The communes (local organisations) were primarily
responsible for the third category. The unsatisfactory progress of
the program led Chairman Mao to modify this pattern of differentiation on the eve of the Cultural Revolution. The nature and scope of
the functions looked after by the bureaucracy were drastically
reduced. The role of the communes was considerably strengthened.

A part of the reason for this shift must be sought in the
leadership's failure to effectively integrate these categories of
functions.[7] The political leadership was new and relatively
inexperienced in managing the bureaucracy in the early Fifties.
The three groups assigned to look after the three categories of
functions differed considerably in their interests and values. For
instance, the bureaucracy was governed by professional considerations and attached much value to quality and expertise. The Party
subcommittee and communes were non-professional in their orientation and more closely identified with the masses. A strong and
sustained effort to integrate the different functions and groups
was clearly needed. The political leadership, however, was
unable to play this integrative role adequately in the Fifties.
Consequently, the interdependence between the three parts was lost
sight of and coordination could not be achieved.

The political leadership under Chairman Mao achieved a more
effective integration of the program only during the Cultural
Revolution. The program strategy underwent some significant

changes during this period. It has been argued that these changes
which limited the program goals and made them more internally
consistent were responsible for the more effective integration that
followed.[8] The political leadership at this stage made the Health
Ministry largely irrelevant and assumed the key integrative role.
At the local level the commune played a similar role by integrating
the preventive and curative services through the medium of the
barefoot doctor.

The Network in Mexico

In the Mexican case, the three divisions of Conafe represented
three different functions. The technical division was concerned
with curriculum planning, teaching materials, and selection,
training, and deployment of instructors. The financial and administrative divisions were concerned with the usual housekeeping
functions common to most organisations. These functions were also
represented at the state level offices of Conafe which had responsibility for planning and implementing the Program in different
regions. Specialists belonging to the functional divisions in
Conafe were deputed to work in the state level offices. Thus
from a simple functional form, Conafe's structure evolved into the
matrix form as state level (regional) offices began to be set up.
Conafe, however, operated with a network of organisations in
the field. Its state level offices collaborated closely with the
state government's Department of Education and the state level
committee presided over by the Governor. In the village, the
community committee played an active role in the program. There
were thus four separate organisations in the Program's organisational structure.
Conafe's integrative mechanism operated at three levels.
(1) At the top, Conafe's board and management committee coordinated
its different functions. The Director General was the key integrator at this level. (2) At the state level, the state committee of
Conafe and the Conafe delegate played a similar coordinating role.
(3) In the rural community, the community committee played an
integrative role. The instructor worked closely with the committee
assisted by the assessor who visited the village periodically.
Thus mechanisms for integrating the relevant functions existed at
all three levels in relation to the rural education program.

Evolution of Structures

What is striking about the organisational structures of the
six programs is that they did not remain static. The structures
seem to have evolved over time and adapted to changing circumstances. All except Masagana-99 and the Chinese Public Health Program,
started with functional structures for the program agencies.
Masagana-99 had a matrix form to begin with, having learned from
the experience of earlier programs. The Chinese Program had a

structure differentiated by service (preventive and curative services) and function (medical education, research, and drugs). The preventive and curative services were related activities for which two different types of organisations were responsible. Both were serviced by the Ministry of Health which performed functions such as education, research, and drug distribution. The other national program agencies we have examined had their focus on a single service or output and had their own staff who performed different functions around this service. However, the range of functions supported by these structures expanded over time in almost all the programs.

Expansion was followed by other structural changes. When the program agencies expanded geographically, regional or provincial offices were set up and a matrix form of organisation was adopted with functional staff reporting to the provincial manager/chief who had responsibility for the area. This was the experience in NDDB, Conafe, BKKBN, and NFAC. In NDDB, regional directors performed this role in relation to the staff from the functional divisions of the board located in the regions. The provincial heads of BKKBN and NFAC also operated within a similar structure.[9] In fact, the matrix form was in operation at the regional level in the lead agencies of all programs except KTDA.

Expansion in the more complex national environments seems to have led the program agencies (lead agencies) to work formally with a network of organisations. Thus NDDB worked with IDC, state dairy development corporations (SDDC) and district cooperative unions (DCU). BKKBN worked with several ministries, the provincial and district heads and their organisations and village community organisations. There were multiple organisations which had formal roles/functions to perform within the program's structure which in effect took the form of a network (See Diagram 10.1). Again, KTDA was the only program whose structure least resembled a network. The multiple, integrative devices used by the programs made the task of coordination of network structures more manageable and reduced its costs. The larger and more complex the network, the more complex and numerous were its integrative mechanisms.

Why did the organisational structures of the programs evolve in this manner? We present below an interpretation and a set of propositions which seem warranted by the evidence from the programs.

The evolution of structures described above can, for the most part, be attributed to the strategies of the programs and the changes in their nature and scope over time. NDDB had a limited functional structure when it defined its strategy in terms of providing technical services to the dairy sector at the request of the agencies involved. The new strategy underlying Operation Flood called for additional functions to be performed by the organisation. The phased expansion of the program to cover the vast regions of India required the setting up of regional divisions organised in matrix style. The diversification of NDDB into the oilseeds sector initiated the process of differentiating the structure by service or output. A similar adaptation is found in BKKBN which also went through the functional or matrix forms as the program expanded. The

diversification of the program (family planning and population
activities) marked the introduction of a structure differentiated
by service. A relatively speedy adaptation of the structure of
the program agency to its strategy seems to have occurred in all
our programs except the Chinese during its early phase.

The performance of development programs is facilitated by
a speedy adaptation of their structures to their
strategies. Successful leaders create or adapt their
organisational structures to reinforce their strategies.

(Proposition 10.1)

In retrospect, the problem with the Chinese program appears to
have been a failure to integrate the three differentiated parts of
the structure which were supposed to offer a range of health
services together. As has been explained, the health bureaucracy,
the Party subcommittee and the communes were not identical in their
values and interests. Strong integrative devices would have been
required to get these disparate groups to work together. In the
next phase, Chairman Mao not only strengthened the integrative role
both at the political level and through the communes, but also
modified the strategy by narrowing the focus of the program. For
example, medical education and research were given reduced emphasis
and the focus was shifted to the delivery of rural health services.
It is important to note that both structural and strategic interventions were used by Chairman Mao in order to cope with the problem
of faltering performance. The widely acclaimed expansion of rural
health care in China followed in the wake of these interventions.
The networks depicted in Diagram 10.1 offer us useful insights
into the linkages with other organisations and the coordinating
role which was performed by the different lead agencies. Achieving
interorganisational cooperation through these networks is clearly a
more complex task than managing the self-contained and hierarchically
controlled structure of a single program agency. The scope of the
network is influenced by the nature of the program service and the
complexity of the environment. Thus if NDDB was not committed to
dairy development through farmer cooperatives, linkages with
district cooperative unions (DCU) could have been dispensed with.
If involvement of village community groups was not critical to the
program strategy of demand mobilisation and service delivery, BKKBN
could have eliminated community groups from the network. Thus, the
complexity of the network structure and the integration mechanisms
associated with it can be traced to the program strategy and the
scope of the program environment. In general, in an environment in
which the technical inputs for the service required by a development
program are under the control of diverse agencies and actors,
program implementation seem to benefit from the formal support and
cooperation of different levels of government (federal, state, and
local), and other organisations, both public and private, which
might facilitate demand mobilisation and service delivery.

Diagram 10.1

Network Structures

National Dairy Development
Program of India

Philippines Rice
Development Program

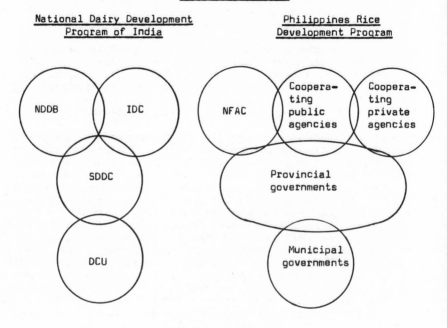

Kenyan Smallholder Tea
Development Program

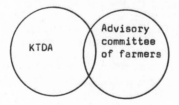

Diagram 10.1, cont'd

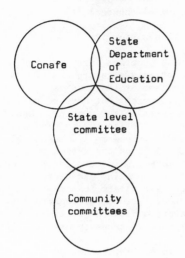

Mexican Rural Education Program

Chinese Public Health Program

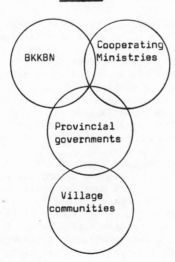

Indonesian Population Program

Large development programs operating in complex environments tend to perform better by relying more on
interorganisational cooperation through the use of
network structures than on hierarchical control.

(Proposition 10.2)

The very fact that services in these programs were expanded and
diversified sequentially (over time) reflects an awareness of the
limitations of the structural interventions at their command. The
leaders of NDDB felt that their structure might not have supported a
diversified strategy in the first few years of the program. BKKBN
could not have expanded into the Outer Islands in the initial stages
in view of the tremendous burden it would impose on its relatively
new structure. Since there were constraints on the extent to which
they could restructure their organisations and the degree of direct
control they could exercise over other cooperating agencies
(network), they responded by limiting their strategies and phasing
their implementation consistent with these structural constraints.
Viewed thus, a process of mutual adaptation between strategies and
structures also seems to have been at work in these programs.

When external or internal forces impose limitations on
structural changes, successful program leaders respond
by limiting or adapting their strategies, consistent
with such constraints.

(Proposition 10.3)

DECENTRALISATION AND SOURCES OF LATERAL INFLUENCE

There is a strong belief that a development program needs a
decentralised structure in order to be effective. The meaning of
decen ralisation is seldom spelt out clearly. Consequently
structural choices are thought of in "either or" terms. Since
structure reflects the mix of functions or tasks to be performed,
it is more meaningful to examine which functions were decentralised
or centralised in each program and search for the reasons why the
mix of centralised and decentralised functions emerged the way it
did in each case. The degree of decentralisation present in a
program can be measured only in the light of such an analysis of
the patterns of authority sharing.

We present below the results of an analysis of a set of
critical decision areas in respect of the six programs. While
this set does not exhaust all decision making areas and functions in
development programs, it covers the key functions and tasks which
are taken into account in determining the pattern of distribution
of authority within the program's structure. Evidence from the case
studies is used to indicate whether in a given program each of the
decision areas (functions) was centralised (C), mostly

centralised (MC) or decentralised (D). "Mostly centralised" refers
to cases where lower levels of the program agency and linked
organisations were involved in decision making, but the top management of the program had the final say as the decisions affected all
constituent units. To illustrate, let us take the function of
resource generation. The Chinese Program is rated (D) as the local
organisations had a major role in raising resources for the
services. The Indonesian Program is rated (MC) as most of the funds
were generated centrally with the communities providing only labor.
KTDA is rated (C) since the program agency generated the entire
funds for its activities. C, MC, D represent different points in
the spectrum of distribution of authority within the program
structure.

Table 10.1 presents some interesting findings on the degree of
decentralisation associated with the different programs. First of
all, the most centralised functions concern areas such as purchase,
technology, production facilities, etc., in which the role of
economies of scale, and the use of specialised knowledge are the
dominant considerations. Authority for these decisions was vested
in the program's top management in all cases. In the Indian program,
the bulk import of milk powder and other dairy aid commodities was
centralised. Dairy plant design and other technological choices
were also centralised decisions even though inputs for these
decisions may have come from different levels in the network. A
similar pattern emerges in the Indonesian Program where the import
and internal supply of contraceptives were centralised functions of
BKKBN. In the Chinese case, production and distribution of drugs
was centrally controlled through the Ministry of Health. In the
Mexican Program, the development of the school curriculum and
production of teaching materials were centrally organised, but in
consultation with groups of instructors. KTDA's nurseries for tea
stumps, and extension technology were under central control. Thus,
wherever common services and technology choices for the entire
program were involved which entailed large scale operations and
highly specialised knowledge, the tendency was to centralise such
services and choices.

Second, in the allocation and control of funds, centralisation
of authority was relatively high in almost all programs except the
Chinese and Mexican. Being large national programs, funds had to
be allocated and activities planned and coordinated across units
and areas. Since most of the funds for the programs were raised
centrally, their allocation also tended to be done centrally to a
large extent. In the Philippine Program where credit was a major
input, centralised planning and over-all allocation of credit were
done through the Central Bank of the country which had indirect
control over the network of rural banks. This involved, however, a
process of discussion at different levels in the network which we
shall discuss in detail in the next chapter. Where there was
sharing in resource generation, the degree of centralisation in
allocations tended to decline. Thus in the Mexican Program where
the communities put up one room schools and met the local costs of
the program, there was a more active role for the local groups

(community committee and state committee) in planning and resource allocation. The same was true in China where the communes raised part of the resources for the local health services and hence shared the responsibility and authority for planning and resource allocation. At the other extreme was KTDA which completely centralised planning and allocation of funds. Its funds were centrally raised and it had no network structure to speak of. Operating in a relatively stable agricultural environment with a regional focus and standard technology, KTDA could plan its activities centrally and get farmers to respond through a system of incentives.

Table 10.1

Patterns of Authority Sharing

	Mexican Program	Chinese Program	Indone- sian Program	Indian Pro- gram	Phili- ppine Program	Kenyan Pro- gram
1. Functioal areas dominated by scale economies (eg. decisions on purchases, technology choices, processing*)	C	C	C	C	C	C
2. Allocation and control of funds	D	D	MC	MC	MC	C
3. Supervision and control of field activities	D	D	MC	MC	MC	C
4. Resource genera- tion (responsi- bility of raising resources)	D	D	MC	MC	MC	C
5. Design of service (specification)	D	D	D	MC	MC	MC
6. Service delivery	D	D	D	D	D	D

* In economic programs, the marketing of the products (eg. crops) may also gain from centralisation because of the scale economies involved.

Third, in contrast to these functions, we observe a greater
degree of decentralisation in some programs as we move to other
areas such as supervision and control and resource generation. This
tendency is clearly noticeable in the Mexican and Chinese programs
where the nature of the environment (inaccessible locations of
community schools, widely scattered communes) and the strategic
decision to seek joint responsibility for resource generation
seem to have caused these functions to be decentralised. KTDA, on
the other hand, performed these functions in a centralised mode
chiefly because it had a more controllable environment and central
mobilisation of funds was feasible. Other programs could be placed
somewhere between these two extremes.

Fourth, decentralisation was the preferred mode in service
delivery in all the six programs. Any other mode would have been
less efficient given the size of the programs and the nature of
their environments. Decentralisation became necessary also because
the involvement of the beneficiary was perceived as useful. The
participation of beneficiary groups in planning and implementing
service delivery was evident in some degree in all programs, though
the Mexican, Chinese, Indonesian, and Indian programs provided a
more active role for them than the Philippine and Kenyan programs.
Design of the service and decision making in relation to adapting
the service at the local level were also decentralised in all cases
except in the three economic programs. In the Kenyan case, the
nature of tea crop and the feasibility of developing standard
extension practices in a relatively homogeneous regional environment
enabled the KTDA head office to prescribe the design of the service
to be offered to farmers. The extension staff were required only
to implement or follow the instructions, with limited scope for
varying the practices or adapting them over time. In the Indian
Program also, the basic design of service at the village level was
prescribed centrally, though the spearhead team had reasonable
decentralised authority to adapt to local conditions and vary
practices as long as the basic design was not tampered with. In
the Philippine Program, the design of the 16 step package of
practices was laid down centrally, though the production technicians
had some flexibility to adapt them to local conditions. At the
other extreme was the Mexican, Chinese, and Indonesian Programs,
where the design of service itself varied from place to place and
different parts and levels in the network had considerable flexibility in adapting to the local conditions. Thus instructors had
much flexibility in designing the service. BKKBN's inputs were not
identical in the conservative Muslim areas of West Java and the
compact Hindu island of Bali. In fact, a major reason for undertaking pilot experiments on a decentralised basis at the initiative
of local functionaires in different parts of Indonesia was to
strengthen their ability to adapt the service to local needs.

The foregoing analysis of the results summarised in Table 10.1
shows that the social development programs in our sample operated
in a relatively more decentralised mode than the economic (agricultural) programs. Both types of programs operated in a centralised
mode with respect to certain key functions. But the structures of

the social development programs (education, health, and population)
seem to be decentralised in relation to more functions than is
ture of the dairy, rice, an tea programs. The explanation lies in
(1.) the nature of the service, its underlying technology and the
need to adapt it to varying beneficiary needs in order to elicit
their response,[10] (2) the need to involve beneficiaries in planning
and implementing the program as a means of creating self-sustained
social change in the absence of the pull effect of any other motivating factor, and (3) the complexity of the environment in terms of
uncertainty, diversity, and scope which renders central information
processing for decision making in important areas ineffective. Of
the economic programs, the Indian and Philippine rogram structures
were more decentralised than that of the Kenyan Program. The
reasons for the relatively centralised structure of KTDA should be
sought in the standardised service and stable technical practices
associated with tea development, the active role of economic
incentives, and the homogeneity and stability of the environment.
If all these programs performed well, it is in part due to their
success in matching their degree of decentralisation to the set of
factors mentioned above.

A second point to note is that the mix of functions (centralised
and decentralised) evolved over time in all the programs. This
evolution was both a function of learning over time as well as
expansion in the size and scope of the program. Thus, in the early
years, the Mexican Program had a relatively centralised structure
which left only a few functions to the state level committee. The
experience gained in operating the state offices and the confidence
built up over time in the ability of the state level committee and
its staff to perform additional functions better led the program
headquarters to decentralise and bestow additional responsibility
and corresponding authority to the field staff. Expansion of the
program clearly accelerated this process. In the Indian Program,
expansion led to the setting up of regional offices with increased
powers delegated to them. Even in KTDA, while most of the extension planning and marketing remained centralised, the creation of
group managers for tea factories on a regional basis reflected a
move towards decentralisation in the wake of the setting up of
several new factories and the consequent system over-load imposed
on the head office by the non-routine problems of factory management. On the other hand, in controlling leaf collection, such
problems were not faced and so it continued to operate in the
centralised mode. In the Indonesian Program, the structure became
more decentralised in the wake of a strategic shift towards the
increased participation of communities in service design and
delivery. In part, this was a response to the demand problem that
faced the program, and also reflected the learning process at work.

The degree of decentralisation appropriate to a development
program is a function of its strategy of service and demand
mobilisation, the need for beneficiary participation, the
scope for reaping economies of scale, and the complexity of
its environment in terms of uncertainty, diversity and scope.

(Proposition 10.4)

Sources of Influence

We have seen that relatively decentralised network structures
characterised all our programs except one. Hierarchical authority
and direct control over the structures were by definition ruled
out in these cases. How then did these programs operate their
structures? What were the lead agency's sources of influence? We
find that a number of lateral influences were deployed to make the
network effective.

Field investigations have revealed five sources of influence
which were used by the lead agencies to make the network structures
operate effectively. First, the lead agency had control over funds
(budgets), scarce supplies (imports or other critical inputs)
or technical assistance, which the linked organisations needed. For
instance, in the Indonesian Program, the budget was controlled by
BKKBN which allocated funds to the cooperating ministries and
provincial governments to finance their tasks in the program. It
also controlled the import and distribution of contraceptive
supplies. In the Indian Program, financial and technical assistance
to the state implementing agencies were controlled by NDDB and IDC.
Second, joint planning and review of program activities by the lead
agency with the linked organisations through common councils/boards
gave it a powerful instrument to gain commitment from members of the
network. NFAC used this device in the Philippines. The Indonesian
Program and Indian Program also used joint planning to create a
common understanding and commitment to program goals and action
plans. NDDB and IDC had a common board and chairman to facilitate
joint action. Third, political support by those in power was used
by the lead agencies to convey to the network the priority attached
to the programs. The Philippine and Indonesian Programs
explicitly used the political clout of the Presidents of their
countries to goad the cooperating agencies to work together
effectively. Political commitment to the program from the top
leadership was an important source of influence in Mexico, China,
India, and Kenya. Fourth, monitoring and review by the Head of
State or other high level bodies gave the lead agencies added power
over the cooperating organisations. In Kenya, more than political
leaders, donor agencies in the KTDA Board played an important
monitoring role. In China where there was no formal information
system, Chairman Mao's personal follow up of the Program spurred
the network to action. Fifth, the demand for the program service
created from below through strategic interventions put pressure on
the network to respond. Thus in the Philippines, the communications
campaign and the work of the production technicians in the field

led farmers to seek loans from the rural banks and inputs such as
fertiliser, seeds, etc., from other agencies. Failure to respond
would have exposed these agencies to severe public criticism. The
demand mobilisation in rural areas by the field workers in Indonesia
put pressure on the Health Ministry clinics to respond and the
provincial governments to coordinate the speedy delivery of contraceptive supplies to the villages. When the spearhead teams
organised village milk cooperatives in India, the state dairy
development corporations had to respond by offering the necessary
support.

Table 10.2

Sources of Influence on Networks

Sources of Influence	Mexican Program	Chinese Program	Indone-sian Program	Indian Program	Phili-ppine Program	Kenyan Program
1. Use of funds/ scarce supplies/ technical assistance.	✓	✓	✓	✓	✓*	✓
2. Joint Planning and review mechanisms.	✓	X	✓	✓	✓	X
3. Strong political support by those in authority.	✓	✓	✓	✓	✓	✓
4. Monitoring/review by Head of State/ high level bodies.	✓	✓	✓	✓	✓	✓
5. Demand creation for services through participa- tion of beneficia- ries/use of incentives.	✓	✓	✓	✓	✓	✓

Note: The symbol ✓ indicates the presence of the source of
influence specified in the table. The symbol X indicates
the absence of the specified source of influence.

* Partial control over funds.

Table 10.2 summarises the role of these diverse sources of influence on the networks of the six programs. The Kenyan Program is also included here though the role of the network in KTDA was rather limited. Table 10.2 shows that joint planning was not an active influence in the Chinese and Kenyan Programs. In the Chinese case, the lack of joint planning was a deficiency in the first phase of the Program when lack of coordination led to major imbalance. Chairman Mao tried to correct it through the Cultural Revolution. Except for these two cases, the evidence is that the five sources of influence were actively used in the different programs to reinforce the working of their network structures.

> A program's lack of direct control over its network structure can be offset by the use of multiple sources of lateral influence such as control over funds, joint planning, political support, monitoring by political leadership, and creation of demand for services from below.
>
> (Proposition 10.5)

ORGANISATIONAL AUTONOMY

Mutual adaptation of strategies and structures and the management of networks in a complex environment call for a measure of autonomy in the program organisations. All the six program agencies in our study had some measure of organisational autonomy though the degree varied from one case to another. In legal terms, Conafe (Mexico) and KTDA (Kenya) had the maximum autonomy. They were set up as seperate legal entities under the national law with provision for funding independently of government, separate policy making boards to manage their affairs, flexibility in regard to recruitment, scales of pay, and other terms of employment and financial practices different from those of government. Thus though governments established these organisations, there was a conscious attempt to bestow upon them "adequate legal autonomy" to enable them to perform their tasks effectively. In Conafe's case, the justification was that rural education required innovative interventions and that conventional government departments had failed in this area because of their rigid structures and practices. A legallv autonomous agency, it was hoped, would perform better in this difficult field. In respect of KTDA, the rationale was that a commercial activity was involved and that risk taking, quick responses, and transactions with financial institutions and donors would be facilitated by a high degree of legal autonomy.

The legal autonomy enjoyed by NDDB (India) and BKKBN (Indonesia) was considerably less than in the case of Conafe and KTDA. While both were established as boards with seperate legal identity, they were not given any formal autonomy in the generation of funds, personnel matters such as scales of pay, and financial practices. As entities which received funds from governments, they were subject to conventional government audit. They had their own policy making boards, but these consisted of senior officials of government for the most part. However, they did enjoy some autonomy in matters of recruitment and their boards' decisions were final for all practical purposes in many policy areas as members represented the concerned ministries at their highest level. Thus in NDDB, the head of the Finance Ministry was a member. This meant that in financial matters when the board took a decision, it did not have to be referred back again to his ministry which controlled expenditure. The composition of the board was used in this case to gain a measure of formal autonomy.

NFAC in the Philippines and the Ministry of Health, the lead agency in China did not enjoy the measure of legal autonomy that any of the preceding program agencies had. NFAC was a council set up in the Ministry of Agriculture by an executive order of President Marcos. While the council consisted of representatives of various ministries and private agencies, it did not have a legal status that bestowed autonomy in terms of funds generation, financial practices, and personnel matters. The naming of the Agricultural Secretary (the Chairman of NFAC), as a "Presidential Action Officer" reporting to the President did give NFAC a measure of flexibility in operations and policy making. The authority given to NFAC to recruit high level personnel on special contract terms and offer incentive pay to the field staff could be interpreted as evidence of a measure of formal autonomy. But NFAC was subject to government audit and other regulations very much like other agencies. In the Chinese case, there is no evidence that the Ministry of Health was treated differently from other ministries in the matter of autonomy. The Chinese Program is a special case and we should seek evidence of autonomy in other parts of the network.

Our analysis of the case studies shows that the effective autonomy enjoyed by the different programs was quite different from the pattern described in the preceding pages. In point of fact, NDDB and BKKBN operated with as much autonomy as Conafe and KTDA though the legal or nominal autonomy of the former was far more limited. Even the Philippine and the Chinese Programs operated with much more autonomy than was warranted by the nominal autonomy enjoyed by their program agencies (NFAC and Ministry of Health). What explains this phenomenon?

There is considerable evidence that program leaders sought to induce autonomy for their agencies when their legal autonomy was limited. They also found ways of involving autonomous groups in the network structure to compensate for the limited autonomy of the lead agencies. In effect, they were inducing or earning autonomy so that their structures could operate more flexibly than was permitted by their limited nominal autonomy.

Take NDDB, for instance. The financial controls and practices of government were found to be irksome and dysfunctional by the NDDB leaders which had to operate in a difficult environment and perform some commercial functions. By setting up IDC as a corporate body, the program increased its autonomy as some of the commercial functions could now be passed on to the new corporation. In addition, NDDB began to charge fees for its services instead of receiving budgetary grants and allocations from the government. The revenue earned by selling the dairy commodities imported under aid were received by IDC directly and not through the government budget. In effect, NDDB thus avoided direct dependence on government funds and earned a significant measure of autonomy in the process. This independence, in turn, gave NDDB increased flexibility in terms of personnel and financial practices though certain basic constraints such as salary scales were binding.

BKKBN's funds came from government sources. Expenditure controls of the government therefore applied to the program budget in general. However, BKKBN leadership was able to induce the government to agree that financial controls (governmental) in their entirety should not apply to the use of foreign aid resources for the program. BKKBN was subsequently authorised to receive aid funds directly for broadly specified purposes. These funds were used for activities which needed fast response and greater flexibility. For example, aid funds were used for the import and distribution of contraceptive supplies. Normal government procedures for import and distribution would have entailed considerable delays. Similarly aid funds were used to support pilot experiments in different parts of the country. Since these experiments were often proposed by regional and local staff, speedy response to them encouraged local initiative and increased the capacity for problem solving at the grassroots. Effective autonomy is also reinforced by good performance. When a program performs well, it is able to earn increased autonomy because superior bodies have greater trust in them and are willing to support and facilitate their work. Thus the Planning Board of Indonesia was more responsive and accommodative towards BKKBN's requests than towards many other agencies simply because it had a more impressive record of performance. Similarly, the government authorised the Chairman of BKKBN to recruit staff directly even though he did not head a ministry and did not have the rank of a minister. This enabled BKKBN to recruit staff speedily and directly. Thus in several ways, BKKBN was able to induce additional autonomy for the operations of the program.

In the Philippines, NFAC was able to earn a part of its autonomy because of the high national priority attahced to the rice program. The cumbersome procedures for receiving budgetary allocations were minimal for NFAC as a result of all the concerned departments using their discretion to facilitate the program's working. Unlike other government agencies, NFAC was permitted greater flexibility in reallocating its budget from one head to another without prior approval. NFAC was also able to offer incentive allowances to its field staff, a flexibility that other field staff in the Ministry did not enjoy. Its effective autonomy was thus expanded as a result of the flexibility it was able to earn after the program got going.

In the Chinese case, the rigidities of the Ministry were in part offset by the direct and forceful interventions of Chairman Mao and the innovative use of communes which enjoyed a high degree of autonomy. This is an example of a linked organisation in the network having a larger measure of autonomy than the lead agency itself. The Chinese Program's success may have been due partly to its extensive use of the decentralised and autonomous communes which integrated health services into their ongoing programs of work. In a sense, the role played by the private agencies as members of NFAC was similar. In the provision of inputs such as fertilisers, pesticides, and credit, private firms and banks operated with greater flexibility and speed than would have been possible if these services were to be provided by conventional public agencies. Thus, in both the Chinese and Philippine Programs, the limited autonomy of the lead agencies was to some extent offset by the greater autonomy enjoyed by other parts of the network structure. The use of community groups by BKKBN and rural cooperatives by NDDB also appears to have had a similar effect.

It is difficult to measure the degree of autonomy enjoyed by a program in precise terms. However, the foregoing analysis shows that all the six programs had moderately autonomous structures though the lead agencies in every case did not possess the same degree of legal autonomy. As we have seen, this is because they were able to induce or earn autonomy through other devices including the use of private or other autonomous agencies as part of the network. Judging the level of autonomy solely by reference to nominal or legal autonomy will therefore be misleading.

The effective autonomy of a development program is a function of its nominal as well as induced (earned) autonomy.

(Proposition 10.6)

Successful program leaders do not necessarily start out with highly autonomous structures. They may induce or earn additional autonomy or compensate for the limits on their autonomy through the use of private agencies (the market mechanism) or community organisations in the network.

(Proposition 10.7)

CONCLUSIONS

In the design and management of development programs, structural interventions are often given inadequate attention. It is not unusual to find innovative and complex strategies being superimposed on weak and rigid structures. The evidence presented in this chapter lends considerable support to the thesis that careful design and dynamic adjustments of structures are important elements in the success of development programs. In concluding this chapter, we shall summarise four lessons which emerge from the experience of our programs.

First, mutual adaptation of program strategies and structures appears to be an essential requirement of success. The Chinese Program's failure to achieve this 'fit' in its first phase and the problems of performance that ensued is an important lesson. That structure follows strategy is part of the conventional wisdom in management. In the field of development, however, it is equally important to bear in mind th t there can be constraints on structural changes and therefore "mutual adaptation" assumes special significance.

Second, it seems that large and complex programs must learn to live with network structures. A national lead agency becomes necessary because of the dominant role of specialised knowledge and scale economies in many programs. Yet one agency cannot possibly provide all the inputs needed even by a "single service" program. Dependence on multiple agencies and actors outside the agency's control thus becomes inevitable. The dilemma can be solved only by deploying a variety of lateral influences some of which were innovatively used by the programs reviewed here. Governments which set up program agencies without providing for such sources of influence have much to learn from this lesson.

Third, it is important to note that the need for decentralisation and beneficiary participation is a function of the strategy and environment of a program. That social development programs require more decentralised and participatory structures than conventional economic programs is an important finding. Decentralisation and participation are costly. A contextual analysis will be an aid to program designers in determining the degree and nature of decentralisation and participation required in specific cases.

Fourth, the role of organisational autonomy in enabling program leaders to adapt and orchestrate planning and implementation has been highlighted by the analysis presented in this chapter. The need for managers to earn a part of their autonomy and search for ways to compensate for the limits on their autonomy cannot be overemphasised. That the more complex a program and its environment the greater its need for effective autonomy is an important lesson for policy makers and program designers.

NOTES

1. See Chapter 8, pp. 117-121.
2. The oilseeds component was added to NDDB's mission only in 1978.
3. This arrangement existed even in the rice program that preceded Masagana-99.
4. This was a structural intervention which was not attempted in the earlier rice programs. (Compare Exhibits 10.1 and 10.2)
5. The production technician also prepared the farm budget and planned jointly with the farmer and worked out his input requirements. He recommended the farmer's loan application to the bank and gave him the chits needed to procure fertiliser and seeds. He also had a role in recommending farmers for training.
6. The only exception was the tea officers who reported through senior tea officers. The latter functioned partly as regional managers. More recently, group factory managers have been created to perform a similar function.

7. A more important reason was the inadequacy of the strategy itself. This question will be taken up later on in this chapter.

8. See Lampton, _op.cit._, Chapter 11.

9. In BKKBN, the structure was differentiated on the basis of services also in 1978.

10. The characteristics of beneficiaries and the nature of social change being sought are such that a pre-packaged design may be less appropriate in social programs. Hence the need to vary the design to suit local conditions.

EXHIBIT 10.1*

ORGANISATIONAL STRUCTURE OF NFAC (1971)

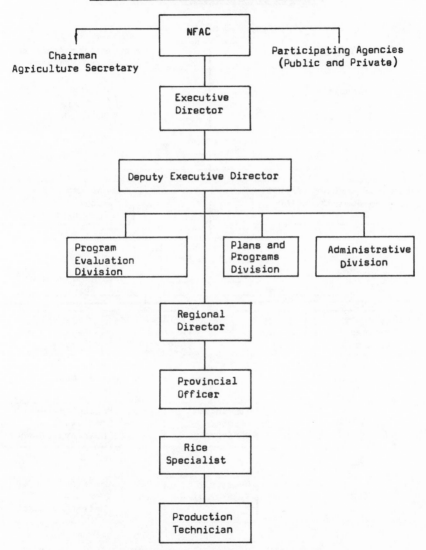

* Exhibits 10.1 to 10.4 are designed to bring out the major changes
over time in the structures of selected program agencies.
However, these are not complete organisation charts nor do they
reflect   every stage in the evolution of these structures.

EXHIBIT 10.2

ORGANISATIONAL STRUCTURE OF NFAC (1977)

```
                          ┌──────────────┐
                          │     NFAC     │
                          └──────────────┘
        Chairman                                Participating Agencies
  Agriculture Secretary                          (Public and Private)

      ╭──────────╮                                 ╭──────────╮
      │ Committee │                                 │ Committee │
      │    on    │                                 │ on Agrl. │
      │  Credit  │                                 │ Research │
      ╰──────────╯                                 ╰──────────╯

                          ┌──────────────┐
                          │  Executive   │
                          │  Director    │
                          └──────────────┘

  ┌─────────────────────────┐          ┌──────────────────────┐
  │ Deputy Executive Director│          │ Deputy Executive     │
  │ Program Administration   │          │ Director             │
  └─────────────────────────┘          │ Field Operations     │
                                        └──────────────────────┘

                    ┌──────────────┐
                    │ Management   │
                    │ Committee for│
                    │ M-99         │
                    └──────────────┘

  ┌──────────┐  ┌────────┐  ┌─────────────┐  ┌─────────────┐
  │ Plans and│  │  MIS   │  │ Agricultural│  │ Administra- │
  │ Programs │  │  Unit  │  │ Program     │  │ tion        │
  │ Division │  │        │  │ Evaluation  │  │ Division    │
  └──────────┘  └────────┘  │ Service     │  └─────────────┘
                            └─────────────┘

                    ──── Regional Coordinator

            ┌──────────────┐      ┌──────────────────────┐
            │ Provincial   │      │ Provincial Action    │
            │ Program      │──────│ Committee            │
            │ Officer*     │      │ Chairman:Governor    │
            └──────────────┘      └──────────────────────┘

            ┌──────────────┐      ┌──────────────────────┐
            │ Production   │      │ Municipal Action     │
            │ Technician £ │──────│ Committee            │
            └──────────────┘      │ Chairman : Mayor     │
                                  └──────────────────────┘
```

* The Provincial Program Officer (PPO) reported both to the NFAC
  Head Office as well as to the Governor.

£ The Production Technician reported both to the PPO and the Mayor.

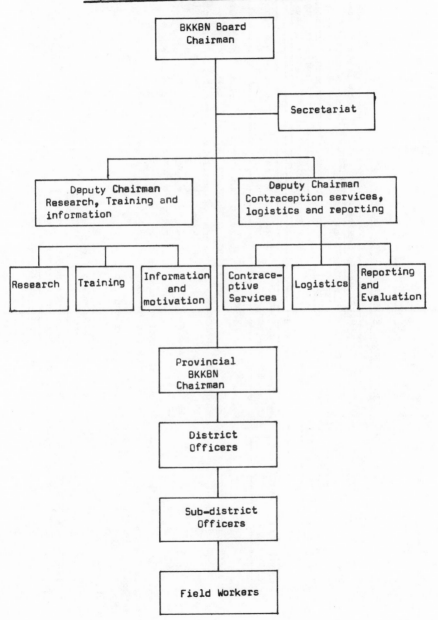

Exhibit 10.3
Organisational Structure of BKKBN, 1972

Exhibit 10.4

ORGANISATIONAL STRUCTURE OF BKKBN - 1978

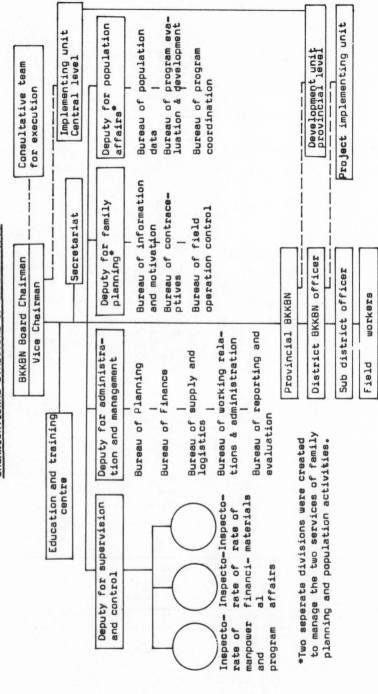

*Two seperate divisions were created
to manage the two services of family
planning and population activities.

11
Process Interventions

Four sets of critical organisational processes relating to participation, human resource development, monitoring, and motivation and their relationships with the program environment, strategy, and structure were described in Chapter 8. The program's organisational structure is the framework within which these processes operate. We shall now proceed to seek evidence on the manner in which the six programs under study evolved and matched the four processes to their environments and internal requirements. The most striking features emerging from this analysis are:

- the influence of the complexity of the program and its environment on the degree of beneficiary participation adopted;

- the dominant role of training as part of the human resource development process in all the programs;

- the simplicity and speed of feedback associated with the monitoring process in most of the programs; and

- the inverse relationship between beneficiary participation and the importance of economic incentives in motivating beneficiaries.

At the end of each section, we shall state some propositions which derive support from the analysis of the process interventions of the programs. A comparative analysis of the evidence from the different programs is attempted in the concluding section.

THE PARTICIPATIVE PROCESS

In the literature on development, peoples' participation is sometimes viewed as an "objective" to be achieved through development programs. Participation of beneficiaries in decision making and action is seen as an end in itself and not as a means to create economic or social services. While there is considerable merit in treating participation as a goal of development, it is pertinent to point out that we are concerned here with the instrumental role of participation. The focus of the participative process is on the functional role it plays in achieving program goals. If participation were to be treated as a goal, it would have been more appropriate to discuss it under "strategic interventions".

The participative process to be discussed below is concerned with goal setting, creation of commitment to plans, allocation of tasks and resources, and service delivery.[1] The process used in these important areas of decision making and action is critical to the integration of planning and implementation in any development program. Thus while we are not comprehensive in our coverage of the participative process, we hope to capture its essence by focusing on three major dimensions. Programs vary in the extent to which the three dimensions described below are present in their processes of decision making and implementation. The role played by beneficiary participation in operational planning and implementation represents one important dimension. The degree of internal autonomy of implementors reflects the flexibility enjoyed by the program staff in areas for which they have responsibility. The role of negotiation is yet another dimension of the participative process. The negotiating process may be used in arriving at joint decisions between beneficiaries and the program staff, and between different levels within the program agency itself. The role of participation in the planning and implementation of different programs is discussed below.

While NDDB was primarily responsible for the overall strategic planning of Operation Flood, it evolved the operational plans for the sub-programs in the different states in collaboration with the concerned state governments. These governments designated the newly created state dairy development corporations (SDDCs) or other agencies to represent them and the farmers who were yet to set up dairy cooperatives according to the Anand Pattern. The agreement was that when district cooperative unions were formed, they would play the representational role in relation to NDDB.[2] This was a compromise agreement as far as NDDB was concerned as the latter was committed to the participation of the cooperative unions in the planning and implementation of Operation Flood. The role of beneficiary participation in these critical processes could be regarded as moderate in the early years of the program. In the second (current) phase of Operation Flood, the agreements with the participating state governments require that the implementing agency will be the farmers' cooperative federation in each state. This step is clearly designed to expand the role of beneficiary participation in the planning and implementation of the program.

We have already commented on the large measure of organisational autonomy enjoyed by NDDB. Other parts of the network were also designed to have a fair measure of autonomy. Thus IDC and SDDCs were set up as semi-autonomous corporations. Cooperatives were voluntary groups which also enjoyed a high degree of autonomy. The network could therefore operate with moderately flexible planning and allocation processes. Equally important was the autonomy extended by NDDB to its grassroots implementors. The spearhead team leaders who engaged in goal setting, formulation of operational plans, and action along with their counterparts at the district level enjoyed a fair measure of flexibility in their decision making processes. They were authorised to incur expenditure, make purchases, and decide personnel matters within certain prescribed limits which enabled them to adapt to local needs expeditiously.

The planning and implementation tasks of NDDB made moderate use of negotiation in gaining commitments from other parts of the network. Questions as to which agency was to be responsible for the implementation of the program in a state, the targets to be achieved, deployment of resources, and the division of tasks among the different agencies were decided through the process of negotiation among the organisations concerned. Thus we find that NDDB's planning and allocation were characterised by a moderate emphasis on beneficiary participation, internal autonomy for implementors and negotiation.

In the Philippine Program, the role of beneficiary participation in planning and implementation was quite limited. There was no organisation of farmers in Masagana-99.[3] The production technicians dealt with individual farmers except in respect of credit for which groups of farmers were required to provide a joint guarantee for loan repayment. This scheme did not work out smoothly and was subsequently abandoned. The implementors of the program at lower levels did enjoy a fair measure of autonomy for operational planning and implementation tasks. The Provincial Program Officers and production technicians in the villages provided inputs for planning and negotiated with NFAC head office in respect of plans and resources. The production technician was empowered to recommend the credit needs of farmers to the rural banks. He had powers to recommend farmers for training. While beneficiary participation in decision making was low, the implementors of the program had a moderate measure of autonomy and room for negotiation which made the planning and implementation of NFAC relatively flexible.

In KTDA, there was a formal role for beneficiaries in operational planning and implementation. It was an advisory role which made their participation rather limited in scope. The growers' advisory committees at the divisional and district levels were consulted on plans, distribution of inputs, and other services by KTDA. There was also a symbolic representation of growers on the board of KTDA. As a program agency, KTDA enjoyed a moderate degree of autonomy, though the structure was managed in a relatively centralised manner. The flexibility in decision making given to the field staff was therefore rather limited. The role of negotiation within different levels in the organisation and in transactions with the beneficiaries was relatively insignificant.

Participation of beneficiaries in decision making processes did not exist in the early years of BKKBN's existance. It was the strategic shift to actively incorporate village communities into the Indonesian Program's network that led BKKBN to emphasise the participative process in planning and implementation. Community leaders played a key role in setting goals and targets for their area. The role of bargaining and negotiation in decision making is strong in Indonesian life. This feature was reflected in the organisational processes of BKKBN. Provincial officers and field workers at the grassroots enjoyed a moderate degree of autonomy. Local officers were encouraged to propose pilot experiments in their areas and to negotiate with the head office for goal setting and resource allocation. Field workers were authorised to adapt to local conditions as in West Java where they would examine women and prescribe pills in the course of their visits to villages.[4]

The role of beneficiary participation in the Chinese Public Health Program was high. The communes which had a major role in the operational planning and delivery of health services were organisations of the people. Since the communes generated a part of the funds for the program, their role in the allocation of resources was also significant. There is evidence that in agriculturally bad years, many communes did reduce their budgets for health services even though the political leadership would have liked them to keep up the tempo. The mix of preventive and curative services to be provided in the local areas was left to be decided by the communes which enjoyed considerable autonomy. Negotiation played a moderate role in operational planning and implementation. Policy guidelines were provided by the Communist Party leadership and technical support and advice by the Ministry. Within this framework, the communes and similar local organisations of beneficiaries seemed to have taken recourse to adaptive planning and allocation processes.

In the Mexican Program (Conafe), participation was a dominant feature of operational planning and implementation. The role of the village communities and state level committees in operational planning was significant. The program strategy which emphasised their role in resource generation strengthened the participatory process. The community committee and local leaders were actively involved in goal setting and resource allocation. The instructor worked closely with the committee and adapted his services to their local needs. The curriculum prescribed by Conafe provided the basic guidelines for the instructor's work. This framework, however, left considerable room for him to improvise and adapt to the special requirements of the children and the community. Thus the instructor enjoyed a moderate degree of internal autonomy. The state level offices and committees of Conafe which raised a part of their resources also had a fair measure of autonomy. The process of negotiation was extensively used by them in their transactions with Conafe head office in respect of goal setting and resource allocation. The dimensions of participation, autonomy for implementors, and negotiation in operational planning, allocation, and implementation had grown stronger in Conafe as it evolved over time.

A comparison of the programs shows that the social development programs differ significantly from the economic programs in the use of the participative process. The active role of beneficiaries, for example, is more evident in the Indonesian, Chinese, and Mexican Programs than in the Kenyan and Philippine Programs. The Indian Program is somewhere in between. The thrust of the first three programs was on social change which called for rather complex inter-

ventions. In the economic programs involving tea and rice, the
stable prices offered for the crops were sufficiently strong to
elicit beneficiary response even in the absence of a participatory
process. Though the Indian Dairy Program is also economic in
nature, it had a strong social change orientation to it, and its
strategic and structural interventions were more complex than those
of the other two agricultural programs. There is a similar, but
less marked contrast between the two sets of programs also in
respect of the use of autonomy and negotiation. In the relatively
more uncertain and diverse environments facing the social development programs (population, health, and rural education), processes
which made use of the internal autonomy of implementors and
offered greater scope for negotiation in decision making facilitated adaptive responses and commitment creation in the field.[5] The
Kenyan Program appears to have had the most stable and homogeneous
environment among the different programs. The cultivation and
processing of tea could be standardised under these conditions,
thus eliminating the need for a highly decentralised structure. The
limited role of negotiation and low autonomy for field implementors
in its organisational process was consistent with KTDA's relatively
centralised structure. The larger Indian and Philippine Programs
with their more uncertain and diverse environments fall between
these two extremes. Thus the nature of program complexity in terms
of strategic and structural interventions and the features of the
environment seems to influence the extent to which the participative
process is adopted by a successful program. These interventions in
turn are reinforced by and are consistent with the latter process.
The evidence from the six programs lends modest support to the
following proposition:

> Program performance is facilitated when beneficiary partici-
> pation, negotiation, and internal autonomy of implementors
> vary in proportion to the complexity of the program and the
> environment.

(Proposition 11.1)

HUMAN RESOURCE DEVELOPMENT

Selection and development processes are meant to assist program
managers in matching their staff and program tasks. Rigid
approaches to recruitment and training, for example, could render
an innovative strategy ineffective simply because the program staff
were ill prepared to cope with its requirements. This is a major
problem in many development programs which are unable to design and
utilise selection and development processes capable of reinforcing
their strategies. How well did our six programs achieve this much
needed "match"?

In NDDB, the Indian Program's lead agency, selection and
development process received considerable support from the top
management. One of the first divisions to be created in the NDDB
was for manpower development. Three features of the selection

206

process deserve to be noted. First, diverse sources were tapped to
identify suitable staff. This is in contrast to the practice in
many programs which depend solely on government departments for
their staff. NDDB, like others, was also subject to government
regulations on salary scales and other terms of appointment. Yet
it used its selection process more flexibly to recruit staff to
match the requirements of its development tasks. Second, NDDB
deliberately used "Amul" as a nursery for recruiting some of its
key personnel and for staff development. Amul's experience was
considered highly relevant to NDDB's mission. The selection process
thus facilitated the task of "matching" by identifying and tapping
sources which were more relevant to the program. Third, the sharp
focus of the process of "matching" led to a de-emphasis on the
practice of deputation of staff from government for specified
periods which generally tended to reduce the level of their
commitment to the program.[6]

Training was the key to the human resource development process
in NDDB. Amul was extensively used for the training of its newly
recruited staff. In addition, NDDB set up its own facilities for
training. Even the secretary of a village cooperative society, who
was the lowest level functionary in the network, was given systematic training. Groups of farmers from different states were brought
to Amul for an orientation as part of an effort to improve their
understanding of and commitment to the program. Training in the
class room as well as on the job was used by NDDB not only to
improve the match between people and tasks, but also to initiate a
learning process that would create confidence, and commitment, and
also encourage sharing of common values among its staff and
beneficiaries.

In the Philippine Program, two features of the selection process
deserve to be noted. First, the Bulacan Pilot Project acted as a
nursery for recruitment, very much like Amul in the Indian Dairy
Program. The technicians in the pilot project were absorbed by NFAC
which played a key role in training the field staff for Masagana-99.
The senior officers involved in the pilot project were also given
important positions in the new program. Second, though government
was the major source of personnel in this program, adequate
flexibility was built into the selection process to permit the
recruitment of senior staff from non-government agencies on special
terms. Even for the field staff, the process was used flexibly to
permit modest departures from the normal government terms of
appointment. Training, as part of the development process, received
considerable attention in NFAC. It has already been pointed out
that the pilot project staff were used as the core group for the
training of the extension staff. University staff and facilities
were also used intensively for training. The training of farmers
in groups was organised in different parts of the country.

KTDA's experience in Kenya was similar to that of the
Philippines Program. Its extension staff were drawn from the
government, but training intensively in KTDA's own training schools.[7]
Its managerial staff were drawn from a variety of sources,
government, private sector, and other countries. Over the years,

the role of expatriates has declined. The selection process was used with considerable flexibility to attract a mix of people whose skills matched the program tasks. Some of the government personnel involved in the original pilot project were absorbed by the new program. Training schools were set up by KTDA for both its own staff and for participating growers. Considerable top level attention was given to training as an aid to human development.

Government was the major source of personnel for the Indonesian Program's lead agency, BKKBN. However, the practice of deputation from other ministries was discouraged. The only other significant source of staff was the private family planning federation which was also tapped by BKKBN. Unlike India, Indonesia's manpower and experience base were extremely limited. BKKBN, therefore, did not have access to the diversity of sources that NDDB had. In respect of the field staff, however, BKKBN departed from the pattern we have seen in other programs. Its field workers were recruited as contract employees and not as civil servants. They were paid a fixed honorarium and had no security of tenure. The selection process was thus used with a measure of flexibility that was not common in other Indonesian programs. Training was an important process by which BKKBN attempted to match its people to the program tasks. It had its own training establishments. It also pioneered the training of local midwives, community volunteers, and leaders of village communities as part of an effort to develop local capacity and commitment.

In the Chinese Program, the role of flexibility in the selection and development process was considerable at the local level. The communes were free to identify their members to be trained as barefoot doctors and health aides. We do not know much about the flexibility of the process within the Ministry of Health. However, training received the highest priority in the program as is clear from the massive deployment of doctors from the cities to the rural areas for training purposes. Teams of highly qualified doctors moved about in different parts of the country, training thousands of barefoot doctors and health aides. A criticism of this process was that it led to the neglect of medical research and high quality medical education. There is no doubt, however, that the focus on training and commitment creation was very strong in the Chinese Program.

Conafe of Mexico effectively used its high degree of autonomy to operate a flexible selection process. Its source of recruitment consisted of both the public and private sectors. Through its flexible compensation practices, it succeeded in attracting experts with professional skills and experience. For specialised needs, it subcontracted the jobs to qualified private experts and consultants instead of recruiting them on a full time basis. In its recruitment of instructors, Conafe departed noticeably from the government pattern. It used a variety of methods, viz., advertising, personal contacts, etc., to attract young people with the right motivation for contract appointments.[8] Though its training programs were shorter compared to the conventional training for teachers, a great deal of attention was given to them. Training was also used as a means to create commitment and a sense of service and to eliminate people who did not seem to match the program's needs. Both in the flexibility with which it used its selection process and the importance it attached to training, Conafe deserves to be rated high.

An important feature that emerges from a comparative analysis of the six programs is the absence of a rigid adherence to conventional recruitment practices of government and exclusive dependence on government as the source of personnel. It appears that all the programs used selection and development processes flexibly and innovated in interesting ways. Among the innovations were the use of pilot projects as a nursery for recruiting staff and training personnel and the appointment of senior staff as well as field personnel on contract terms. The evidence presented above supports the proposition that flexibility in selection and a sharp focus on training are associated with high levels of program performance.

> Program performance is facilitated by the program management's flexibility in staff selection, and a strong emphasis on training and commitment creation.

(Proposition 11.2)

THE MONITORING PROCESS

Collection, analysis, and use of information are at the heart of the monitoring process. An information system, formal or informal, is therefore, the foundation of the process. Monitoring processes differ in respect of three characteristics : the degree of complexity in information, the speed of feedback, and the mix of formal and informal sources of data gathering. We analyse below the monitoring processes of the six programs in terms of these dimensions.

NDDB used a relatively simple information system as an aid to its monitoring process. Each district union/dairy was required to send in a monthly report to NDDB on a set of key indicators relevant to the progress of the project. The report called for data on milk procurement, fat content, prices paid to farmers, sale proceeds, village society membership, mobile veterinary services, artificial insemination services, etc.(See Exhibit 11.1). This formal one page report was the primary input received by the head office for monitoring purposes. A similarly simple and brief report was sent monthly to the district union by the district supervisors who visited the villages. The basic source of information for the entire program was the village society. The data collected at this level were simple, directly related to the society's activities and did not involve any special survey or complex estimation procedures.[9] Reports were also received from the urban dairies on a monthly basis. Monitoring of program tasks such as erection of dairy plants and the operation of milk grids was done through the regional offices of NDDB. The monitoring unit in the Chairman's office collected the data on the progress of the program as a whole. Periodic reporting to the Board and the

Ministry of Agriculture, and review by the steering committee were
based on the monitoring unit's analysis.

Fast feedback to the field was a feature of NDDB's monitoring
process. Quick processing of the simple and brief reports from
the districts facilitated speedy feedback which the field personnel
could use to make corrections and adaptations. This process was
greatly aided by the frequent field visits by senior managers and
experts who used a variety of informal sources and discussions with
the field staff and farmers to supplement the information gathered
through formal reports. Such field visits and discussions with
SDDCs and state government officials also aided conflict resolution
and informal problem solving on the spot without delays. This was
especially useful for dealing with non-routine problems which were
unlikely to be detected through the formal monitoring process.

The Philippine Program set up a simple information system which
required the production technician in the field to submit a monthly
report to his Provincial Officer on the progress of the tasks
entrusted to him   The provincial officer aggregated the data from
the technicians and sent a summary report to NFAC. (See Exhibits
11.2 and 11.3). The financial institutions were also required to
report to NFAC because of the high priority attached to credit as
a program input (See Exhibits 11.2 and 11.3). These reports were
brief, one page statements which the field staff could fill from
their records. Production technicians were required to maintain
work sheets on each of their farmers to facilitate this task. Each
technician reported on planting and harvesting operations, credit,
and crop production in his village. The banks reported on the
number of loans, area financed, loans released, and repayments
received. In respect of crop production, the production technician
had to make an estimate. This was an area in which biases crept in,
for obvious reasons. NFAC eventually made its own estimates of
such biases (through field visits and audits) and made internal
adjustments for them in its aggregate estimates.

The production technicians delivered their monthly reports by
hand, mail, or radio to the provincial program officer who in turn
collated them and forwarded the data to NFAC headquarters. The
data were processed speedily by the central information unit which
was quick to send its feedback to the field. Computerisation of
data processing aided quick identification of problems and action
to rectify them. NFAC staff also undertook frequent tours to the
rice growing areas for inspection, discussion, and problem solving.
Given the short production cycle and constraints on communication,
they found the mix of formal and informal sources of information
extremely useful for monitoring program activities.

KTDA's monitoring process was aided by a centralised information
system which received monthly reports from tea officers on extension
services, leaf officers on leaf collection, and factory managers on
tea processing. The reporting format was simple and brief. The
leaf officer, for example, reported on the number of growers selling
leaf, total weight of green leaf collected and delivered, maximum
and minimum delivery everyday, and measures of leaf quality. The
information collected was readily available with the officer and

focused on key indicators of the operations. Computerised data processing at the head office of KTDA facilitated speedy feedbak to the field on problems and corrective actions. Field visits by senior officers were used to gather additional information, but not as much as in the Indian and Philippine Programs. The more recent appointment of group managers for factories on a regional basis reflects the growing importance being attached by KTDA to field visits to solve problems using both formal and informal sources of information.

The Indonesian Program was known for its very efficient, but simple information system. The one page monthly clinic report was the basic input of the information system. Data on new acceptors by method used, types of services provided, and stocks of supplies were reported by the clinic regularly (see Exhibit 11.4). These reports were sent to BKKBN headquarters by mail and processed within a matter of days. Each administrative level was given a feedback on the trends indicated by the data analysis. The feedback reports showed subordinate units ranked by performance, and classified by the different indicators mentioned above. This system permitted local officials to compare their district's progress with that of others and a basis on which to negotiate for additional resources and assistance.

The monitoring process also made use of field visits and cross-checks by senior officials to minimise exaggerated claims by clinics. The checking of clinic reports against the tear off sections from acceptor records which were also sent to the central office every month enabled analysts to spot false claims. Apart from the program leadership's interest in monitoring, an important reason for the success of this information system was its clear focus on manage-rially relevant data without getting bogged down in gathering demo-graphic data for research purposes.

We do not have adequate data on the monitoring processes used by the Chinese and Mexican Programs. In the Mexican Program, the monitoring process operated with relatively fast feedback between the state level offices and headquarters, but the frequency of contact with the schools and instructors was much less. In the Chinese case, it would seem that the formal information system played a less important role than in the other programs. Local communities were most actively involved in both these programs and shared financial responsibilities too. Much of the monitoring appears to have been left to the local authorities which may have used informal rather than formal processes for monitoring, given the limited area covered by them. The need to report regularly to headquarters may have been reduced as a result.[10] In the Mexican case, assessors who visited schools did carry information back to the state offices and from there to the headquarters. But problems of communication and accessibility seem to have made feedback less frequent. The Chinese Program also may have faced similar problems in monitoring communes directly. Hence the hypothesis that political channels and other informal means may have been used by the leadership to monitor the progress of the program. The Ministry of Health may have had its own information system to monitor its hospitals, institutions, and drug distribution. We do not, however, have any data on this aspect of the program.

Of the six programs, four clearly support the proposition that simple information systems with fast feedback and which use a mix of formal and informal sources are an aid to the monitoring process which in turn facilitate program performance. The development of a small set of key indicators which reflected the progress of the program was a part of this exercise. Though the information system appeared to be simple and limited in the types of data sought, its design called for considerable sophistication. The identification and selection of the most relevant indicators invariably call for a great deal of skill and understanding. A remarkable feature was the detailed attention given to the design and operation of the process at the lowest level. It seems that local conditions and resources were taken into account in designing manageable information systems. The two programs which show limited evidence of a formal process with fast feedback happen to have left a major part of the responsibility for control to their local communities, which depended very much on local resources. It is possible that the need to report to the lead agency was minimised under this institutional arrangement. If so, the absence of a formal system with built in provision for fast feedback would not have hurt their performance.

> Successful development programs utilise monitoring processes which are simple, yet speedy in terms of feedback. Their information systems make use of both formal and informal sources.

> (Proposition 11.3)

MOTIVATION PROCESS

In this section, we propose to analyse the experience of the six programs in the use of incentives to influence the behaviour of beneficiaries and program staff. While the training and monitoring processes we have discussed in earlier sections have a motivational dimension, incentives, both economic and non-economic, constitute the most direct and powerful means available to development programs to elicit the cooperation of their staff and beneficiaries. The types of incentives designed and the manner in which they were used in the six programs are discussed below.

The basic services provided by the three agricultural programs were economic in nature. The program leaders of NDDB, NFAC, and KTDA recognised at the very outset that economic gain was the primary motive behind the farmers whom they wished to attract. In the Indian Dairy Program, there was a conscious effort to create farmer organisations to play an active role in the program. As a result, NDDB was also interested in motivating farmers to cooperate for their common good and not merely for direct economic gain.[11] The strategies of the three programs had provided for the award of attractive and stable prices and prompt payments to the farmer. The internal processes used by the program agencies to translate these strategies into action had much in common.

In NDDB, the process involved was twofold. First, the spearhead teams working in the districts were demonstrating to the people that the economic incentives were real. The initial process of credibility building was aimed at convincing the farmer that the program could really give him tabgible economic benefits. Second, the streamlined system for paying a stable price to the farmer for his/her milk on a daily basis as part of the village cooperative's operations reinforced his economic motivation. Fat testing (quality control) in the presence of the farmer, regular supervision of the society's work and audit of society accounts were other aspects of the process which made the system credible and sustained client motivation.

Both the Philippine and Kenyan Programs operated similar processes. The National Grains Authority's ability to buy surplus rice from the farmer and pay him a good price with promptness was an important part of the motivation process in the Philippines. The speed with which the farmer's loan request was processed by the production technician and the rural bank reinforced this process by giving him adequate funds to carry on his operations till the harvest was over. It is interesting to note that the Indian Program did not provide credit to the farmer as the latter was paid in cash on a daily basis. The belief was that the need for credit was reduced to the extent that the farmer got his daily payment without fail. KTDA also had an efficient process, though centrally operated, for determining the payments due to tea growers and ensuring that they received their payments promptly.[12] If the internal processes were slow and inefficient in coping with changing conditions, policy statements on price would have sounded hollow and farmer motivation would have been adversely affected. Though economic motivation dominated these three programs, non-economic incentives were also used to influence the response of beneficiaries. Both in the Philippines and Kenya, annual competitions, shows, and awards for farmers with the highest yields were organised regularly. This is a case of using "recognition" as part of the motivation process.

In the three social development programs, the appeal to beneficiaries was non-economic in nature. In Indonesia, processes for mobilising the support of key actors such as Islamic leaders and local elders were aimed at motivating public response. In recognition of this work, village chiefs in Bali were invited to visit the successful East Java program. A system of presenting awards to communities which excelled in family planning work was introduced to create increased public motivation. Individual material incentives for family planning acceptors were experimented with, but not found effective. The goal was to recognise and support cooperative action which was believed to hold the key to improved performance. In China, ideological commitment among the people was created through political and educational processes. In Mexico, the accent was on the mobilisation of communities through visits and increasing their motivation through participation in setting up and managing the schools. Thus where social or collective gains were expected from a program, the focus of the motivation process was on non-economic incentives.[13]

In regard to the motivation of program staff, there is evidence of the use of a mix of economic and non-economic incentives in almost all the programs. The staff of the program agencies in all cases except the Chinese, received somewhat better monetary remuneration and fringe benefits than most other civil servants in their countries. Except for the field staff in the Philippines, there was no attempt to link monetary incentives directly to performance. The production technicians in the Philippines were given an incentive payment in proportion to the repayment of loans by farmers to the banks. In other cases, the process of evaluation was used to link performance to career development. Promotion or greater responsibilities were given to those with a better record of performance than others in the Indian, Indonesian, and Mexican Programs. But incentive pay or allowances were generally offered as lumpsum payments. In the Philippines, a higher salary scale was given to the production technicians working in Masagana-99 as compared to those working on other crops. They were also given a higher status by redesignating them as "technologists".

Surprisingly, in the three social development programs, the implementing staff at the grassroots were recruited as temporary or part time employees. As has been mentioned earlier, they had no security of tenure and were paid a fixed honorarium or stipend. The barefoot doctors in China, who worked part-time, did not receive any monetary payment, but were awarded "work points" instead. In Indonesia, mid wives in the Outer Islands who performed well were sent for IUD-insertion training in Bali. Program managers in the field were given public recognition for their work and additional funds for their program activities. Innovative ideas were generated within the program and not borrowed from abroad.[14] Thus, the thrust of the motivation process of the Indonesian Program was on finding ways of recognising its better workers by giving them non-monetary awards, higher training, and other incentives adapted to their social and cultural values. In all the programs except KTDA, the lower level implementing staff enjoyed a fair measure of internal autonomy, which according to some observers, might have increased their motivation and job satisfaction. Through training conferences and field visits the social development programs have attempted to create and sustain a sense of commitment and spirit of service in the implementing staff. Their emphasis on the use of non-economic incentives for motivating staff seems to have been greater than in the three agricultural programs which were primarily economic in nature. Staff members who were interviewed in five out of the six programs attached considerable importance to the ability and commitment of their top program leaders as an important motivating factor. This exercise could not be done for the Chinese Program.

In brief, we find that the nature of the program strategy and service had much to do with the mix of economic and non-economic incentives used by the programs in motivating their beneficiaries and staff. The processes used were such as would reinforce the program strategies and facilitate service delivery. It is important to note that the motivation process even in economic programs made

use of non-economic incentives and that in the social development
programs, the role of non-economic incentives was dominant in
motivating both the beneficiaries and the staff.

> The compliance and cooperation offered by the staff and
> beneficiaries of a development program is influenced by
> the mix of incentives used to motivate them. Beneficia-
> ries will respond to economic incentives when they
> perceive direct economic gains from their participation
> in the program. When non-economic or collective gains
> are perceived, positive response by beneficiaries will
> call for an increased use of non-economic incentives
> such as recognition, status, and a sense of challenge and
> commitment.

(Proposition 11.4)

> When program outcomes cannot be related directly to the
> individual efforts of the program staff, a mix of
> generalised economic incentives and non-economic incen-
> tives will be in order. The motivation process should
> focus relatively more on non-economic factors such as
> commitment to a cause, recognition, and autonomy for
> implementors in programs whose dominant concern is
> social rather than economic change.

(Proposition 11.5)

PROCESS INTERVENTIONS : SOME PATTERNS

The key features of the four processes in relation to each
program are summarised in Table 11.1 based on the analysis presented
in the preceding sections. In order to facilitate comparison, a
program is rated high, moderate, or low in relation to each feature
listed in the table. Some interesting patterns emerge from a
comparative analysis of these ratings.

First, it appears that human resource development and monitoring
are the two processes which operate with considerable uniformity
across the six programs. Thus training was given a great deal of
emphasis in all the programs. There was evidence of the use of
simple information systems in five out of the six programs. A
plausible explanation of these phenomena is that most developing
countries are limited in their manpower skills and capacities to
manage development activities especially at the grassroots. Training
is essential to develop their human resources and match them to the
needs of programs. The top management concern for training and the
special attention given to developing skills and commitment at lower
levels was a unique feature of all our programs. There was no market
from where programs could have bought the required skills. Without
some flexibility in selection and investment in training to develop
skills and create a sense of commitment, a program could not have
made its strategy work. Similarly, given the paucity of skills and

Table 11.1

Rating of Programs by Process Feature

Process	Indo-nesian	Chinese	Mexican	Indian	Phili-ppine	Kenyan
PLANNING & ALLOCATION:						
Beneficiary participation	H	H	H	M	L	L
Autonomy of implementors	M	H	M	M	M	L
Negotiation	H	M*	H	M	M	L
HUMAN RESOURCE DEVELOPMENT:						
Flexibility in staff selection	H	*	H	H	M	M
Focus on training	H	H	H	H	H	H
MONITORING:						
Simplicity of system	H	@	H	H	H	H
Speed of feedback	H	@	M	H	H	H
Use of informal means	H	M	M	H	H	M
MOTIVATION:						
Economic incentives for beneficiaries	L	L	L	H	H	H
Economic incentives for staff	M	L	M	M	H	H

H = High;   M = Moderate;   L = Low;

* based on partial information
@ not known

facilities at lower levels and in the field, a complex information system would have been unmanageable. The design and use of simple systems was a recognition of this basic reality. The priority attached to the monitoring process reflects the program leaders' interest in using information to correct errors and improve performance.

Second, there is considerably greater variation in the emphasis placed by different programs on the different dimensions of the integration and motivation processes. In specific terms, it is significant that where economic incentives played a greater role, in motivating beneficiaries, the role of beneficiary participation was relatively low in planning and implementation. Where the role of participation was high, the use of economic incentives was moderate or low. The Philippines and Kenyan Programs were low with respect to the role of participation, but high on the use of economic motivation. The Indonesian, Mexican, and Chinese Programs were high on the role of participation and low on the use of economic incentives.

In the preceding pages, this pattern was explained in terms of whether the program was economic or social in nature. The inverse relationship between the use of economic incentives for beneficiaries and the degree of beneficiary participation in planning and implementation could be viewed also as a partial substitution of the two processes. Where individual economic incentives were strong enough to generate beneficiary response, a program might succeed even if beneficiary participation is limited. Where economic motivation is weak, beneficiary participation could play a useful role in eliciting increased public response. This is not to deny the importance of participation in the development of people. Our argument is that a program which has no individual economic incentives to offer to its beneficiaries (better prices, higher incomes etc.) must pay even greater attention to participative processes than others which can provide such incentives.

The processes we have discussed in this chapter are closer to implementation and action than the strategic and structural interventions analysed in earlier chapters. The experience of the six programs shows how they supported and reinforced these interventions. In doing so, they did depart from the standardised and rather rigid processes and systems which are common in government. Take, for example, the concept of functional and vertical integration which was an essential part of the strategies of some of our programs. Since this complex integration of inputs required the cooperation of diverse agencies, the major structural intervention employed was the creation of a network with multiple integrative mechanisms and sources of lateral influence. These interventions would not have been effective if the planning and allocation tasks of the program were not characterised by an appropriate degree of participation and negotiation. Flexible selection and training of staff facilitated cooperative action by them in order to achieve integration. The careful use of a mix of incentives influenced the behavior of the staff and beneficiaries towards achieving the strategy. The monitoring process helped to rectify errors and

ensure that integration was being achieved as desired. The
different processes which departed somewhat from the government
pattern supported and reinforced the strategic and structural
interventions. It appears that their compatibility with these
interventions was an important reason for program success.

The design and operation of the different processes discussed
in this chapter have a direct bearing on the efficiency with which
development programs are managed. Participation of beneficiaries in
program planning and implementation could lead to a better design of
service and improved public response. These factors have a major
influence on the efficiency of resource utilisation and unit cost of
service. Careful monitoring with fast feedback does contribute to
improved efficiency through early detection of errors and realloca-
tion of scarce resources. The use of incentives, both economic and
non-economic, tend to have a positive impact on the efficiency of
resource utilisation. Thus processes which match a program's
strategy and structure might have a direct influence on the efficiency with which it is managed. While measuring and comparing costs
and efficiency pose severe problems in many development programs,
an evaluation of processes could offer some useful indirect
evidence on this important dimension of performance.[15]

In conclusion, it is pertinent to point out that the implementation of programs involves some internal processes which have not
been explicitly treated in this chapter. Thus, budgeting and
performance evaluation are important processes in translating
strategies into action. Both can be used to influence the behavior
of the staff in desired directions. While we have not discussed
them separately, it should be noted that the budgetary process is
built into the tasks of planning, allocation, and control. Performance evaluation is implied in the discussion of the monitoring and
motivation processes. A detailed investigation of budgetary
planning and control, and evaluation processes was not undertaken in
this study. Further explorations of how these specialised processes
and their mechanics aided the broad organisational processes
discussed in this chapter are clearly in order.

NOTES

1. These are the most important aspects of the planning and
implementation of development programs.

2. In some states, this transfer has already taken place. NDDB
had to negotiate long and hard with SDDCs on the timing of the
transfer in some cases.

3. There was a lone representative of the National Federation
of Farmers in NFAC. This was no more than a symbolic representation.

4. It is unusual for field workers to be given this degree of
discretion to adapt to local conditions. They were also given
appropriate training to play this role.

5. Even if structures are autonomous and decentralised, it does
not mean that programs necessarily encourage beneficiary participation or negotiation. There are cases where these dimensions are
ignored and therefore a mismatch occurs between structure and process.

Explicit attention to decision making processes thus becomes necessary.

6. For some jobs, NDDB did recruit persons with experience on deputation from government. But this was not the norm.

7. In both the Philippines and Kenyan Programs, large numbers of field staff were required. Given the nature of the programs, they could not be given permanent employment. The arrangement therefore was for the staff to return to their parent departments when the program's need for them was over or when the program itself was terminated.

8. The decision to select staff on a contract basis was influenced by the discouraging experience with the tenured federal teachers who were sent to teach in the rural areas.

9. Systematic and continuous audit of accounts of the cooperative union provided a cross check on the information system. This function was performed by the Cooperative Department of the state government.

10. When operational problems are being solved at the local level, there is no need to refer them upwards. Nor is there any need for those at the top to receive and process the relevant information. The load on the information and monitoring process is to this extent reduced.

11. Though cooperation leads to eventual economic gain for all, individual farmers may not perceive this as such at the outset.

12. KTDA also provided credit to the farmers indirectly through the sale of tea stumps at subsidised prices. The subsidy was recovered from farmers over a period of time. This incentive also acted as a motivating factor.

13. It is recognised that health and educational services do bestow economic gains on beneficiaries. But these gains are not immediate and illiterate beneficiaries do not see them in the same light as the gains from economic activities.

14. For example, the community incentive scheme promoted by one external donor did not make much headway in Indonesia.

15. Among our programs, rates of return and cost data were available only on three. Even in these cases, inter-program comparisons are not easy.

Exhibits

NATIONAL DAIRY DEVELOPMENT BOARD
MONTHLY REPORT FROM UNION/RURAL DAIRIES (M2)

Exhibit 11.1

Name of the Union/Milk Plant	
Month	Date of issue

A. MILK PROCUREMENT

Procurement from		Total quantity in the month ('000 Kgs.)	Average		Producers' price (Rs./Kg.)		Maximum procurement on any single day ('000 Kgs.)	Remarks, if any
			Fat%	SNF%	Fat	SNF		
Societies:	Cow milk							
	Buff.milk							
Other agencies:	Cow milk							
	Buff.milk							

B. USE OF CONSERVED COMMODITIES

Commodities used for	Total during the month in MT		
	SMP	Butter oil	White butter
Recombination			
Making products			
Commodities received during the month			

C. MILK MARKETING

Milk sold directly in towns (name)	Packaging	Total quantity during the month ('000 litres)	Average		Consumer's price(Rs./L)	Milk supplied to other dairies (name of dairy)	Total quantity during the month('000 L)	Average		Price (Rs./L)
			Fat%	SNF%				Fat%	SNF%	

Exhibit 11.1, cont'd

D. PRODUCTS MANUFACTURED

Product	Quantity (MT)	Average Fat%	SNF%	Selling price (Rs./Kg.)	Other products	Quantity (MT)	Average Fat%	SNF%	Selling price (Rs./Kg.)
1 White/Table butter					4				
2 Ghee					5				
3 SMP					6				

E. FARMERS' ORGANISATION AND MILK PRODUCTION ENHANCEMENT INPUTS

Primary societies organised: Anand Pattern ☐ Conventional ☐

No. of societies registered: Anand Pattern ☐ Conventional ☐

No. of functional societies: Anand Pattern ☐ Conventional ☐

No. of farmer-members: Total ☐ Women ☐

Cattle feed manufactured during the month (MT): ☐

No. of societies marketing cattle feed: ☐

Cattle feed sold during the month (MT): ☐

Sale price (Rs./Kg.): ☐

No. of artificial insemination sub-centres:
1. Frozen semen: ☐ ☐
2. Liquid semen: ☐ ☐

Liquid Nitrogen produced during the month (L): ☐

A.I. performed since inception ('000):
     Cow   Buffalo
1. F.S. ☐ ☐
2. L.S. ☐ ☐

Calves born since inception ('000):

	Cattle		Buffalo	
	Male	Female	Male	Female
	☐	☐	☐	☐

No. of societies covered under animal health programme: ☐

No. of societies with veterinary first-aid: ☐

No. of mobile veterinary clinics functioning during the month ('000 cases): ☐

	Routine		Emergency	
	No.	Cases	No.	Cases
	☐	☐	☐	☐

Area under fodder crops (hectare): ☐

No. of minikits supplied since inception: ☐

No. of demonstration farms functioning: ☐

pifc:ktm:tno:220681.

221

Exhibit 11.2

Masagana 99 Summary Report from Production Technician to Provincial Program Officer

Cumulative from......... to.........

Production Technician ....Municipality.......Province

Financing Institution......

Note: Your report for the month must be received by Provincial Program officer not later than the 3rd of the following month.

SUPERVISED FARMERS WITHOUT CREDIT

1. Number of farmers   .... farmers
2. Area Planted (Irrigated)   .... ha
3. Area Planted (Rainfed)   .... ha

Harvest Operation

4. Area Harvested (Irrigated)   .... ha
5. Total Production (Irrigated)   .... cav.
6. Area Harvested (Rainfed)   .... ha
7. Total Production (Rainfed)   .... cav.

SUPERVISED FARMERS WITH CREDIT
Planting Operation

8. Number of farmers   .... farmers
9. Area planted (Irrigated)   .... ha
10. Area Planted (Rainfed)   .... ha

Harvest Operation

11. Area harvested (Irrigated)   .... ha
12. Total Production (Irrigated)   .... cav.
13. Area Harvested (Rainfed)   .... ha.
14. Total Production (Rainfed)   .... cav.

PROBLEMS

15. .... Lack of seeds
16. .... Slow credit approval/release
17. .... Fertiliser unavailable
18. .... Pesticides unavailable
19. .... Weedicides unavailable
20. .... Water supply inadequate
21. .... Flood, typhoon, drought
22. .... Pests and disease
23. .... Labor shortage
24. .... Drying/storage
25. .... Marketing/pricing difficulties

Exhibit 11.3

Masagana - 99

Report of Financing Institutions to Provincial Program Officers
Cumulative From .... To.....

Financing Institution............. Province...........

Instructions: 1. Report should be cumulative by Phase.
2. Report should be submitted to the Provincial Program Officers not later than the 5th of each succeeding month

PHASE

	I	II	III	III	IV	V	
			Masagana Plus DS[2]	Direct seeding only		Masagana Plus DS[2]	Direct seeding only
A. Total number of loans (Farmers)							
B. Total area financed (hectares)							
C. Total loans approved (P)							
D. Total loans granted/released (P)							
E. Total loans matured/Due[1] (P)							
F. Total Loans Repaid (P) (Principal only)							
G. Total Loans Restructured[1] (P)							

Various financial institutions in the province support the Masagana 99 program. The three organisations involved are: 1. The Rural Banking System, 2. The Philippine National Bank and 3. The Agricultural Credit Administration.

The field offices (Rural Banks, PNB and ACA Branches) make a monthly report to the PPO in their province on Form 5 summarising the status of loaning operations

Note: 1. Loans restructured should not be included in matured loans (due for repayment)
2. Direct seeding.

Exhibit 11.4

National Family Planning Program
Monthly Clinic Report

```
Name of Clinic  :
Address         :
Clinic Status   : 1. Department of Health 2. Armed Force
                  3. Other Government Agency  4. Private
Clinic Type     : 1. Simple
                  2. Complete

Clinic open this month :      times
Total                  :      hours

Clinic Code Number     :
Report for month of    :
```

A. ACTIVITIES IN THE CLINIC

    1. Total new acceptors visit to this clinic:
        1. Pill   ... (Col.5)
        2. Intra Uterine Device   ... (Col.6)
        3. Condom   ... (Col.7)
        4. Vaginal tablets   ... (Col.8)
        5. Vasectomy   ... (Col.9)
        6. Total ligation   ... (Col.10)
        7. Injection   ... (Col.11)

                                 Total   ...

    II. Total revisits for some contraceptive method (visit)
        i. Pill
            a. To obtain more pills   ... (Col.12)
            b. Complaints   ... (Col.13)
            c. Others   ... (Col.14)

        2. Intra Uterine Device
            a. Routine checking   ... (Col.15)
            b. Complaints   ... (Col.16)
            c. Expulsion   ... (Col.17)
            d. Extraction   ... (Col.18)
            e. Re-insertion   ... (Col.19)
        3. Condom   ... (Col.20)
        4. Vaginal tablets   ... (Col.21)
        5. Others   ... (Col.22)

Exhibit 11.4 (Continued)

B. Activities outside the FP Clinic:
    1. Total persons contacted on house visit
        a. Finding new acceptors   ...
        b. Providing contraceptives   ...
        c. Other purposes   ...

    2. a. Total referral cards distributed
           to acceptor candidates   ...
        b. Total candidates that became acceptors   ...

    3. New acceptors who were referred by
        a. Relative/friend   ...(Col.23)
        b. Other acceptor   ...(Col.24)
        c. Health worker   ...(Col.25)
        d. FP field worker   ...(Col.26)
        e. Indigenous midwife   ...(Col.27)
        f. Self referred   ...(Col.28)
        g. Other   ...(Col.29)

    4. Total group summons   ...
        b. Total attendeance   ...

    5. Total new acceptors all methods) recruited by
       Medical Mobile Team.   ...(Col.30)

C. Only for Post-martum Clinic
    1. Type of new acceptor
        a. Immediate   ...(Col.31)
        b. Direct   ...(Col.32)
        c. Indirect   ...(Col.33)

    2.a.Total deliveries   ...
      b.Total abortions   ...

Stock of contraceptives	End of last month supply	Received this month	Issued this month	End of this month supply
1. Pill strip	...	...	...	...
2. IUD size B	...	...	...	...
size C	...	...	...	...
size D	...	...	...	...
3. Condom	...	...	...	...
4. Vaginal tablet	...	...	...	...
5. Other identify	...	...	...	...

E. Acceptor Card (K/IV/KB) sheets
F. Other information

12
Learning From Success

Our analysis of the strategic, structural, and process interventions in the six development programs is now complete. In view
of the small sample of programs under study, it is hazardous to
generalise about strategic management from their experience.
Instead, the findings of the study have been used to generate a set
of propositions on the major categories of interventions and their
orchestration as an aid to enriching our understanding of the
linkages between performance and strategic management. This is
consistent with the basic objective of the study which was to learn
from success by identifying and analysing the management and insti-
tuional interventions associated with a set of high performers among
development programs. We have indeed been able not only to identify
a variety of critical interventions, but also discover certain
underlying patterns which seem to be associated with success. This
study has merely scratched the surface of an important, but neglected
area in the management of public organisations. Other more detailed
and specialised studies of a broader range of programs are needed to
establish the links between these patterns and performance.

INNOVATIONS

As the case studies show, our six programs did face serious
problems in the course of their development. Their relative success
in moving towards congruence should not be interpreted to mean that
their leaders had hit upon a grand design that led to permanent
harmony and order. They had to cope with conflicts and face setbacks
some of which have been documented in the cases. What is significant
is that they were adaptive and innovative in their responses, and
deliberate in their choice of interventions. A more detailed analysis
than has been attempted in this book is required to fully understand
the dynamics of their management. Even our limited study, however,
has many important lessons to offer to those engaged in designing and
managing development programs. To bring these into sharper focus,
we shall first pull together the major innovations and common
features of the strategic management of the six programs which emerge
from our analysis. The role of the government in facilitating the
strategic management of these programs will be examined in the second

section. We shall then present some evidence on the management
problems of low performers. The final section will be devoted to
a discussion of the implications of the study for public policy
and management.

Our six case studies have unfolded a wide range of management
innovations most of which could not have been projected from the
experience of low performers. Some of these innovations are program
specific whereas others are found in several programs. The deployment of spearhead teams by the Indian Dairy Program, the concept of
the barefoot doctor in the Chinese Health Program, provision of
credit without collateral in the Philippine Rice Program and the
use of young people as instructors in the Mexican Rural Education
Program are examples of program specific innovations. The strength
of the spearhead team lay in its interdisciplinary nature, the
internal autonomy its members enjoyed,and its sharply focused
mission to build credibility among farmers and demonstrate how
viable farmer organisations could be created. The barefoot doctor
concept was an imaginative and cost effective response to the
problem of large scale health service delivery using local resources
and organisations. The provision of credit without collateral
reflected an unconventional move to mobilise farmer response to the
program through the supply of an input which was a missing link in
the integration strategy. Young instructors on contract terms
represented a bold departure from the traditional approach of the
Mexican Education Ministry and effectively matched the environment's
unique features and the program's goal.

A number of interventions which have been discussed in the
preceding chapters were highly innovative and common to several
programs. Take, for example, the deliberate linkages forged
between pilot projects and national programs. In four programs,
pilot projects and experiments were designed as learning devices
which facilitated the replication of more realistic and adaptive
program services on a national scale. They were used as nurseries
for selecting and training program staff. In many countries,
national programs are launched in a hurry without any concern for
developing and testing the relevance and feasibility of the service
being replicated. It is also true that pilot projects are sometimes
initiated without any serious commitment to developing services or
products to be replicated through larger programs. However, it is
important to note that while pilot projects are a powerful device
to design and test new service concepts, they cannot possibly offer
adequate guidelines for large scale structural interventions. They
are, by definition, small in scale and can generally do with simple
structures Hence,the structural requirements of replicating a
service on a national scale cannot be learnt from their limited
experience. Blowing up the pilot project structure is unlikely to
help in most cases.

The strategy of functional and vertical integration was yet
another innovation, especially in the economic programs. Many
programs have performed poorly because of their inadequate attention
to the integration of the relevant inputs and its failure to make
up for the inability of beneficiaries to achieve such integration on

their own. In contrast, the strategy of functional and vertical
integration was attempted in our programs precisely to compensate
for this deficiency. Similarly, demand mobilisation using community
participation in some of our programs was an innovative intervention. In the social programs which had no direct economic gains to
offer, the involvement of communities in operational planning and
implementation acted as a powerful means for mobilising beneficiary
response. Many more examples of innovations such as the use of
networks, design of simple information systems, and imaginative use
of non-economic incentives could be cited. Suffice it to say that
there is considerable evidence of innovative behavior on the part
of the high performers in our study.

CONGRUENCE : THE COMMON THEME

The major lessons to be learnt from the present study, however,
are not confined to the several innovations reviewed above. Rather,
they pertain to certain patterns which emerge from our analysis of
the different types of management interventions. First, in spite
of the diversity ofthe sectors and countries involved, the programs
seem to have much in common in respect of several ritical interventions. The initial focus on a single goal or service, sequential
diversification of goals, phased program implementation, organisational autonomy, the use of network structures, the use of simple
information systems with fast feedback, and flexible selection and
training processes are common elements of the strategic management
of our programs.

On the other hand, another set of interventions in these
programs reveal a different pattern altogether. In respect of the
participative process, for example, programs followed diverse
approaches. Though there was a basic similarity in the strategy of
functional and vertical integration, the nature of the integration
attempted varied among the programs. The program agencies also
differed in their degree of decentralisation and the mix of
incentives they used for motivating the beneficiaries.

An Interpretation

What accounts for this paradox? The similarities among the
interventions which we first described are likely to tempt the
reader to conclude that a standard recipe for success is in the
making. Yet the differences in other critical interventions show
that we have a paradox here which deserves closer scrutiny. To
sharpen the focus on the differences, we present below a set of
key management interventions corresponding to the Indonesian
Population Program (BKKBN) and the Kenyan Smallholder Tea Development Program (KTDA).

230

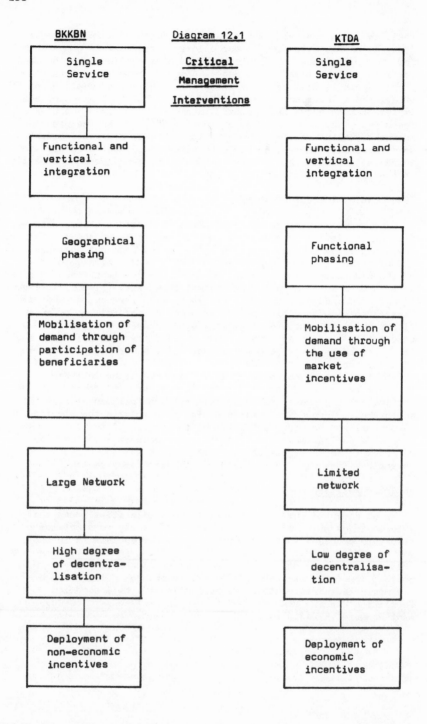

BKKBN

Single
Service

Functional and
vertical
integration

Geographical
phasing

Mobilisation of
demand through
participation of
beneficiaries

Large Network

High degree
of decentra-
lisation

Deployment of
non-economic
incentives

Diagram 12.1

Critical
Management
Interventions

KTDA

Single
Service

Functional and
vertical
integration

Functional
phasing

Mobilisation of
demand through
the use of
market
incentives

Limited
network

Low degree of
decentralisa-
tion

Deployment of
economic
incentives

In the diagram above, we have not depicted the complete set of interventions associated with these two programs. It does, however, represent a mix of interventions drawn from the preceding three chapters. Some of them are identical in both programs and others are dissimilar. The first two boxes depict interventions which seem identical. The remaining have very little in common. An important explanation for the similarity between programs in the first two interventions lies in the similarity in important dimensions of the environment. The environment was sufficiently complex that both programs opted for a single service strategy. The uncertainties on the demand and supply sides were such that both programs focused on a single service. The type of integration of inputs they adopted matched the goals they selected and the requirements of the beneficiaries in their environments. But the nature of inputs they integrated was not identical. While vertical integration meant market linkages for KTDA, in BKKBN's case, the vertical inputs were the services of the provincial and local governments in terms of demand mobilisation and service delivery. The two programs differed considerably in the remaining interventions. Though both were regarded as successful programs, they differed in the type of program phasing, strategy of demand mobilisation, scope of network, degree of decentralisation and the use of incentives. In each case, however, the entire set of interventions were mutually compatible. The Indonesian Program was aimed at social change and had no direct economic appeal to its beneficiaries. Its demand mobilisation therefore made extensive use of beneficiary participation. Given the large size of the country, it had to phase program implementation geographically. Again, the size of the country, diversity of the relevant agencies and the need for local adaptation of service necessitated the use of a large network and a high degree of decentralisation. The use of non-economic incentives to motivate beneficiaries and staff was consistent with the need to facilitate collaborative action through a decentralised network in a socially sensitive area.

Some features of the environment and the nature of the program service were quite different in the Kenyan case. The unfamiliarity of the Kenyans with tea processing and marketing and shortage of manpower led KTDA to phase the program functionally by first focusing on extension, tea cultivation, and leaf collection. The availability of the inputs needed for integration under the parent Ministry of Agriculture (except for the construction of roads) meant that the network structure could be more limited in its scope compared to that of the Indonesian Program. The relatively lower degree of diversity in the Kenyan Tea environment and the stability of extension practices made it unnecessary for KTDA to decentralise as much as BKKBN did. The use of economic incentives in motivating farmers was consistent with the program strategy of functional and vertical integration with its strong emphasis on economic returns.

An important lesson that follows from this comparison is that program success requires a high degree of "congruence" among the strategic, structural, and process interventions initiated by program leaders. This was true of both the Indonesian and Kenyan programs. That some of their major interventions were not identical reflects the differences in certain dimensions of their environments and program strategies. A similar analysis of the remaining programs provides further evidence in support of the same proposition. Program performance is thus influenced not only by the individual innovations and interventions, but perhaps even more importantly, by the congruence or fit among the entire set of interventions in the specific context of the program environment. The appropriateness of any one type of management intervention can be judged only in relation to the larger set of interventions of which it is a part. Perhaps a major reason for the failure of many development programs lies in the blind tendency of their leaders to standardize all interventions, and the negative interaction effects created in the process.

The creation and orchestration of congruence constitute the core of strategic management. Development programs seem to succeed when their top leaders and managers are able to practise strategic management. While in the present study we have not examined the role of program leaders in detail, it is pertinent to point out that putting the pieces together is their function. They create and orchestrate congruence by learning and adapting, not by following a "blueprint" approach which assumes all elements as given and inflexible.[1] Governments can make or mar this critical role of program leaders as we shall see in the next section.

ROLE OF THE GOVERNMENT

What role did the governments of the respective countries play in facilitating the strategic management of our programs? Those who manage development programs have often complained about the rigid manner in which governments tend to impose goals and targets on them and their lack of involvement in the planning process. An analysis of the experience of our programs shows that the governments which set them up played a significantly different role. We were unable to examine the Chinese experience in this regard for lack of data. The following observations, therefore, apply only to five out of the six programs.

Specification of Objectives

First of all, there was a formal statement of objectives given to every program by its government in the form of a legislative enactment, resolution or order. These were broad statements permitting the program agencies to pursue multiple goals and activities. In no case is there evidence that a government rigidly specified the operational goals and strategy of a program. Instead, the approach seems to have been to let the specification be influenced by the environment as perceived by the program leadership. The Kenyan Program was the only exception where, at the political level, there was prior strategic thinking about the program direction. In the Kenyan case, even though the government had specified the promotion of five crops for the original program agency, it agreed, in the light of experience, to limit the program's scope to one crop, namely, tea. This clearly reflects the positive response by the Government of Kenya to the feedback given by the program leadership.

Planning and Implementation Dichotomy

Second, the degree of flexibility given by the government to a program leader in evolving his strategy is an important indicator of the political commitment behind the program. It represents an important pre-condition for program performance. Top level political support ensures commitment of resources, financial, physical, and human to the program and facilitates the processes of conflict resolution and negotiation with external actors which program leaders have to manage continually. The sequence of decisions leading to the operation of the program is significant in terms of the constraints on program design and implementation it imposes. A policy decision to set up a program may be followed by the establishment of a new agency with broad objectives whose leader is asked to design the program and oversee its implementation. Alternatively, the basic policy decision may be followed by a specification of the program goals and plans by the sponsoring ministry or department and the establishment of an agency to implement it. Key personnel may then be appointed to manage the program which has already been designed and approved. The route chosen to initiate the program will determine the nature and intensity of the constraints under which the program leadership will have to operate.

The degree of political commitment and the sequence of decisions leading to a program's origin will also determine the manner in which power will be shared between the sponsor and the program authority. The imposition of additional constraints means reduced discretion and less freedom and authority for those who bear the constraints. Significant political support implies greater trust and hence a willingness on the part of the sponsor to share power with those responsible for the program. In turn, this willingness to share power leads to fewer constraints and greater autonomy for program managers.

The sequence of decisions and actions that intervene between the original policy decision of the government initiating a development program and the outcome of the program may proceed in one of two ways.

Routes A and B represent the two paths which governments usually take in planning and implementing development programs. The two models differ in the sequence followed from Stages 2 through 5. In Route A, the specification of the program's goals and plans follows the appointment of the top managers in the program agency, whereas in Route B program managers are appointed to implement a program which has already been formulated. The model adopted for initiating a program may have a decisive influence on the program outcome and performance. Route A permits a closer integration between design and implementation than Route B. Those involved in managing the program will also be involved in designing and planning the program in Route B and consequently the possibility of integration and mutual adaptation will be much greater in A than in B.

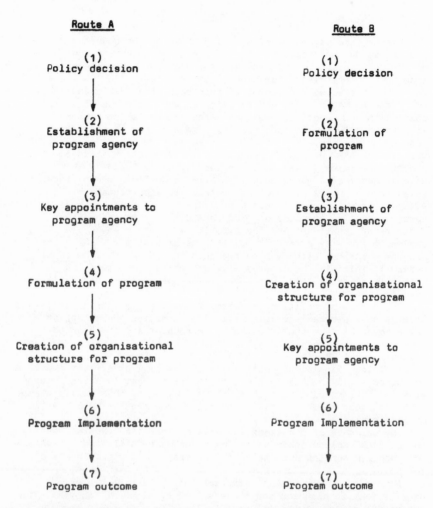

In five out of our six programs the dichotomy between planning and implementation was found to be minimal (China was excluded for lack of data). That their governments followed Route A rather than Route B may well have facilitated this outcome. Once a broad mandate was given by the government, it was the program leaders who were responsible for planning the strategy and implementing it. In India's National Dairy Development Board (NDDB), its chairman and his group played a decisive role in formulating the strategy

of Operation Flood and had primary responsibility for its diffusion.
In the Philippines, it was the Agriculture Secretary and his group
who planned the strategy of Masagana-99 and played the lead role in
its implementation. In five out of six cases, the formal creation
or restructuring of the program agencies was closely followed by
the appointment of program leaders. The initiative for defining
and evolving the program strategy was left to the program leaders
who were thus responsible for both planning and implementation.
This seems to have given the leaders greater flexibility to
orchestrate these two processes and a sense of "being in charge"
with its obvious implications for improved motivation to achieve
results. Governments seem to have approved the strategy deployed
developed by them instead of handing over program designs to
them.

This pattern differs significantly from those observed in
many countries and programs. Governments sometimes tend to import
program strategies or formulate them through internal groups
without any reference to those likely to manage them. Strategy
and implementation thus become disjointed and make mutual adaptation between the two difficult in such programs. This problem
seems to have been avoided in the programs we have reviewed. In
the Chinese Program which had some problems in this respect, the
health bureaucracy was not supportive of the new strategy. The
political leadership therefore left only a limited role to the
bureaucracy in planning and implementation. The major participants
were the political cadres and local organisations. Implementation
by a bureaucracy which was not involved in or supportive of the
program strategy would have been dysfunctional.

The Monitoring Role: Third, an important function performed by
the government in most of our programs was in monitoring their
progress and performance. The Heads of State or ministers concerned were actively interested in the results being achieved and
asked specific questions about their progress periodically. In
Indonesia and the Philippines, the Heads of State reviewed the
progress of the programs on a regular basis. In Mexico and Kenya,
Ministers who were chairmen of the boards of the program agencies
reviewed their progress. In the Chinese case, where we do not have
detailed information on the monitoring aspect, we do know that
Chairman Mao took a personal interest in the implementation of the
health strategy. He may have used political channels rather than
the bureaucracy for monitoring purposes. Political commitment thus
meant not only the initial support given to a program, but also
monitoring it so that a sense of accountability was built in to
counterbalance the autonomy given to those who managed it. Clearly,
there was recognition on the part of the political leadership
in the countries involved that the development tasks entrusted
to the programs under study required structures and processes
different from those common to the conventional activities of
government. Interestingly, both the economic and social programs
lent themselves to certain tests of performance, which though
imperfect, facilitated balancing their autonomy with accountability.

236

 Stability of leadership: A fourth role played by the governments was in providing stability,commitment, and continuity of
program leadership. We have seen how in five out of six cases,
attention was given to the early identification and appointment
of program leaders. In four out of the five cases, only one of
the program chief executives left his program at the end of four
years. Others stayed for longer periods and some are in position
even today. At least in these programs, the governments concerned
did not encourage the easy entry and exit of the top managers which
the civil service tradition has institutionalised in development
programs in some countries. Coping with and adapting to complex
environments call for stable, committed,and competent top managers.
Congruence would have been difficult to create and maintain if the
program leadership changed too frequently. It was not charisma
as much as their continuity on the job and commitment to program
tasks which enabled them to keep track of and orchestrate the
different components of strategic management.

 Political commitment as a pre-condition for program success
assumes a special meaning in light of the foregoing discussion.
The different roles described above were a manifestation of the
political commitment of the governments concerned to the programs
under review. The significance of this commitment lies in the
conditions it created for the practice of strategic management by
program leaders.

EVIDENCE FROM LOW PERFORMERS

 The conclusions and propositions presented in this book are
based on the experiences of a small sample of high performers. One
obvious limitation of the study is that we do not have comparable
evidence from an analysis of low performers. Is it possible that
similar patterns of management intervention are found among low
performers too? Anticipating this question, we noted in Chapter 1
that studies of failures were plentiful, and that there was need to
redress the imbalance by probing the experiences of high performers.
Unfortunately comparisons are not easy as studies of low performers
have not been done using the framework of strategic management.
The evidence from low performers presented below, therefore, tends
to be partial and piece-meal, though suggestive in the contrasting
patterns they reveal.

 Problems of strategy have been commented upon by several
authors. Having stated the importance of promoting growth with
equity, many integrated projects seemed to have had no strategy
for combining the inputs necessary to achieve this goal. Here is
an assessment by two authors who surveyed several integrated rural
development projects:[2]

 A major constraint on implementing integrated rural development strategies is the difficulty of determining the
 most effective combination of inputs for promoting growth
 with equity .... Although much has been written about
 techniques for increasing agricultural production, little

is known about the best combinations of technical, social,
economic, and administrative functions for promoting rural
development.

Problems of strategy have been severe even in single sector
programs. A major difficulty appears to be in creating linkages
among the components of strategy. In a regional evaluation of one
of India's national programs for livestock development, an analyst
reports:[3]

> In the name of integrated, intensive, coordinated approach
> there is emerging a tendency to take up many schemes
> simultaneously. But in the process of implementation there
> is often no logical, systematic integration of activities
> over time and space. There is no correct perception of the
> linkages of various schemes. In the integrated approach,
> there is a great danger of losing sight of the primary task
> or core activity which is the soul of the program. More
> often than not the primary task gets secondary importance
> because it is difficult to achieve it and 'soft' activities
> take precedence and are emphasized. For example, failure
> on the breeding front was generally obscured by a dense fog
> of statistics about achievements on linked activities.
> The main reason seems to be that the empirical basis of
> assumptions regarding linked activities in an integrated
> approach is often vague and undefined.

Inadequacies of organisational structure have been repeatedly
pointed out in studies of low performers. Problems of coordination
among participating agencies have received much attention. A World
Bank review of rural development projects has highlighted the lack
of appropriate structural interventions:[4]

> The newer multisectoral projects, in particular, suffered
> from problems of coordination among participating agents
> and their project related activities. In a South Asian
> country, for instance, it was found that the prolifera-
> tion of ministers and agencies directly involved both in
> planning and execution of rural development activities
> results in a lack of focused, well-structured and coordi-
> nated efforts to deal with the problem. At times the
> lack of coordination appears to be intentional; for example,
> when local officials resent the special attention given to
> Project Management Units. In other cases, the problems of
> coordination are so great that project designers seek ways
> to avoid the need for such coordination.

Over centralisation of structures is another problem area. It
is unfair to characterise overcentralisation solely as a structural
issue. Centralisation of planning and decision making in general
is part of the working culture of many low performers. The
experience of India's nutrition program is a case in point. A

leading authority in the field has summed up his diagnosis as
follows:[5]

> We are also beginning to learn that nutrition and other
> welfare programs among poor communities cannot succeed
> if they are carried out as highly centralised operations.
> There must be effective decentralisation not only with
> respect to responsibility for implementation, but also
> with regard to decision-making. The Nutrition Program over
> which we have spent millions of rupees largely failed
> for this reason. The pattern of the program must be
> tailored and adapted to suit local needs and must be
> based on the felt needs of the community.

Problems of organisational processes have also received
considerable attention from those who have analysed the performance
of low performers. In a survey of the problems facing integrated
rural development programs in the Third World, a UN report
commented on the inadequacies of monitoring and control as follows:[6]

> Inadequate monitoring and evaluation of project results
> is another common problem in program implementation.
> Every program administrator needs to know how much
> measurable progress is being attained in the implemen-
> tation of the program. He needs to know for his personal
> satisfaction and to be able to introduce relevant inputs
> that should be considered in the continuing review and
> modification of program objectives and other program
> configurations. The organisational imperatives of data
> retrieval and evaluation in these regards are critical
> to program success and may never be ignored.

A review of rural development programs and projects in Africa
sums up the problems of human resource development as follows:[7]

> Trained manpower poses a particularly severe constraint
> to the expansion of rural services in African countries.
> Substantial investment in manpower training of field
> level and administrative staff is, therefore, necessary
> if rural development programs are to reach a mass of the
> low income rural population.

Admittedly, this is a small sample of the conclusions of authors
who have examined the management problems of low performers among
development programs. But these observations are indicative of
the strategic, structural, and process related problems faced by
poor performers. It is clear that the innovative interventions we
have come across in the six programs represent the opposite side of
the coin. Even if a program has strengths in some dimensions of
strategic management, one inappropriate intervention in a critical
area is enough to create a mismatch and weaken its state of
congruence.

Evidence from our case studies reaffirm the conclusions reported above. Several of our programs have experienced ups and downs in terms of performance. Some of them had predecessors which did not do well. An analysis of their experience also shows that performance improved when strategic, structural, or process interventions were redesigned and adapted to suit the environment and redefined program goals. NDDB, for example, eventually followed a strategy of integration of inputs very different from that adopted by earlier programs for dairy development. When NDDB found that the response to its passive strategy of technical assistance was poor, it moved deliberately towards the more aggressive strategy of "Operation Flood" the results of which were strikingly different. BKKBN went all out for community participation after it experienced a plateauing of public response. The shift in strategy had a positive impact on program performance. The slow progress of the Chinese health strategy due to the uncoordinated structure in the early years has already been commented upon. It was only after attempting some significant structural interventions and strategic shifts that the Chinese Program's performance improved dramatically. NFAC's network structure and sources of lateral influence were distinctly superior to the weakly coordinated structure of some of the preceding rice programs which were plagued by inter agency conflicts. The new structure matched the more comprehensive strategy adopted by NFAC and led to a distinctly superior performance. These longitudinal experiences also support the proposition that when a program performs poorly, a realignment of its management interventions to match the changed conditions tends to cause performance to improve. The evidence from our programs thus reinforces the findings of authors who have investigated the problems of low performers.

IMPLICATIONS FOR PUBLIC POLICY AND MANAGEMENT

The development program is the unit of analysis in our study. Our primary focus , therefore, has been on the interventions of program leaders in the context of a specific program. There is no doubt, however, that the experiences we have analysed and the findings we have highlighted have important implications for policy makers and top administrators in developing countries as well as international donor agencies who play a major role in initiating, financing, and evaluating development programs.

Planning for Strategic Management

The empirical evidence on the management of the six successful development programs presented in the preceding chapters supports the thesis that strategic management is complementary to the roles played by political commitment and resources in program performance. The case studies have provided in rich detail the interrelated interventions which seem to fit the conceptual framework of strategic management discussed in Chapter 8. The experiences of these programs and of several low performers referred to in this chapter also lend support to the notion that performance suffers when elements of strategic management are missing or mismatched. It would seem, then, that policy makers and top administrators stand to gain from the practice of strategic management in their development programs. The strategic management approach could well be used as a diagnostic tool in analysing the ills of programs and as an aid to the search for improving performance.

There is a danger, of course, that the strategic management approach might become yet another ritual, mechanically adopted and uncritically applied by ill informed persons. Undoubtedly, standardising this approach and the combinations of interventions it implies is against the spirit of the basic concept. On the other hand, it may be highly instructive to raise a set of relevant questions about strategic management at the initial stage of project/program appraisal which may well complement the conventional techno-economic analysis attempted by planners. The environment-strategy-structure-process spectrum has many critical dimensions which could be probed systematically through a series of questions to be adapted to the needs of different types of programs. Similar questions could also be raised when the evaluation of projects/programs is undertaken, especially if the purpose of the exercise is to facilitate improved performance. The strategic management approach may thus provide some useful guidelines for the design, management, and evaluation of development projects and programs.

Political Compulsions and System Overloads

Large, multi-goal programs are initiated in many developing countries with little attention paid to the problems of strategic management. Political compulsions of national leaders and some-times the preferences of large donors seem to reinforce this tendency. Technical feasibility may well be the overriding consideration in these cases. On the other hand, our case studies show how much attention is demanded by aspects such as demand mobilisation, beneficiary diversity, integration of inputs, use of networks, mobilisation of key actors, community participation, and the use of non-economic incentives in motivating beneficiaries even for a single service. It is true that the programs analysed by us were, for the most part, in their developmental or entrepreneurial phase. Once they stabilise and mature, their management is likely to become less complex. An important lesson of our study, however, is that overloading the system in its initial phase is not a good strategy unless compensating structural and process interventions are feasible and environmental complexity is limited.

As noted in Chapter 1, private and public management differ in their degree of control over the choice of goals and means and the resources available to them to influence the course of implementation. Private managers tend to exercise greater control over their choice of goals and means and have at their disposal more potent sources of influence (over motivation and compliance) than public

managers. As development programs become more complex, these
limitations become more severe and hamper the managers' ability to
create and maintain the state of congruence needed for successful
program performance. If the structure-process limitations facing
a program cannot be eliminated and problems such as inter-agency
coordination in networks persist, then, the program strategy must
take into account the reality of the situation. The failure of many
large integrated rural development programs could be attributed to
a lack of awareness of this problem or a reluctance to face the
choices involved squarely. There are four alternative ways of
addressing this problem. First, if the program is given a greater
measure of autonomy, managers may be able to adapt the different
variables better and move towards a congruent combination. Second, a
part of the complexity of integration could be eliminated by organisations of beneficiaries playing a more active role. When beneficiaries are well organised and participate actively, they are able to
lighten the burden of the program manager by taking over a part of
the integrative role. Third, the program may offer multiple
services only in one area or region at a time, rather than all over
the country simultaneously. A variant of this approach is the
creation of separate local or regional programs that reduce the
complexity of management. Fourth, multiple services may be
sequenced over time on a national basis. First, a single basic
service is offered and as it stabilises, the second service is
added. Over time, the entire spectrum of services is offered. This
is a case of sequential diversification. In brief, the strategic
management approach underscores the point that the more complex
development programs will pay a heavy price in terms of performance
when they ignore the managerial implications of the choice problem
referred to above.

Government's Role : A Shift in Focus

Development programs cause a number of unintended consequences
some of which militate against the larger goals of development.
Industrial programs, for example, have led to urban congestion and
pollution. To take a specific case, it was alleged that India's
Dairy Development Program aggravated the problem of malnutrition in
rural areas. It is a moot point whether the individual program
concerned could have anticipated such problems and taken action to
deal with its second generation problems. To the extent that these
are due to externalities which could be taken into account at the
design stage, program strategies should certainly be encouraged to
seek answers to and bear the costs of such problems. On the other
hand, if it is difficult to anticipate them and coping with them
adds to internal conflicts, a better approach will be for the
government to search for remedies in the broader context of the
country and let the existing programs pursue their basic goals.
Thus a dairy program that offers a good price for milk is bound to
encourage farmers to sell an increasing share of their milk. If
this leads to rural children getting a reduced supply of milk, the
answer may lie in the government taking this phenomenon into account
in formulating alternative remedial measures rather than intervening

to reduce the milk price or limit the sale of milk by rural farmers.
An important role of the government will then be to monitor the
operations and performance of its diverse development programs and
identify areas in which new interventions are needed to cope with
the second generation problems caused by the original program.

Of necessity, public interventions tend to bestow monopoly power
on program organisations and networks which have no competition to
content with. A single, large agency to deal with a sector, sub-
sector or commodity may be appropriate in the early development
phase of a program when private alternatives may not exist or are
inadequate. On the other hand, as programs reach maturity, their
monopoly power may well go against the interests of beneficiaries.
Costs of services may go up, and quality and responsiveness to the
public may decline. Meanwhile, if beneficiaries have developed the
capacity to manage the services on their own, or at least play an
enlarged role in service planning and delivery, government could
play a stretegic role in facilitating the divestment of services by
program agencies. A program could be so designed that it moves from
one service to another related service, having passed on the former
to a beneficiary organisation or other private or cooperative
agencies if such alternatives are available. The point is that a
program or its service need not live for ever. Managing its life
cycle to match the development of beneficiaries should be a part
of the government's developmental responsibility.

Viewed thus, the role of the government shifts from routine
monitoring of procedures and interventions in the operational
decisions of programs to the monitoring of program performance,
coping with the external effects of programs,and influencing the
choice and divestment of program goals. This shift of focus
obviously calls for skilled personnel within government who understand not only the politics and techno-economics of programs,but
also the basics of strategic management. Top administrators in
every ministry which has a portfolio of programs will need to be
supported by a small group of persons with appropriate skills to
strengthen their capacity to play the new roles and reinforce the
strategic interventions of the program managers in the field.

Linking Pilot Projects to National Programs

Pilot projects have been an enduring fashion in the field of
development. Yet there are countries which have become
"graveyards" of pilot projects with little success in replicating
or extending the new services on a larger scale. In Chapter 9,
we highlighted the conditions under which learning from pilot
projects was internalised effectively by several large programs.
It is important to draw attention to them again for the simple
reason that governments have a considerable influence on the manner
in which pilot projects are planned and utilised.

How can the linkages between pilot projects and national
programs be improved? Three types of interventions are in order.
First, the conventional practice of isolating pilot projects and
experiments from national programs needs to be discouraged. Where-

ver possible, there should be a beneficiary for a pilot project
in the form of an actual or potential national program. Preferably,
those who are likely to manage the program should be actively
involved in the project with a commitment to learn from it. Second,
experiments should be encouraged in the field as a device for
continued learning and local adaptation even after a national
program has been launched. In other words, a pilot project is not
to be thought of solely as a pre-program effort. It is a means of
adapting to the environment, stimulating local initiative, and
developing innovative ideas throughout the life of the program.
Third, pilot projects are a device not only for generating and
testing ideas, but also a nursery for developing trained personnel.
If a pilot project preceded a program, it is possible that some of
those who participated in the project could be given appropriate
roles in managing the new program. This is an effective way for a
program to internalise the learning from a pilot project that
preceded it. In short, governments ought to seek ways and means
to integrate pilot projects with national programs organically
rather than view the two as discrete parts linked indirectly
through administrative fiat.

Development and the Weaker Sections

A set of development programs does not necessarily usher in
the development of a country. The problems of equity and the
neglect of the weaker sections which have received much public
attention in recent years reflect this concern. Why do the weaker
sections of beneficiaries fail to benefit from development
programs? The present study though limited to six programs sheds
some light on this important question.

First of all, when a program does not explicitly define
intended beneficiaries, it tends to focus on a standardised service
which invariably fails to meet the needs of the weaker sections.
Program designers are often carried away by the technology underlying the service. But technology does make some assumptions about
the capacity and skills of the beneficiary. Designers seldom check
to see whether these implicit assumptions are valid for the environment in which the program is to operate. It is well known, for
instance, that rural water supply programs tend to define their
service as the installation of pumps. This may well be in order if
the beneficiaries are educated citizens with willingness and ability
to use the facility. A close look at the beneficiaries and the
barriers facing them might have helped design the service differently.

Second, as a response to the first problem, programs have been
designed to focus exclusively on weaker sections. It has been
noticed in such cases that the intended beneficiaries are unable
to take advantage of the program although nominally the service
is meant for them. As explained in Chapter 8, the basic problem
here lies in the program's failure to pull together the inputs
relevant to the weaker sections and integrate them in a manner that
compensates for their inability to do so on their own.

244

An agricultural program may provide high yielding seeds and extension, but not credit and marketing support. Under these conditions,
the richer farmers will find the latter inputs on their own, but
the weaker sections may fail to take advantage of the program
service precisely because of their limited access to these inputs.
Rural development programs which offer assets such as cattle to
poor beneficiaries but fail to provide the related inputs need to
sustain them are committing the same error. It appears that
careful attention to the nature and scope of integration of inputs
is an essential pre-condition for benefiting the weaker sections.

Third, our study shows the critical role of demand mobilisation
in facilitating an equitable distribution of the benefits of
development. It is the elites who are willing and able to take
advantage of most program services without any effort on the part of
programs to mobilise them. But for the weaker sections, lack of
information and education about the program are a major hurdle.
Rural water supply may fail to benefit weaker sections because no
one has informed and educated them about its advantages. In many
cases, beneficiary participation could be a powerful means of
mobilising response. In other cases, direct incentives may provide
an answer. In brief, the capacity of weaker sections to share the
benefits of development programs can be agumented through a deliberate strategy to mobilise their demand.

While broader policy interventions and institutional reforms
have a major role to play in achieving a more equitable distribution of the benefits of development, there is no doubt that the
strategic management of development programs could also work towards
this end. A clear focus on weaker sections in the design of
service, careful integration of inputs to match the needs of the
intended beneficiaries, and deliberate efforts to mobilise their
response are dimensions which deserve special attention in this
context. Program leaders as well as policy makers in government
ought to give high priority to these strategic interventions if
they are committed to a more equitable distribution of the benefits
of development.

NOTES

1. D. Korten, "Community Organisation and Rural Development :
A Learning Process Approach". Public Administration Review,
September-October, 1980, pp. 480-511.
2. D.A. Rondinelli and K. Ruddle, Urbanization and Rural
Development : A Spatial Policy for Equitable Growth (New York :
Praegar, 1978), p.72.
3. V.R. Gaikwad, A Study of Key Village Scheme in Bhavnagar
(Ahmedabad : Indian Institute of Management, 1974), p.56.
4. W.E. Smith, et.al. op.cit. p.2.
5. C. Gopalan, "Thirteenth Jawaharlal Nehru Memorial Lecture",
Teen Murti House, New Delhi, 1979.
6. UN, Public Administration Institutions and Practices in
Integrated Rural Development Programs (New York, 1980), p.19.
7. U. Lele, op.cit. p.182

Index